MODERN MEXICO

A Volume in the Comparative Societies Series

Y0-AER-405

MODERN MEXICO

A Volume in the Comparative Societies Series

WILLIAM CANAK
Middle Tennessee State University
Murfreesboro, Tennessee

LAURA SWANSON
Middle Tennessee State University
Murfreesboro, Tennessee

SERIES EDITOR HAROLD R. KERBO

Boston   Burr Ridge, IL   Dubuque, IA   Madison, WI
New York   San Francisco   St. Louis
Bangkok   Bogotá   Caracas   Lisbon   London   Madrid   Mexico City
Milan   New Delhi   Seoul   Singapore   Sydney   Taipei   Toronto

McGraw-Hill

A Division of The **McGraw·Hill** *Companies*

MODERN MEXICO

This book is printed on acid-free paper.

1 2 3 4 5 6 7 8 9 0 DOC/DOC 9 0 9 8 7

ISBN 0-07-034431-0

Editorial director: *Phillip A. Butcher*
Sponsoring editor: *Jill Gordon*
Editorial coordinator: *Amy Smeltzley*
Marketing manager: *Sally Constable*
Project manager: *Kimberly D. Hooker*
Production supervisor: *Scott Hamilton*
Senior designer: *Laurie J. Entringer*
Compositor: *Shepherd Incorporated*
Typeface: *11/13 Palatino*
Printer: *R. R. Donnelley & Sons Company*

Library of Congress Cataloging-in-Publication Data
Canak, William L. (William Leigh)
    Modern Mexico : a volume in the comparative societies series /
William Canak, Laura Swanson.
        p.   cm.
    Includes index.
    ISBN 0-07-034431-0
    1. Mexico—Social conditions.   2. Social structure—Mexico.
3. Social interaction—Mexico.   I. Swanson, Laura.   II. Title.
HN113.C28   1998
306'.0972—dc21   97-38941
                                                                    CIP

http://www.mhhe.com

In one of the early scenes of the movie *Reds*, the U.S. revolutionary journalist, John Reed, just back from covering the beginning of World War I, is asked by a roomful of business leaders, "What is this War really about?" John Reed stands and stops all conversation with a one word reply—"profits." Today, war between major industrial nations would disrupt profits much more than create money for a military industrial complex. Highly integrated global markets and infrastructures support the daily life of suburban families in Chicago and urban squatter settlements in Bombay. These ties produce a social and economic ecology that transcends political and cultural boundaries.

The world is a very different place than it was for our parents and grandparents. Those rare epic events of world war certainly invaded their everyday lives and futures, but we now find that daily events thousands of miles away, in countries large and small, have a greater impact on North Americans than ever before, with the speed of this impact multiplied many times in recent decades. Our standard of living, jobs, and even prospects of living in a healthy environment have never before been so dependent on outside forces.

Yet, there is much evidence that North Americans have less easy access to good information about the outside world than even a few years ago. Since the end of the Cold War, newspaper and television coverage of events in other countries has dropped dramatically. It is difficult to put much blame on the mass media, however: international news seldom sells anymore. There is simply less interest.

It is not surprising, then, that Americans know comparatively little about the outside world. A recent *Los Angeles Times* survey provides a good example: People in eight countries were asked five basic questions about current events of the day. Americans were dead last in their knowledge, trailing people from Canada, Mexico, England, France, Spain, Germany, and Italy.* It is also not surprising that the annual report published by the Swiss World Economic Forum always ranks American executives quite low in their international experience and understanding.

---

*For example, while only 3 percent of Germans missed all five questions, 37 percent of the Americans did (*Los Angeles Times*, March 16, 1994).

Such ignorance harms American competitiveness in the world economy in many ways. But there is much more. Seymour Martin Lipset put it nicely in one of his recent books: "Those who know only one country know no country" (Lipset 1996, p. 17). Considerable time spent in a foreign country is one of the best stimulants for a sociological imagination: Studying or doing research in other countries makes us realize how much we really, in fact, have learned about our own society in the process. Seeing other social arrangements, ways of doing things, and foreign perspectives allows for far greater insight to the familiar, our own society. This is also to say that ignorance limits solutions to many of our own serious social problems. How many Americans, for example, are aware that levels of poverty are much lower in all other advanced nations and that the workable government services in those countries keep poverty low? Likewise, how many Americans are aware of alternative means of providing health care and quality education or reducing crime?

We can take heart in the fact that sociology in the United States has become more comparative in recent decades. A comparative approach, of course, was at the heart of classical European sociology during the 1800s. But as sociology was transported from Europe to the United States early in the twentieth century, it lost much of this comparative focus. In recent years, sociology journals have published more comparative research. There are large data sets with samples from many countries around the world in research seeking general laws on issues such as causes of social mobility or political violence, all very much in the tradition of Durkheim. But we also need much more of the old Max Weber. His was a qualitative historical and comparative perspective (Smelser 1976; Ragin and Zaret 1983). Weber's methodology provides a richer understanding of other societies, a greater recognition of the complexity of social, cultural, and historical forces shaping each society. Ahead of his time in many ways, C. Wright Mills was planning a qualitative comparative sociology of world regions just before his death in 1961 (Horowitz 1983, p. 324). Too few American sociologists have yet to follow in his footsteps.

Following these trends, sociology textbooks in the United States have also become more comparative in content in recent years. And while this tendency must be applauded, it is not enough. Typically there is an example from Japan here, another from Germany there, and so on haphazardly for a few countries in different subject areas as the writer's knowledge of these bits and pieces allows. What we need are the textbook equivalents of a richer Weberian comparative analysis, a qualitative comparative analysis of the social, cultural, and historical forces that have combined to make relatively unique societies around the world. It is this type of comparative material that can best help people in the United States overcome their lack of understanding about other countries and allow them to see their own society with much greater insight.

The Comparative Societies Series, of which this book is a part, has been designed as a small step in filling this need. We have currently selected 12 countries on which to focus: Japan, Thailand, Switzerland, Mexico, Eritria, Hungary, Germany, China, India, Iran, Brazil, and Russia. We selected these countries as representatives of major world regions and cultures, and each will be examined in separate books written by talented sociologists. All of these basic sociological issues and topics will be covered: Each book will begin with a look at the important historical and geographical forces shaping the society, then turn to basic aspects of social organization and culture. From there each book will proceed to examine the political and economic institutions of the specific country, along with the social stratification, the family, religion, education, and finally urbanization, demography, social problems, and social change.

Although each volume in the Comparative Societies Series is of necessity brief to allow for use as supplementary readings in standard sociology courses, we have tried to assure that this brief coverage provides students with sufficient information to better understand each society, as well as their own. The ideal would be to transport every student to another country for a period of observation and learning. Realizing the unfortunate impracticality of this ideal, we hope to do the next best thing—to at least mentally move these students to a country very different from their own, provide something of the everyday reality of the people in these other countries, and demonstrate how the tools of sociological analysis can help them see these societies as well as their own with much greater understanding.

Harold R. Kerbo
San Luis Obispo, CA
June 1997

Mexico and the United States should know each other well. Much of the western United States was once part of Mexico. Today they share a 2,000-mile border and have merged their economies with Canada under the North American Free Trade Agreement. An estimated 1997 $120 billion (US) in bilateral trade complements billions more in investments by U.S. corporations and individuals. Millions of Mexican immigrants, temporary and permanent, legal and illegal, live and work in the United States. Within a decade citizens of Latin ancestry will compose the largest government-defined minority in the United States, and the majority of these Hispanics trace their ancestry to Mexico. Millions of U.S. citizens regularly visit Mexico as tourists and thousands choose Mexico as a retirement haven where their pensions and social security dollars go a long way. U.S.–Mexican trade and investment patterns document the emergence of a regional market for goods, capital, and labor. Waves of sport, food, and music wash across the border in both directions.

Why then is Mexico such an enigma to most people living in the United States? If we examine a holiday celebrated in both countries we may gain some insights. In the United States, the holiday (holy day), like Christmas, has become profoundly detached from its religious origins. Halloween, All Hallows Eve, the night before All Saints Day, has become a Disney-flavored secular celebration sanitized by parent groups and public officials. Stores and television trumpet candy, costumes, and other commodities so widely that the event seems to be one celebrating the opportunity to consume unusual goods. Trick-or-treating rounds are now carefully chaperoned and often end at sundown. Not so Mexico.

Mexicans, as their famous writer Octavio Paz notes, celebrate "The Day of the Dead" and relish the opportunity to embrace it with fervor and enthusiasm unimaginable in the United States. Their entire society is caught up with deeply rooted ethnic and regional customs that draw Mexicans to remember the dead, especially dead children. Visions of "La Muerte," a skeletal lady representing death, are everywhere. Food comes in the form of bones and coffins specially baked. "Pan de muerto," death bread, comes with bits of simulated bone on top. Elaborate home altars are built to honor dead relatives and the altars become laden with decorations ranging from food to liquor. At cemeteries Mexicans may be found tending to grave sites, cleaning stones, weeding, and festooning graves with flowers and creative colorful adornments. Picnics at the cemetery include tequila, grand heartfelt song fests, firecrackers and rockets, and even the occasional mariachi band. Vigils for the dead often last all night.

As with their dead, Mexicans cherish history with a knowledge and intimacy wholly unfamiliar north of the border. Unlike in the United States, Mexican's sensibilities run directly from the era prior to what Stannard (1992) terms an "American holocaust" as he so aptly terms the Spanish conquest and colonization of Mexico. After independence, Mexican culture was relatively unaffected by the waves of European and Asian migration that swept across the United States in the nineteenth and twentieth centuries. Mexican identity, in contrast, was shaped by a long insulated process that produced a sense of national identity wholly distinct from the complex patchwork of race, ethnicity, and religion marking U.S. culture. In its place we find Mexico's "cosmic race" blending Amerindian indigenous peoples, Spanish, and small numbers of Africans and Asians. Coursing through this amalgam we see continuities of Amerindian life, Spanish language and institutions, and Roman Catholicism.

Spain's centuries of colonial rule over Mexico produced a society with extremely concentrated land ownership and a vast gulf between a small concentrated elite and a large population of peasants. In the United States, only one region, the South, ever produced an economy and culture with some similarities. Like the American South, the Mexican elite has maintained a harsh and suspicious view of lower classes. Mexico's landed aristocracy, and later its industrial and political elite, viewed both Amerindians and most *mestizos* as not up to the process of self-rule and modern life. The southern elite of the old Confederacy and Jim Crow years held similar views of blacks and poor rural whites. Nevertheless, both elites recognized the need to modernize and catch up with the world and both have viewed industrialization as the path. In each case the road to modernization required massive capital investment, but these two elites regarded market risks as unacceptable. Thus, they each sought to modernize with foreign investment or, in the case of the United States, northern investment. Foreign investment demanded stability—stability was achieved with an iron fist.

In a world of democracy, relatively open markets, and equality, stability may be achieved through consensual values, voluntary organizations, and broad-based commitment to civic culture. In a world with little opportunity and brutal domination by a small entrenched elite, it was hard to attract immigrants who sought economic opportunity, political freedom, and religious acceptance. Neither Mexico nor the American South offered any of these. Thus, both reached the middle twentieth century with a strong sense of self-identity, but little influence from without and a relatively narrow set of institutions defining civil culture. In both cases, also, the years from World War II until the century's end would bring great transformations as integration with the global economy brought pressure for economic, political, and social change.

In 1997, one may assert that Mexico is becoming a cipher to Mexicans themselves. Mexico is, in a word, changing. Until the 1980s, Mexico's economy seemed to be buffered from the world by high tariffs and a large state-owned industrial sector. But government programs funded by foreign loans from banks; U.S., European and Japanese governments, and international agencies caught Mexico in a web of debt that crushed those buffers. Mexico went through an abrupt transformation as its political elite sold off state-owned industries, reduced or eliminated taxes on imports, and lobbied hard to merge Mexico's economy with those of the United States and Canada. If they had suspected the result, collapse of 70 years of one-party political rule, they may have been more cautious.

Political and economic change have been complemented by social change. For over one hundred years following the Mexican-American War (1846–48), most Mexicans viewed the United States with resentment and suspicion. In the 1980s one would commonly walk through Mexico City and encounter numerous murals, street theater groups, and political demonstrations condemning "American" imperialism and exploitation of Mexico and Latin America. As Alan Riding notes in his broad-ranging evaluation of Mexican society, *Distant Neighbors,* "The emotional prism of defeat and resentment through which Mexico views every bilateral problem is not simply the legacy of unpardoned injustices from the past." Indeed, Mexicans saw their cart hitched to the driving force of the U.S. economy, but were deeply suspicious that they would always be exploited.

The 1990s have brought great changes in the U.S.–Mexican cultural relationship. Spanish is now the most frequently spoken and taught language in the United States (after English). Economic integration has accelerated the flow of people, goods, information, and capital. In Mexico, until recently only the middle class openly emulated U.S. values and lifestyles. Ironically, Mexico's middle class experienced severe economic dislocations during the 1980s and early 1990s. And U.S. consumer culture has flooded through the gates opened by the 1994 North American Free Trade Agreement. McDonald's and Taco Bell proliferate throughout urban areas. U.S.-style enclosed malls draw Mexicans away from small locally owned shops as brand names and styles familiar in the United States capture the fancy of Mexico's youth culture.

Is Mexico becoming what the English weekly news magazine *The Economist* terms "Amexica the Beautiful" or will Mexico remain "So far from heaven, so close to the United States"? In this book we attempt to present information on a range of social institutions and processes. We aim to provide students with tools to begin their own informed questioning of Mexican culture, social structure, and political economy. Chapter 1, "The Place, the People, and the Past," maps out a basic profile of Mexico's geography, population, and history. Chapter 2, "Politics and Political Institutions," reviews important aspects of Mexico's distinctive and rapidly changing political culture and government. Chapter 3, "The Mexican Economy," focuses on the major sectors of industrial, financial, and commercial activity, but also considers the impact of the North American Free Trade Agreement, the treaty that merges Mexico's economy with those of the United States of America and Canada. Chapter 4, "Mexican Stratification and Mobility," reviews Mexico's class structure, but also considers regional patterns of inequality. Chapters 5 through 9 examine other basic characteristics of Mexican society and culture, the family, religion, education, race and ethnicity, and gender. Chapter 10, "Population," reviews core demographic structure and processes, including fertility, mortality, and migration. In addition, we evaluate Mexico's government policies targeting family planning. Finally, Chapter 11 presents information on important social problems facing Mexico and the urban and rural social movements that express a range of challenges to institutionalized authority.

We know this supplementary textbook, aimed at undergraduate university students, does not provide a comprehensive knowledge of Mexican society. Our goal is to provide a foundation that complements the information and analysis methods students must master in a range of social science courses. Our references and the "Webliography" appendix at the end of the book

CONTENTS

Chapter 10

Population 141

Chapter 11

Social Problems and Social Movements 157

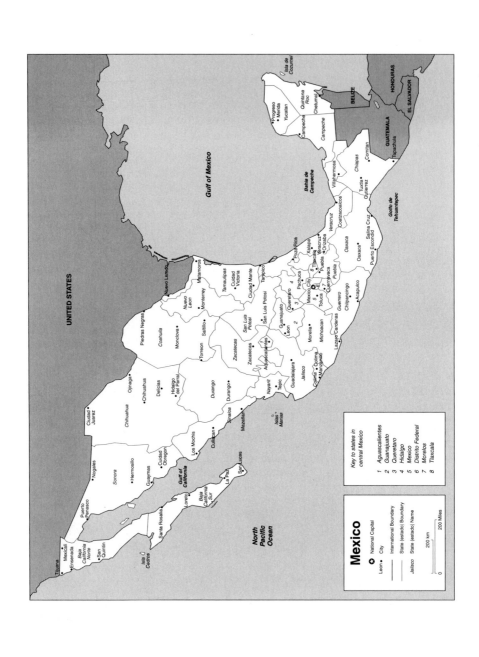

Mexico

- ⊕ National Capital
- León • City
- ——— International Boundary
- ——— State (estado) Boundary
- Jalisco State (estado) Name

Key to states in
central Mexico

1 Aguascalientes
2 Guanajuato
3 Querétaro
4 Hidalgo
5 Mexico
6 Distrito Federal
7 Morelos
8 Tlaxcala

0   200 km

0   200 Miles

UNITED STATES

Gulf of Mexico

North
Pacific
Ocean

Gulf of
California

Bahía de
Campeche

Gofo de
Tehuantepec

GUATEMALA
BELIZE
HONDURAS
EL SALVADOR

Tijuana
Mexicali
Ensenada
Baja California Norte
San Quintín
Isla Cedros
Santa Rosalia
Loreto
Baja California Sur
La Paz
San Lucas
Nogales
Puerto Peñasco
Sonora
Hermosillo
Guaymas
Ciudad Obregón
Los Mochis
Culiacán
Sinaloa
Mazatlán
Islas Marias
Tepic
Nayarit
Guadalajara
Jalisco
Colima
Manzanillo
Lázaro Cárdenas
Michoacán
Morelos
León
Guanajuato
Querétaro
Pachuca
Mexico City
Toluca
Cuernavaca
Guerrero
Acapulco
Chilpancingo
Puerto Escondido
Oaxaca
Oaxaca
Puebla
Puebla
Orizaba
Veracruz
Xalapa
Poza Rica
Tampico
Ciudad Mante
Ciudad Victoria
San Luis Potosí
San Luis Potosí
Aguascalientes
Zacatecas
Zacatecas
Durango
Durango
Torreón
Coahuila
Saltillo
Monclova
Piedras Negras
Nuevo León
Monterrey
Nuevo Laredo
Matamoros
Tamaulipas
Ciudad Juárez
Chihuahua
Chihuahua
Ojinaga
Delicias
Hidalgo del Parral
Coatzacoalcos
Salina Cruz
Villahermosa
Tuxtla Gutiérrez
Chiapas
Comitán
Tapachula
Campeche
Campeche
Mérida
Progreso
Yucatán
Quintana Roo
Chetumal
Isla de Cozumel

The Place, the People, and the Past

Mexico is one of three nation-states comprising the North American continent, and its topography, culture, and history are intimately entwined with its northern neighbors, Canada and the United States of America. No other large Third World nation shares such geographic proximity, economic integration, and political intimacy with advanced First World nations.

Most students in the United States and Canada, however, lack even rudimentary knowledge of Mexico's climate and landscape, its people, or their remarkable history. Stereotypes contain images of tropical resorts like Cancun or Acapulco, millions of illegal immigrants at the border, or U.S. corporations searching for cheap labor.

In this chapter, we establish a factual knowledge base for students. We profile Mexico with the three themes shared by other books in this series: "The Place," "The People," and "The Past." We emphasize those elements of Mexico's place, people, and past that are linked directly to the topics students will encounter in later chapters. We also introduce concepts and terms that may be unfamiliar to undergraduate students. These concepts and terms appear in **bold print** and are defined in the glossary at the end of this book. In addition, throughout all chapters we introduce students to Spanish words we think are important for their vocabulary. These words appear in *italics,* and their definitions can also be found in the glossary.

THE PLACE

Modern Mexico's territory stretches from a 2,000-mile northern border with the United States to a southern border of 600 miles with Guatemala. Its Yucatan peninsula thrusts into the Gulf of Mexico and shares a brief 160-mile border with Belize. To the south extend the several countries of Central America that form an isthmus linking the North and South American continents. The 760,000 square miles of national territory of the United States of Mexico (*Estados Unidos Mexicanos*) make Mexico the third-largest nation-state in Latin America after Brazil and Argentina and one of the world's 10 largest nations. With a western coast on the Pacific Ocean and an eastern coast along the Gulf of Mexico and Caribbean Sea, Mexico is directly linked to Atlantic and Pacific markets and politics.

As with any large land mass stretching north to south across many latitudes and from sea level to volcanic mountain chains, Mexico has strong regional differences in climate and topography. Thrusting into the Caribbean, the Yucatan peninsula's lush tropical jungles and beaches contrast with the arid deserts and hot highland plateaus and valleys that mark Mexico's north. Temperate zones are restricted to the mountainous areas over 8,000 feet in elevation. The rugged geography and climate limit agricultural potential. They also present extraordinary impediments to Mexican efforts at developing transportation and communication between regions. Much of Mexico lacks sufficient rainfall to support highly productive agriculture. In the arid northern region near the United States, widespread export agriculture focusing on fruits and vegetables requires extensive irrigation. Mountains cover nearly one-fourth of Mexico and have a temperate but high-rainfall climate. Finally, in the southern region bordering Guatemala and extending east into the Yucatan peninsula, a high-rainfall tropical climate and fertile soils have supported plantation agriculture since the 19th century (Lima-Dantas 1985).

Mexico once contained extensive fertile agricultural land, but it lost much of it to the United States in the 1848 Treaty of Guadalupe Hidalgo ending the Mexican-American War. This sparsely settled region stretched from Texas to California, and the central government, based in Mexico City, had exercised marginal control over it. In what remains of Mexico's north, high-yield agricultural production on large-scale plots has developed with the help of foreign investment and government-subsidized development of roads and irrigation.

Mexico's geological diversity contains a wealth of minerals. Much of Mexico's colonial history was shaped by the abundance of gold and silver, much desired by Spaniards. Significant deposits of lead, zinc, copper, and sulfur have been exploited, too. And in the 1970s, discovery of large oil deposits shaped Mexican economic and political life as the political elite thought it had discovered a cornucopia to finance development policies without sacrifice or taxes. Despite a wealth of minerals, Mexico's population remained poor during the colonial period and remains poor today.

THE PEOPLE

Most researchers and even the Mexican government divide Mexico into distinct regions. The north Pacific region includes the states of Baja California, Baja California Sur, Sonora, Sinaloa, and Nayarit. This region is mostly arid desert. Its population was small until recent decades, when tourism and export industrialization along the border encouraged large-scale migration northward by Mexicans looking for upward economic mobility. The northern region extends from the Sierra Madre Occidental mountain chain to the Gulf of Mexico. Chihuahua, Coahuila, Durango, Zacatecas, and San Luis Potosí cover 40 percent of Mexico, but only 20 percent of Mexicans live there (Lima-Dantas 1985).

The Sierra Madre Oriental mountain chain joins the Sierra Madre Occidental to define Mexico's north. On the high plateau between them sit central Mexico and Mexico City, the Federal District. Fifty percent of all Mexicans live in central Mexico, many in Mexico City, the largest city in the world. Two northeastern states, Nuevo León and Tamaulipas, contain an important seaport (Tampico) and a concentration of heavy industry centered around the city of Monterrey. The North American Free Trade Agreement (see Chapter 3, "The Mexican Economy") has helped integrate this region with the U.S. border economy as assembly plants based here expand rapidly. The Gulf coast states of Veracruz, Tabasco, and Yucatán are small and lightly populated. The southern Pacific region, much of it once part of Guatemala, contains coastal and mountainous regions. Rural, poor, and home to indigenous Amerindian groups only marginally integrated with Mexico's mainstream society, the southern Pacific states of Chiapas, Oaxaca, and Guerrera remain culturally, economically, and politically quite similar to Central America. Thus, one is not surprised to find it the site of revolutionary social movements discussed elsewhere in this text (see Chapter 11, "Social Problems and Social Movements").

Extremely uneven economic development underlies Mexican **regionalism.** National government programs barely touch the poorest regions. In recent years, responding to social protests and widespread international condemnation, the federal government, based in Mexico City, decentralized some political functions by giving municipal governments greater autonomy. For purposes of comparison, most sociologists and economists divide jobs into three major groups: a primary sector (food production and distribution, such as fishing and farming, and mining); a secondary sector (manufacturing, utilities, and construction); and a tertiary sector (services). In Mexico, as in most of the world system, tertiary sector employment has been growing most rapidly and is the largest sector in the 1990s. Nevertheless, Mexico's extremely uneven development leads other sectors to dominate job growth in some regions. In the northern and central regions, secondary sector employment growth has been rapid. Tropical plantation agriculture dominates the south and east.

These sectoral differences are paralleled by great differences in regional wealth and income. With an official minimum wage set at about U.S. $5 per day, most Mexicans' salary is below U.S. $10 per day. In the south, poor rural peasants, often landless, live outside the money economy. Nearly one person in five has no measurable income. The population along the northern border and in the central region near Mexico City has the highest percentage

Modern Mexico remains a Third World economy. Hard labor and family define the only safety net available to most Mexicans. (Courtesy of the Inter-American Foundation; photographer, Philip Decker)

CHAPTER 1

earning over $25 per day, roughly 8 to 10 percent (Instituto Nacional de Estadística, Geografía e Informática 1990).

The majority of Mexicans trace their heritage to two profoundly different groups. As a *mestizo* nation, modern Mexico's culture derives from the forces unleashed when Spanish *conquistadores* encountered and decimated one of the world's greatest societies. Mexico's unique culture is both an alloy and a compound of Spanish and native Amerindian cultures. The result is something unique and new, but that also retains intact important elements of each. For most Mexicans, the alloy is distinctly more Amerindian than Spanish. At its core, modern Mexico's culture is more deeply and self-consciously influenced by Amerindian values and sensibilities than any other major Latin American nation. Among the smaller countries only Peru, Paraguay, Guatemala, and Bolivia retain national cultures with strong consciousness of their original peoples. In these smaller countries traditional Indian culture, while strong and viable, is marginalized from the dominant political and economic institutions. Mexican regionalism is also reflected in the physical and cultural composition of the population. While still *mestizo*, the population in the north Pacific and northern regions has a typical skin color, height, and facial characteristics quite distinct from the population in the south Pacific region.

Perhaps 5 to 10 percent of Mexicans speak an Amerindian language as their primary or only language. Mass media, formal schooling, and migration patterns are reducing this population. Nevertheless, Amerindian identity and culture, especially in the south, retains its integrity as 5 million Mexicans speak some 25 distinct Amerindian languages (Siembieda and Rodríguez 1996). As Levy and Székely (1983, p. 11) note:

> Different Indian groups concentrate in different regions, mostly in southern and central Mexico. Descendants of the Mayas are concentrated in the south and the Yucatán, Zapotecs and Mixtecs in Oaxaca, Tarascans in Michoacán, fiercely independent Yaquis in Sonora, and Aztec descendants in various parts of Mexico. Different groups have their own languages, customs, dances, music, and clothing.

Beyond the *mestizo* core of Mexico's population, one finds ethnic diversity in the current of African slaves brought during colonial times to work in the coastal economy. Blacks and black–*mestizo* Mexicans are concentrated in the Caribbean region around the city of Veracruz. Asian immigrants from China and Japan can also be found in small numbers as an urban population. Both blacks and Asians integrated into Mexico's *mestizo* "cosmic race," but as elsewhere, Mexicans of Chinese and Japanese descent often occupy professional and entrepreneurial positions.

We cannot consider Mexico's population without reference to the United States and the millions of legal and illegal Mexican immigrants who live and work there. Although lost to Mexico in the 19th-century wars with the United States, the region stretching from Texas to California has formed a deeply integrated regional economy on both sides of the modern border. Mexicans have lived and worked in the United States without controversy until the 1970s. The U.S. Bureau of the Census estimated that the 1984 U.S. population included 9.5 million Mexican-Americans, some 60 percent of all Hispanic-Americans. Large-scale legal and illegal migration to the United States has produced an expatriate population whose remittance of savings is an important factor sustaining the Mexican economy. In recognition of this expatriate population's economic influence and increasing political organization, in 1996 the Mexican government made it possible for Mexicans to hold dual citizenship. The 1980s and 1990s have brought a little-noticed countermigration of retirees and pensioners from the United States. Seeking warm weather and lower living costs, over 1 million U.S. citizens have settled in Mexico, some of them illegally. Some 4 million U.S. citizens travel to Mexico annually. Despite their long border, highly integrated economies, and considerable contact through migration and tourism, Mexican culture, politics, and economic life remain an enigma to most of the U.S. population.

The gulf separating these two societies derives from a profoundly different sense of national and cultural history. The writer Octavio Paz, Mexico's own Nobel Prize recipient, speaks of two visions of Western Civilization: the United States as shaped by the Protestant Reformation, and Mexico shaped by the Spanish Counter-Reformation. Latin Americans and Mexicans stereotype the United States as the epitome of efficiency, technology, rationality, and strength. U.S. culture is also stereotyped as shallow, devoid of esthetic complexity, and emotionally immature. For many Mexicans, self-image revolves around images of lassitude, ineptness, poverty, and victimization. In the United States, popular rhetoric embraces renewal, innovation, and a bridge to the future. In Mexico, modern culture always expresses awareness of Mexico's ancient pre-Columbian past and centuries of colonial oppression.

Thus, Mexico and the rest of North America express contrasting histories, cultures, racial composition, and economic well-being. These differences disguise a remarkable and important point: The

United States and Mexico are already profoundly integrated and mutually influential. National Football League preseason games in Mexico play to sellout crowds. Baseball is equally popular in both cultures. U.S. markets sell more salsa than ketchup, and nachos rival hot dogs at baseball games. Taco Bell, McDonald's, Burger King, and a myriad of U.S. consumer goods inundate Mexican markets. Cities throughout the United States now contain substantial Mexican-American populations that strongly influence contemporary urban culture. For example, in 1997, a "heartland" city like Nashville, Tennessee, estimates its Mexican immigrant residents at over 40,000, soon to be the largest minority group in the region. The 1994 North American Free Trade Agreement will end all tariffs within 15 years, encouraging greater integration of the two economies. Finally, Mexico may even begin to achieve a semblance of pluralist political competition after more than 70 years of virtual one-party rule (see Chapter 2, "Politics and Political Institutions").

In the following sections of this chapter, we will discuss the significance of Mexico's ancient history, the holocaust that followed the Spanish conquest, and the long colonial period that preceded independence. Then we will review the stages of economic and political development that followed. Through these latter eras were built the economic, social, and political institutions of modern Mexico. It is essential to recognize, however, that since the moment of encounter with Spanish *conquistadores*, Mexico has been part of a developing world system. That **world system** developed a **division of labor** based on unequal military and political power, unequal trading relations, and distinctly different patterns of social structure. New regions were incorporated into the world system as colonies of the expanding European nation-states. In colonial regions such as Mexico, markets, private property, and wage labor developed under tight regulation by colonial administrations. The primary responsibility of the colonial administrations was to maintain the production of raw materials destined for Europe. The administrators also guarded the authority of the Spanish state and Roman Catholic church. Thus, Mexico and Latin America developed for several hundred years under colonial rule, linked to the developing capitalist world system but stripped of autonomy and yoked to the carriage of Spanish and Portuguese colonial regimes. As a result, their history has been completely different from the experience of industrial powers in Europe and very different from Japan, for example, which was able to maintain its autonomy before beginning industrial capitalist development in the 1830s.

THE PAST

Preconquest Mexico

Asian migrants to North America first arrived in the lands we call Mexico in, roughly, 40,000 BC. Hunters and gatherers were present there as late as 8,000 BC, but over the next millennium a drier climate changed the ecology of plants and animals upon which they depended. Adapting to this new environment, these early cultures began to domesticate such plants as corn and beans. Agricultural civilization set the stage for a complex **division of labor** with technological advances, architecture, and a civic–religious institutional infrastructure that produced the great pyramids, much as we see in ancient Egypt.

By 200 BC, the end of the era anthropologists designate the Formative period, we witness the emergence of Teotihuacán, located to the east of modern-day Mexico City, as a site of religious and secular authority. During the ensuing Classic period stretching to AD 900, this agrarian civilization rapidly developed literacy, advanced mathematics, and technologically sophisticated arts, crafts, and science. Today, one can visit the architectural products of this civilization and view its grandeur in the great buildings at Teotihuacán, the Temple of the Sun at Pelenque, or the Pyramid of the Niches at El Tajín. Through the Classic Mayan period, this agricultural economy supported a complex system of **social stratification** in which the ruling class of priests, artisans, and intellectuals resided in urban religious centers. They developed advanced writing systems, calendars, and an empire that ruled numerous tribes. Typical of such agrarian societies, a **polytheistic religion** legitimated this stratification system, and religious symbols and deities were dominant themes in the decorative arts that survive. By AD 900, however, this great civilization, which produced elaborate architecture and urban development, including engineering feats such as extensive reservoirs, lakes, and irrigation systems, began to fragment and decline (Miller 1985).

Some sites, like that of Tikal in today's Guatemalan jungle of El Petén, were home to over 100,000 Mayans. Archaeologists have begun to unravel the warp and weft of this society's daily life using recent breakthrough translations of Mayan hieroglyphics. We do not yet fully understand what combination of overpopulation, bad climate, food shortages, or other factors produced a great change in this society, but about AD 900 the Classic period gave way to 600 years of societal development ruled by a warrior caste. Under its rule, religious practice was transformed to embrace violent and aggressive gods and human sacrifice. Extensive warfare produced widespread social disruptions and shifting alliances. Security, loyalty, and tribute from defeated tribes defined the core dynamics of this culture (Meyer and Sherman 1995). This violent military–religious culture produced something remarkable: With knowledge gained from long-distance trade with the Incas of the South American Andean mountain region, it carried metalworking crafts, painting, and architecture to heights of skill and beauty rivaling those of any society or epoch. By the 12th century AD, Mexico's Central Valley, site today of Mexico City, saw the settling of various Náhuatl-speaking peoples, especially the Aztecs. Upon their arrival in the 14th century AD, the Aztecs saw an eagle with a snake in its beak as it perched on a cactus. Modern Mexico's flag contains an image of this vision. Indeed, Mexicans today face constant reminders of ancient grandeur in the surviving architecture of massive buildings and other cultural products. Thus, they share with societies such as Egypt, China, and India a palpable reminder of past glories lost under colonial rule and **peripheral** status in the new world system.

Through alliances and wars, the Aztecs consolidated their supremacy over surrounding peoples. Continual war and the brutality of Aztec dominance, however, demanded escalating numbers of prisoners for human sacrifice. This produced an empire rife with fear, suspicion, and resentment. The empire was comprised of semiautonomous city-states that paid tribute to the Aztecs not in money but in food, jewels, precious metals, and other goods in addition to soldiers and slaves. This fragmentation and internal division would later be exploited by the Spanish.

The Conquest

The year 1492 witnessed more than Columbus's first voyage. In Spain, 800 years of Moorish (Arab) rule ended under the assault of Christian armies. With their control of Spain consolidated, Ferdinand and Isabella were free to launch expeditions manned by soldiers to whom they were eager to give tasks beyond Spain's borders. In part, the Age of Discovery that followed was motivated by a variety of factors. Ottoman control of land routes to Asia blocked trade. The Portuguese, Spain's seafaring competitors, were already well established along the West African coast. New navigational technologies built confidence and used knowledge gained by sailors who ventured far into the Atlantic seeking favorable currents and winds when returning from Africa. Ancient maps became available and showed the world as a sphere with all land masses depicted, excepting the New World. In sum, these factors encouraged the search for a western route to Asia (Skidmore and Smith 1992).

When the young Spaniard Hernán Cortés landed his 508 soldiers and 16 horses in the Yucatan in early 1519, they encountered numerous peoples whose suffering under Aztec domination made them eager to ally with the Spanish. Marching toward the Central Valley and Aztec capital of Tenochtitlán, Spaniards encountered a world beyond imagination. Situated in a body of artificial linked lakes were numerous villages and large cities, Central Mexico's population approached 25 million. At its heart sat an island larger than New York City's Manhattan Island, where some 350,000 Aztecs lived in an orderly, clean, healthy, and well-fed society. By the Spaniards' own accounts, Aztec palaces, horticulture, and public infrastructure were advanced far beyond anything Europe offered. A vast and complex mercantile trade of goods and food was regulated by government officials. The urban plan linked architecture and street patterns to celestial movements so that religion and cosmology were synthesized with everyday life (Stannard 1992).

One century after Cortés arrived, all this great empire and complex society was gone, its wealth looted and population dead from war, disease, famine, and exhaustion in what Stannard (1992) has termed an "American Holocaust." Central Mexico's population fell by almost 95 percent within 75 years following the Europeans' first appearance—from more than 25 million people in 1519 to barely 1.3 million in 1595. And Central Mexico was typical. Even using moderate estimates of the pre-1492 population, in southeastern Mexico the number of inhabitants dropped from 1.7 million to less than 240,000 in a century and a half. In northern Mexico, over a somewhat longer period, the native population fell from more than 2.5 million to less than 320,000. Wherever the invaders went, the pattern was the same (Stannard 1992, p. 86). Smallpox, typhoid, measles, mumps, diphtheria, influenza, and other diseases for which the Amerindian population had no resistance weakened and decimated the population. The Spanish troops, armed with superior technology and military strategy, often slaughtered thousands of sick and defenseless women and children in a single day, a level of genocide almost beyond comprehension in its extent and brutality.

The Colonial Period

Modern Mexico's *mestizo* culture taps deeply into preconquest history and subsequent colonial history synthesized Amerindian and

Spanish societies. This synthesis, however, emerged under the rule of Spaniards who ferociously exploited ever-diminishing numbers of Amerindian workers in mines and *haciendas* (large estates) dedicated to one principal goal—enriching the conquerors. *Conquistadores* became entrepreneurs. Under the tutelage of the colonial administration, Spaniards were transformed into mine owners, *hacendados,* and merchants. The Spanish crown authorized a system of labor controls that were brutally exploited throughout the colonies. One system, the *encomienda,* required Amerindians to work without payment on lands owned by the *conquistadores.* The *encomienda* was viewed by Spain as a means to bring Amerindians into more intimate and constant contact with Christians, thereby leading to their eventual conversion to Roman Catholicism. Another labor control system, the *repartimiento,* obligated Amerindians to work 45 days a year but with wages. Arriving Spaniards, eager to make their fortune, manipulated this system by advancing wages to ensnare Amerindians and then trap them in forms of **debt peonage.** This was functionally a form of slavery because once contracted, the workers were never able to pay off their debt (Lima-Dantas 1985).

Early in the colonial period, a church–state alliance developed in which the Pope granted the Spanish monarch the right to supervise establishing the church in the New World. Supported by fees, taxes, and Amerindian labor on church-owned estates, the spread of Roman Catholicism became a cornerstone of colonial culture. In Mexico, a 1531 vision of the "Virgin of Guadalupe" was accepted and used to promulgate an elaborate **amalgamation** of preconquest Amerindian religious identity with Roman Catholicism, creating a distinctly Mexican religious culture that continues today (see Chapter 8, "Religion in Mexico"). This blending of cultures had more secular expressions. The Aztec custom of *compadrazgo* was rooted in militaristic and religious culture that required strict obedience and loyalty to those in authority. Used by the Spanish to reinforce and legitimate their dominance over Amerindian labor, today we find modern Mexican economic, political, and social organization patterned on **patron–client** relations of responsibility and loyalty very similar in structure and function.

A mid-16th-century discovery of massive silver deposits in northern Mexico produced new immigration and the rise of a mining economy. Demand increased for commercial agriculture and laborers. Thus, the export mining economy multiplied its effects on the development of markets in New Spain, the name attached to Mexico by the Spanish colonial bureaucracy. To rule over this rapidly developing but very distant economy, Spain created a representative of the monarchy, a viceroy (vice king). Viceroys enjoyed considerable autonomy and ruled over a complex hierarchy of bureaucratic officials and administrators who closely supervised and regulated land, labor, and markets.

Spain's monarchy viewed its colonies as possessions that existed solely to enrich and strengthen the crown. Known as **mercantilism,** this political philosophy legitimated policies enforcing strict control of trade and a 20 percent tax on commerce. Land grants enticed Spaniards to migrate to Mexico (New Spain), but the agricultural economy that developed served one primary goal—the mining economy. Given vast silver deposits, Mexico's colonial economy produced wealth that flowed back to Spain and then, through trade, became part of the rapidly emerging dynamic capitalist manufacturing economies of northern Europe. Mexico became part of the rapidly integrating world system of trade as Mexican silver was shipped to Asia where it bought silk and spices (Cockroft 1983). In Mexico itself, however, Spanish merchants with commercial monopolies granted by Spain traded goods at very unfavorable prices. And what remained in Mexico was mostly in the hands of Spanish mine owners, *hacendados* (large landowners), and colonial bureaucrats.

Colonial Mexico's social structure revolved about the poles of race and class. Under the colonial legal system whites, *mestizos,* and Amerindians had distinct rights and responsibilities. As is the case in modern Mexico, virtually all the elite migrated from Europe or were whites born in the colonies. *Mestizos* and Amerindians were excluded from upper-class status. Individual Amerindians could not own property and paid special taxes. *Mestizos* competed for lower-level occupations but lacked access to jobs in the colonial administration. In a society built on race and class, privilege was legitimated by the Roman Catholic church's social services, its educational activities, and promotion of religious doctrines that stressed eventual equality before God.

The 18th century brought great changes in Spain and paved the road to independence for Mexico in 1821. When the Bourbons gained control of Spain's monarchy in 1701, Spain's mercantilist trading monopolies and heavy taxation began to be confronted by rising European competitors who sought access to colonial markets. Backed by governments whose military strength was now supported by a more fully developed capitalist economy and dynamic technological progress, English, French, and Dutch traders began to expand smuggling operations. In response, Spain effected a series of policies known collectively as the Bourbon reforms.

In brief, the Bourbon reforms were aimed at liberalizing trade, allowing more colonial ports to trade directly with Spain, increasing intercolony trade, and ending contraband trade by allowing tightly regulated trade between Europe and Latin America. The Spanish Crown, in turn, hoped to expand its dwindling revenues by taxing the increased trade. Once released from the bottle of regulation, the genie of free trade was a great incentive to Mexican merchants. Economic activity grew quickly, embracing a broad range of manufacturers, and mining output doubled during the last quarter of the 18th century. Mexico's colonial elite invested heavily and exports surged. Rapid economic expansion, however, increased the cost of food and other goods, especially for poor wage workers. A mandatory church tax of 10 percent led to greater social inequality and even greater land concentration. Large landowners and merchants used the financial obligations of poor colonists to gain access to more land or drive down wages. The colonial elite, however, were themselves constrained by the colonial administration. Spain sought to increase the efficiency of tax collection, repress any competing authority, and strengthen military control over its far-flung empire.

Colonial elites chafed as Spanish judges replaced those born in New Spain (Mexico). Spain expelled Roman Catholic Jesuits from Latin America and thus gained their property and eliminated a potential rival for power. The Jesuits controlled education, missionary activities, and fiscal administration of church economic activities. Thus, as the colonial economy boomed, the seeds of discontent and eventual revolt were sown in the increasingly intense social inequality between classes, the social inequality that relegated colonial elites to a lower status than those born in Spain, and relentless political control of a centralized **authoritarian** state.

Independence

Several factors produced early-19th-century independence movements throughout Mexico and Latin America. In Mexico, inflation, drought, agricultural collapse, and administrative problems produced instability and increasing resentment. Dramatic changes in Spain began to have profound consequences in Latin America and New Spain (Mexico). Allied with France's revolutionary regime in 1796, the Spanish naval fleet was decimated at Trafalgar in 1805. Napoleon Bonaparte invaded Portugal and then conquered Spain in 1808. In New Spain, loyalists to the old monarchy seized control and declared loyalty to the old Spanish state, now exiled to Seville. Over the next 13 years, Mexico experienced tremendous violence, social disorder, and physical destruction. Popular armies of *mestizos* and Amerindians loyal to Ferdinand marched on Mexico City with calls for an end to privilege and racial discrimination. They were defeated, but guerrilla groups continued fighting until 1821. The violence was so extreme that roughly 12.5 percent of Mexico's 4 million inhabitants died between 1810 and 1816 (MacLachlan and Beezley 1994, p. 3).

Violence and disorder throughout Mexico were rooted in the lack of jobs and poverty. Conspicuous wealth was present, too, derived from trade, special relationships with the government, and land speculation available only to the elite. Thus, the years leading to Mexico's independence shared many parallels with today. Economic growth and relaxation of trade controls led Mexicans to have high expectations. Faced with violence and widespread destruction, however, under the leadership of Agustín de Iturbide, a *criollo* born in the colonies, the *criollo* elite forged an alliance with guerrilla bands led by Vincente Guerrero in Oaxaca. Under the "Plan of Iguala" guerrilla bands flocked to join the new army.

Independence from Spain, however, did not produce peace, prosperity, or stability. A secure nation-state would not emerge before the late 19th century. Thus, the 18th century produced sovereignty but not legitimacy; a state but not a nation. Over the next century, Mexico lost approximately half its territory, had foreign troops on its soil, and suffered episodes of widespread regional conflict. Mexico's elite forged a pact between conservatives, who favored traditional social organization (mercantilism and religious conservatism), and liberals, who sought free markets, were **anticlerical,** and wanted to end protections for Amerindians and workers. Holding the lower classes and Indians responsible for the violence, they labeled them a negative influence and pursued repressive policies. Under this new consensus, the liberal and conservative elite, *criollos,* turned to Europe for Mexico's future. Hoping to offset the perceived "negative" influence of Amerindian culture, they proposed numerous policies aimed at encouraging European immigration. Few came, as most European immigrants went to the United States.

Mexico's 1824 Constitution gave considerable power to the federal states. In Mexico, as elsewhere in Latin America, 19th-century politics expressed a fundamental conflict between two elite groups—liberals, who supported a loose federal style of government, and conservatives, who supported a stronger central government. The army and Roman Catholic church were also important political actors. The army demanded scarce resources from a national economy ravished by civil conflict. The Roman Catholic church controlled vast resources. Liberals viewed a strong central government, powerful military, and lack of religious toleration for non-Catholics as examples of Mexico's backwardness. Thus, Mexican politics remained a source of conflict and instability, but the conflict was between elite groups; most Mexicans, poor, illiterate, and disorganized, had no voice in the debate and no influence over the outcome.

In the mid-19th century, regional elites led revolts against the central government in Mexico City. Texas, far from Mexico City, lightly populated, and virtually without administration, became home to numerous immigrants from the United States. Seizing the opportunity, settlers declared independence. Hoping to secure its "manifest destiny," the United States annexed Texas in 1845. The Mexican-American war that followed was disastrous for Mexico. At the treaty of Guadalupe Hidalgo ending the war, the United States paid a mere $15 million for Mexican territory that today comprises the states of Arizona, California, Colorado, Nevada, New Mexico, and some land now part of Utah and Wyoming (Lima-Dantas 1985).

Civil War and Nation Building

Humiliated by their defeat, Mexican elite factions turned on each other once again as liberals and conservatives blamed each other for the loss. Beginning in 1858, Mexico's civil war racked the nation as liberals and conservatives fought to control the state. By 1860, victorious liberals reigned over a country decimated by conflict. Mexico's infrastructure was in ruins, trade was nil, and foreign creditors were at the treasury demanding payment on debts. To back up these creditors, Britain, France, and Spain landed troops at Veracruz. The French troops captured Mexico City and set up a puppet government under a plan devised by Napoleon III. Ferdinand Maximilian Joseph of Austria was invited by the conservative Mexican elite to assume the crown. He accepted, but on his arrival the conservative cause was not well served and he failed to repeal laws the liberals had enacted in earlier years. Liberals sought U.S. help, but, ironically, the United States was embroiled in its own Civil War. When it ended, the United States sent troops and military support to help Benito Juárez's fight against the French. The French withdrew and the ill-fated Maximilian was executed. Mexico was once again a sovereign nation-state, but facing the last quarter of the 19th century it was wracked with obstacles to progress.

From 1876 until the Mexican Revolution of 1910, however, Mexico consolidated a fragmented republic, implemented much of Mexican **liberalism**'s plan, and brought the national government center stage, declaring "liberty, order, and progress" under the banner of rational, scientific social engineering. As in the past, while elites and professionals benefited, the cost of progress fell on the poor. When General Porfirio Díaz became president in 1876, he dedicated his regime to realizing progress though dependence on the United States. Mexico and the United States became "inseparable trading partners," anticipating the formal economic integration that finally would be secured a century later through the 1994 North American Free Trade Agreement.

Díaz openly courted U.S. government support and U.S. private investment. He also sought to establish himself as the personification of Mexico's "revolutionary" modernization process. The years of Díaz's rule came to be known as the *Porfiriato* and remain a powerful image for Mexicans. In Japan and the United States, these years were marked by great economic changes in the form of industrialization and urbanization. Mexico also saw important economic changes.

First, there developed an integrated regional economy that incorporated both sides of the northern border. Mexican migration north was an important component of this new economy. Second, Mexico reestablished its worth in international credit markets and began to attract foreign investment. Foreign loans and investments allowed Mexico to expand transportation, especially railroads, with exports to the United States increasing fast. Extractive industries, mining and oil production, grew quickly (MacLachlan and Beezley 1994, p. 99).

Volatile "boom and bust" cycles hit individual industries as world market demand surged and declined. The export–import economy lacked a well-developed national market to balance it. When foreign demand went down, Latin American economies collapsed. When demand for particular exports went up, investors in booming economic sectors became rich. Wages, however, remained low because there was no incentive to increase workers' pay. The Mexican government subsidized industry while it neglected those policies, especially education and land reform, that might have helped build a domestic economy independent of exports.

Third, Mexico's urban and transportation infrastructure improved and its cities gained some modern urban services. Finally, Mexico developed a commercial banking system aimed at facilitating foreign investment, but in the social and political culture that defined Mexican life, this physical and organizational infrastructure never achieved the level of functioning common to advanced market societies where a domestic mass market of widespread high-wage labor produced savings and development independent of foreign investment (MacLachlan and Beezley 1994).

The social and political structure during Mexico's *Porfiriato* saw large landowners at the top. This small elite denigrated traditional Mexican culture and identified with Europe as culturally superior. They were joined by Mexico's small middle class and influential foreign investors. The vast majority of Mexico's people lived a precarious existence devoid of social respect or political influence. With the economy oriented toward exports, **structural dualism** gave Mexico's peasants and urban workers no economic leverage. Child labor was widespread, and labor unions were repressed. Illiterate, destitute, and marginal, the poor constituted 90 percent of the Mexican population.

A unique Mexican institution, the *camarilla,* emerged as an organizing principle of Mexican society (see Chapter 2, "Politics and Political Institutions"). Founded in regional patriarchal family structures, the *camarilla* system formed a pyramid of authority, loyalty, and obligations extending up to the president and down through presidential selection of candidates and judges to control political life. Nineteenth-century *camarilla* politics were extended to other groups, and by the 20th century would involve organized labor, peasant organizations, and student groups. Porfirio Díaz may have been president and virtual dictator for several decades, but his political power operated within the strict limits set by the *camarilla* system. Each state was dominated by organized elite groups who struggled for local dominance, and Díaz functioned only with their support.

The Mexican Revolution 1910–1917

Porfirio Díaz's regime grafted political modernization onto Mexico's social and economic institutions. Mexico, however, had not yet developed a national elite class; regional organization and conflict defined the social fabric. Mexico's military, stripped of power during the 19th century, lacked adequate resources and training. The economic policy focus on export crop production undermined food production for domestic consumption. By century's end, Mexico was importing food to feed urban and rural workers. Food prices skyrocketed, and malnutrition was rampant. When international recession (1906–08) collapsed foreign demand for Mexican exports and restricted credit, the bust hit hard at all levels of Mexico's society but worst at the urban poor and landless rural peasant.

While demands for social reform built through the early 1900s, revolutionary conflicts began in 1910, when small-scale regional guerrilla groups rose up to challenge political authority and economic elites. Rural mobilization and violent conflicts would run through Mexican life for 26 years until President Lazaro Cárdenas nationalized cotton plantations and founded *ejidos* (see Chapter 3, "The Mexican Economy") as a communal organization of popular farm ownership extending land access to Mexico's rural poor. Once again, Mexico suffered great loss of life and destruction to property, with an estimated 500,000 to 2 million casualties and refugees from violence who fled north to the United States (MacLachlan and Beezley 1994, p. 253).

As with most revolutions, Mexico's found its early leaders in young, well-educated elite idealists who challenged Díaz's dictatorship in the name of liberal democracy. One, Francisco I. Madero, came from a wealthy family whose fortunes in cattle and mining were complemented by political connections and power in the state of Coahuila. Educated in Europe and at the University of California–Berkeley, the young Madero challenged Díaz in the 1910 presidential campaign. Díaz won reelection following widespread violent suppression of opponents. Madero then called for armed insurrection, declaring the election a fraud. Díaz shocked his opponents when he resigned and left Mexico, thus setting a precedent for many latter-day Mexican presidents. In the ensuing election, Madero was elected with great popular support and expectations for democracy.

Support, hopes for democracy, and the peace quickly collapsed. Madero, once elected, failed to understand the violent potential of his enemies. In 1913, his own military chief-of-staff Victoriano Huerta, with support from the United States through Ambassador Henry Wilson, assassinated Madero. Huerta, however, offered only a return to Díaz-style rule. When he assumed power, opposition movements erupted throughout Mexico. The Revolutionary years produced great popular military leaders—Emiliano Zapata in the south and Pancho Villa in the north. Zapata led landless peasants in the southern state of Morelos in a movement to reclaim traditional lands. Villa's opposition formed around the interests of ranchers and cowboys. Rather than seeking land reform and a return to small subsistence farming, Villa wanted to expropriate the large *haciendas* and under state control produce jobs and money for his military (Skidmore and Smith 1992).

The United States failed to continue support for Huerta, and he resigned in 1914 after condemning the United States for its betrayal. Opposition forces, however, were unable to consolidate their wide-ranging movements and interests. One group, led by an elite politician named Carranza, set up a separate government based in Veracruz. Now the battle was joined between the former opposition factions. In the end, buoyed by support from urban workers and benefiting from a stalwart military commander, Álvaro Obregón, Carranza forged a new national government based on the Mexican Constitution of 1917. The Constitution became the foundation of Mexican 20th-century government when convention delegates produced a document with strong support for Mexican peasants and urban workers. Nevertheless, in the end, Zapata was murdered and Villa defeated and pushed into a marginal rural resistance that posed no threat to the national government in Mexico City. By 1923, Villa fell to assassins, joining Zapata as an icon for Mexico's rural and urban poor.

Through the 1920s, first under President Obregón, himself assassinated in 1928 by a religious zealot, and then a series of two-year presidents, Mexico's political elite began to consolidate into Mexico's "official" party, the *Partido Nacional Revolutionario* (**PNR**), later renamed the *Partido Revolutionario Institucional* (**PRI**). The PRI dominated Mexican political life for 70 years, operating with virtually no competition until the late 1980s. Ironically, the major current opposition party, the **PAN** (Party of National Action) formed immediately after the Revolution, representing business interests that opposed strong government control of the economy.

Mexico's Miracle

The Revolution began with conflict between elite factions. The late 1920s brought formation of a new political elite that monopolized political office for the next 70 years. Much of the old elite, however, retained its economic and cultural status despite widespread violence by government and grassroots social movements.

Cárdenas's 1934–40 regime, facing international depression and domestic financial collapse, lay the foundation for Mexico's modern state. Mexico's political elite turned away from policies that marked the PRI's original development goals. Agrarian reform, support for Amerindian people, and social programs for urban working-class groups remained part of the PRI's revolutionary rhetoric. Economic policy, however, once again emphasized subsidies to industrial growth and commercial agriculture. Beginning in the late 1930s, Mexico experienced relatively continuous high rates of economic expansion, roughly 6 percent per year for over three decades. It had to do so in order to keep up with population growth, as the population more than doubled between 1937 and 1970. In Mexico and Latin America overall, the decades after World War II witnessed a profound alteration in the national fabric as virtually every country experienced rapid urbanization. By the late 1970s, Mexico was more urban than rural.

Economic expansion meant jobs. Investment in roads, mass transportation, and irrigation systems provided employment, too. Nevertheless, Mexico's "social pact" with its vast poor urban and rural population developed under an umbrella of protectionist trade policies and large-scale government ownership of major economic sectors. Mexico's "miracle" was deceptive. It reinforced and elaborated the **dual economy** of earlier eras. A small insulated elite became wealthier and remained socially and culturally distant from Mexico's working class in a society based on low wages and social stability. That social stability was maintained by the pervasive *camarilla* political culture when the impoverished working class was quiet. It was maintained by violent repression when students, peasants, or working-class groups protested in the streets.

As Mexico's miracle decades reached the 1970s, economic growth and low inflation were matched with increasing inequality and deteriorating living standards. The World Bank grouped Mexico with the "Asian Tigers" (Hong Kong, Indonesia, Malaysia, Singapore, South Korea, and Thailand), countries saluted for their rapid modernization and future prospects.

Debt, Crisis, and Austerity

Instead of reaching "take off" to higher living standards and a balanced economy, however, Mexico's development trajectory stepped off a cliff in the 1980s. Mexico through the 1970s depended on foreign investment and foreign credit to finance government programs.

These policies left Mexico with enormous debts and vulnerability to international markets. Caught in a squeeze between declining exports and restricted credit, Mexico's heavy debts quickly produced a government financial crisis that reverberated through the society (see Chapter 3, "The Mexican Economy"). For most Mexicans, the 1980s were a "lost decade." Average wages plummeted and poverty levels soared. Since 1982, Mexico has been transformed by its debt crisis. The PRI's "old ways" of running the country lost any claim to legitimacy, but it remained strong enough to enforce dramatic changes in social and economic policy. Economic crisis and population pressures built up a tremendous expulsive force for Mexican migration to the United States. While Mexico had been among the most heavily government-controlled and -owned capitalist societies, Mexico's elite responded to its 1980s crisis by privatizing government-owned industry, paying off foreign debts, and opening Mexico's economy to global competition.

In sum, Mexico has become an archetype of what is called **neoliberal reform.** Mexico's elite has committed the nation's future to complete integration with the international economy. Private business gained much greater influence, and Mexico joined Canada and the United States in a regional free trade area (**NAFTA**). The gamble is that Mexico's future development will be led by manufacturing export industries built by foreign investors. These economic and social changes have placed great pressure on Mexico's cultural and political institutions. With millions of Mexicans living and working in the United States yet retaining close family, financial, and political ties to Mexico, rural and urban cultures must cope with forces of global modernization "from below." Recognizing this powerful influence, in 1996 the Mexican government granted Mexicans the right to hold dual citizenship with the United States. Integration and fiscal crises have also forced Mexico's "official political party," the PRI, into competition with other parties, thus undermining its unquestioned dominance. Much as the Liberal Democratic Party of Japan was forced into a more pluralist multiparty environment, so the PRI's control of national and local politics has been undermined by internationalization.

Increased democracy at Mexico's national level, however, will continue to confront the entrenched political power of local leaders. It is difficult to judge whether the challenges facing Mexico will lead it to greater democracy and higher standards of living or see it revert once again to authoritarian repression of civil and human rights to protect the interests of economic and political elites (Otero 1996). Economic integration with the United States and the political influence of Mexicans living there may yet produce a more democratic society with possibilities of greater economic equality and political liberty for Mexicans. If this does not occur, demands for civil rights and economic justice, expressed by groups ranging from the rebels in southern Mexico to opposition parties, may produce another era of widespread conflict and destruction.

CONCLUSION

We cannot understand modern Mexico without knowing its epic ancient history, volatile economic development, and unique culture. For contemporary Mexicans, Mayan and Aztec society, centuries of colonial exploitation, and turbulent independence meld to form a mythic lens that reveals and distorts their everyday sense of identity. The 1990s are compelling Mexican culture to turn its vision to the future. A break with the past and reframing of Mexico's relations with the United States derive from the impact of global economic integration and massive migration to the north.

Some things never change. Mexico's geography and climate remain. Mexico's history created institutions and social processes that will shape the 21st century. The impact of population pressures, racial and ethnic composition, social inequality, and political institutions usually change slowly. Nevertheless, the meaning of Mexico's past may be reinterpreted. Ideologies of nationalism, male dominance, and institutional monopolies by the Roman Catholic church and Institutional Revolutionary Party (PRI) may not be able to sustain themselves when economic and political development demand change. The road to sustainable high-income economic development and political pluralism faces many obstacles. Not the least of these are widespread political corruption, military and police abuses of human rights, and the pernicious effects of a huge drug economy. Rural and urban social movements find fertile soil where exclusion and exploitation define most Mexicans' everyday lives. Had it not been for high levels of migration to the United States and resulting inflows of dollars sent to relatives, Mexico might have collapsed into anarchy by now. It still may.

Politics and Political Institutions

Mexico's political system defies simple categories. Peruvian novelist and Nobel Prize winner Mario Vargas Llosa told a 1990 Mexican national television audience, "Mexico is the perfect dictatorship." His hosts were not charmed. The facts are that from 1929 until the July 1997 congressional elections, the Institutional Revolutionary Party (known by its Spanish initials PRI) dominated political life at the federal, state, and local levels. Despite regular elections, some researchers viewed Mexico as evolving toward full democracy, but still far from it. The evolution gained speed as the "midterm" 1997 elections produced a geological shift in the terrain of Mexican politics. Cuauhtémoc Cárdenas, leader of the leftist **Democratic Revolutionary Party** (PRD), decisively won Mexico City's mayoral race. Until 1997, the mayor was appointed by the president of Mexico. The PRI lost its majority in both houses of congress and the governorship of its most industrialized state, Nuevo Leon. At the local level, opposition parties now govern 40 percent of Mexicans. Thus, in some respects, good government reformists, pragmatic business leaders in the north, and grassroots community groups have combined to present an alternative to Mexico's "perfect dictatorship."

Many social scientists, however, continue to regard Mexico as **authoritarian** due to violent government suppression of public demonstrations, independent unions, and **peasant** groups. One prominent researcher concludes that Mexico fits in the "rapidly expanding category of hybrid, part free, part authoritarian systems" (Cornelius 1996, p. 25). Mexico's political system is becoming more competitive, but elections are not necessarily fair or honest. Government commitment to political stability and labor discipline lacks the balance of support for human rights. Electoral fraud is widely regarded as ubiquitous, and selective repression of dissidents may include torture and murder by police and military.

POLITICAL STRUCTURE

On its surface, the political system of the United States of Mexico is structured much like that of the United States of America—a presidential system, three autonomous branches of government, checks and balances defined in the Constitution, and federalism with considerable state and municipal autonomy. In practice, however, Mexico is very different from the United States. The 1917 Constitution created a federal structure that emphasized local autonomy in the form of a *municipio libre* (a *municipio* is roughly equivalent in size and responsibility to county government in the United States). *Municipios* are governed by an *ayuntamiento*—a council—headed by a *presidente municipal*—mayor—who is elected to a three-year term. However, the *presidente municipal* is hand-picked by the PRI party elite, congressmen, and governors for the state (Cornelius 1996, p. 30). In recent years, opposition parties (discussed below) such as the Autonomous National Party (PAN) have begun to nominate their candidates at public conventions, and pressure has mounted for the PRI to conform.

President Zedillo (1994–2000) claimed he would not interfere in the party's 1995 candidate selection processes for governorships, but local political bosses protected their turf and little change occurred. Political centralism, the hallmark of Mexican political life under the PRI, continues despite pledges by every incoming presidential candidate to reduce it. In part, political centralism resists change because it is institutionalized. Each level of government depends on resources from above and loyalty from below. Thus, entrenched political bosses refuse to relinquish their authority, and with good reason. For example, the 1995 election for governor of the small (1.5 million population) impoverished southern state of Tabasco, won by the PRI candidate, was widely labeled a fraud. After the election, opposition parties documented PRI payments of U.S. $70 million in order to fix the election ("Mexico: Survey" 1995).

THE POLITICAL ELITE

The Mexican political elite, especially at the national level, is comprised of individuals almost exclusively from middle-class and higher economic backgrounds. Local and state political life may include former peasants and working-class individuals, but even here the European minority dominates. Mexico City, the focus of national political and economic life, produces a disproportionate number of leaders. Postgraduate education has become a key credential for access to elite political life. For example, Mexico's past two presidents, Salinas and Zedillo, have doctoral degrees from Harvard and Yale, respectively. As evidence that party politics, kinship, and *camarilla* relationships (discussed below) determine political careers, President Zedillo is the 5th Mexican president with absolutely no previous electoral experience. This so-called new class of technocrats, who rise to administrative and political power with no direct electoral experience, contributes to Mexican voters' widespread conviction that while the PRI remains in control, elections will be counterfeit. *The Economist* ("Mexico: Survey" 1993) concluded about Mexico, "Government is conducted by an unelected bureaucratic elite accountable only to the president."

This **technocrat** new class is not unique to Mexico. During the 1980s debt crisis, many Latin American nation-states found themselves facing a united front of creditors. In order to gain access to credit and investment, Mexico's government was compelled to negotiate with private banks in the United States, Europe, and Japan; lending institutions such as the World Bank and International Monetary Fund; and other governments. This situation greatly increased the power of internationally educated technocrats, members of the Mexican elite who had credentials and personal contacts Mexico needed for these negotiations.

Unlike the PRI elite of the 1930s when the president's cabinet was drawn from throughout Mexico, by the 1980s more than half the leadership called Mexico City home ("Mexico: Survey" 1995). This centralization of authority in Mexico City followed the increasing geographic concentration of economic power. For Mexico's political elite, being close to power became a means to economic wealth. Thus, many Mexicans echo the observation, "a poor politician is a bad politician."

MEXICAN POLITICS AND THE UNITED STATES

From the earliest days of Mexico's independence, the United States has played a role in Mexican politics. Attributed to Mexico's long-term 19th century dictator Porfirio Díaz, the often-repeated lament, "Poor Mexico! So far from God, so close to the United States!" has provided the title to more than one book. Much of Mexico's original territory was seized by the United States in the Mexican-American War of the 1840s. The states of Arizona, California, Nevada, New Mexico, Texas, and Utah were once part of Mexico, and this loss of sovereign territory rests at the heart of Mexicans' often resentful and suspicious attitudes toward their northern neighbor.

Cultural distance and suspicion, however, have not limited the development of a deeply integrated border economy or the continued intensification of trade and investment patterns. A broad array of U.S. industries has relocated in Mexico to take advantage of low wages, lax environmental regulations, and tax incentives resulting from treaties. Contemporary Mexican politics are influenced by the perception that these foreign investments look for social stability, low wages, government subsidies and incentives, including government development of the infrastructure desired, and a weak regulatory environment. The search for foreign capital to develop Mexico's modern economy echoes the strategy of Porfiro Díaz (1876–1910) during his dictatorship. Political goals, therefore, call for establishing an image of Mexican economic and political stability, a high priority for foreign investors.

Mexico's dependence on foreign investment and foreign markets for economic development has enhanced U.S. influence on Mexican politics. Mexicans living and working in the United States have become an important source of income and investment bolstering the Mexican economy. Mexican politicians, especially those from opposition parties, have reached out to this constituency seeking allies to challenge the PRI. U.S. federal government influence became institutionalized in 1993 through approval of the **North American Free Trade Agreement (NAFTA),** which integrated the Canadian, U.S., and Mexican markets. Then, in 1994, the United States helped to bail out Mexico from a new financial crisis by providing U.S. $12.5 billion in bilateral loans, credit swaps, and creation of currency stabilization funds. The U.S. government help came with requirements for accountability and a more open budget process. This implied criticism of Mexican government corruption has encouraged opposition parties to solicit inquiries from the U.S. and Canadian media regarding government involvement in the drug economy, electoral fraud, and suppression of human rights. Thus, the Mexican government allowed foreign observers to evaluate practices at recent national elections. Those observers found widespread PRI control of polling places and violations of established procedures (La Botz

1995). Despite U.S. political influence, the entrenched politics of stability and **corporatism** remain the day-to-day reality of Mexican political life.

POLITICAL PARTIES

The Institutional Revolutionary Party (PRI) has dominated Mexican political life since 1929. Through war and peace, booms and busts, disasters and revolts, population growth and falling standards of living, the PRI controlled Congress and every state governorship until 1989. It is an odd party, careful to conserve its power, but capable of radical policies and even more radical policy switches. Strong leaders dot party history, but none have become dictators, in part because Mexico's Constitution prohibits presidents from succeeding themselves. More important than the Constitution, however, is the underlying power of the *camarilla* system and its complement, the class of government bureaucrats. The Mexican elite political culture and practical system thus grants presidents great autonomy during their six-year reign. Some observers refer to Mexican presidents as *de facto* dictators. They rule for six years, then they are gone.

The PRI's presidential selection process brings to mind Winston Churchill's 1939 radio broadcast description of Russia: "It is a riddle wrapped in a mystery inside an enigma." No campaigns or presidential primary marks this landscape. Efforts to predict the party candidate are only speculations. The selection process is termed *dedazo* (*dedo* means finger in Spanish), and this term refers to the selection of a successor by each outgoing president. Through *dedazo*, Mexicans have institutionalized the *Porfiriato* (referring to Mexico's 19th-century dictator) model of a powerful leader who directs the nation.

The party's organizational structure reflects the **corporatism** and **clientalism** common to Latin American political life. By formally incorporating unions, peasants, and other "popular" interest group organizations (mostly representing the middle class) into the party, the PRI has co-opted and controlled potential sources of opposition. Differences are settled quietly and privately in a structure of highly centralized power that reaches straight back through post-Revolutionary Mexico and colonial rule to the Aztecs ("Mexico: Survey" 1995).

This pattern of political interest representation is known as *corporatism.* For many Mexicans, the distinction between the government and the party has been virtually meaningless. Privileged access to the media and government subsidies for PRI election campaigns stacked the deck against any opposition. Before the 1982 debt crisis began, PRI's corporatist structure allowed it to co-opt much of the population.

Since the crisis, austerity policies mandated by foreign creditors (banks, international agencies, and foreign governments) have undermined the structure of loyalty–resource exchanges. Sectoral organizations linked to the PRI were challenged by independent unions and social movements who were allied with opposition political parties. In this climate of declining support, the PRI began to open up party membership to individuals unaffiliated with organized sectoral organizations (unions, peasants, popular groups), and local party officials gained more control over candidate selection in their municipalities. Earlier, even local candidates were handpicked by the political elite in Mexico City. Nevertheless, federal candidate selection for the Congress and presidency remains firmly rooted in the hands of *camarillas* and the political elite.

PRI changes have come in response to public opinion and challenge from opposition parties. Seeking to survive in this new climate, the PRI has begun to formally disengage its party organization from that of the government. Local candidates now increasingly must be credible and demonstrate some competence beyond party loyalty. PRI's restructuring reflects the practices of opposition parties such as the **PAN** (National Action Party). Whether these changes will produce a change in the authoritarian, corporatist, and highly centralized presidential authority of PRI rule remains to be seen. Mexico's budget remains highly centralized. Over 80 percent of taxes are collected by the federal government, then distributed to local areas through agencies not accountable to local officials. Thus, opposition party gains at the local level may not express a true shift in power away from the PRI. However, the July 1997 midterm elections cannot be ignored. Gains in local, state, and congressional elections now place the majority of Mexicans formally under the leadership of PAN, PRD, and other parties opposed to the PRI (Bagley and Quezada 1995).

OPPOSITION PARTIES

Until the late 1980s, Mexico's opposition parties were ineffectual organizations that provided a forum for dissidents but channeled anti-PRI social groups into government-controlled arenas. They were given a voice and a few seats in Congress where they could denounce government policies. Yet they served also to strengthen the PRI's claims to widespread support by presenting the PRI with token opponents who focused discontent on electoral processes (Cornelius and Craig 1991).

PRI control of Mexican government and political life has been so thorough that several opposition parties, such as the People's Socialist Party (PPS) and the Authentic Party of the Mexican Revolution (PARM), have been controlled through clientalistic practices exchanging resources for support. These groups broke with the PRI in 1988, six years into Mexico's debt crisis and the austerity policies that produced a drastic decline in wages and standards of living for most Mexicans. They provided crucial support for an opposition presidential campaign. Leftist opposition parties formed a temporary coalition supporting Cuauhtémoc Cárdenas, son of a former president and a social democrat attractive to unionists and peasant groups.

After the election, Cárdenas formed a new party, the Party of the Democratic Revolution (PRD), which staked out a position on the left of Mexican politics. However the coalition did not hold. PRD offers a political image and rhetoric supporting core economic policies substantially different from the PRI or PAN. In short, PRD refutes the legitimacy of those neoliberal economic strategies (see Chapter 3, "The Mexican Economy") that have depressed the standard of living for most Mexicans. PRD itself has been the target of repression, and it claims that since 1990 over 300 party members have been murdered by the police and military ("Mexico: Survey" 1995).

Until the July 1997 midterm congressional and local elections, the National Action Party (PAN) has presented the only consistent opposition during PRI's near 70 years of rule. PAN's support base and policies have been very similar to those of Christian Democratic parties elsewhere in Latin America. Catholic intellectuals opposing government hostility to the Roman Catholic church and urban middle-class professionals make up most of the party. PAN's organizational focus and clearly stated policy stands made it the leading opponent to PRI. The PRI's increasingly neoliberal policies of the 1980s, however, undercut many of PAN's criticisms by adopting them.

In 1989, a PAN candidate became the first non-PRI governor since 1929. Frustrated by over five decades of political opposition, PAN's 1989 victory in Baja California marked a geological shift, according to some observers. Since then, PAN has won three more state elections and placed governors in Jalisco, Guanajuato, and again in Baja California. Some regard these events as a PRI tactic of allowing victory in order to gain credibility with foreign creditors and PAN support for domestic programs. But PAN governors such as Vicente Fox, governor of Guanajuato, have generated national followings. Fox, a tall, striking figure given to cowboy clothes, autonomy, and unflinching commitment to ethical and efficient government, looks much like turn-of-the-century progressives and reformers in the United States.

PAN mayoral victories during the 1980s brought an end to PRI promises of more open elections. In subsequent years, PRI candidates regained local power, but under a cloud of suspicion regarding electoral fraud. PAN's own supporters may constitute its greatest limitation as they seek economic policies aimed at helping Mexico's middle class but show little concern for values of democracy, equity, or community. Many PAN supporters would resist efforts to broaden the party's appeal to Mexico's less privileged population. PAN's geographic strength is in cities of the north and center—it has not developed a national program that incorporates rural and southern regions.

ELECTIONS AND VOTING PATTERNS

Electoral fraud is the historical hallmark of Mexican elections at local, state, and federal levels. In the late 1980s, groups challenging PRI electoral corruption began to protest and publicize instances of fraud. They challenged the president to implement reform, and Salinas responded with several acts such as overturning election outcomes. But the interventions appeared arbitrary and capricious. Thus, public confidence in democracy and the validity of elections remains low. In the 1990s, Mexicans have witnessed through mass media the impact of free and fair elections on the societies of Eastern Europe and South America. Mexican elections, however, remain more like those of Central America, where unfair and fraudulent election procedures predominate even when opposition parties exist and contest elections (Domínguez and McCann 1995, p. 174). Thus, Mexico's electoral system has limited the transition to a fully democratic political life where opposition parties may govern when they win elections.

Less than 10 percent of Mexicans believe that elections are free and fair, but in the context of Mexico's widespread economic and social problems, political corruption is not ranked as a top concern.

Voter turnout, however, does seem linked to perceptions of endemic election fraud. Between 1958 and 1982, the percentage of the voting age population who failed to register to vote fell from approximately 28 percent to 15 percent, while abstention rates for registered voters also fell, from 48 percent to 36 percent (Domínguez and McCann 1995, p. 160). These declines suggest that Mexicans' attitudes toward democracy have changed even if their views of Mexican politics remain cynical. In large part, changes in literacy, the role of the Catholic church, women's expanded role outside the home, and the rise of opposition political parties have all contributed to greater political participation rates. According to the Council of Freely Elected Heads of Government, a group founded and led by former U.S. President Jimmy Carter that is held in high esteem across the Americas for election monitoring, "While positive, the electoral reforms taken as a group fell short of establishing a foundation that would give all parties and all the people of Mexico confidence that a genuinely free and fair election would occur in August 1994" (Domínguez and McCann 1995, p. 179).

Nearly all Mexicans receive most of their official information about politics from television—only 8 percent say they use a medium other than television to obtain political news. Mexico has one dominant television network, Televisa, which is heavily influenced by the official party, the PRI. For example, during the 1988 elections Televisa's flagship channel, following charges of electoral fraud by PRI, presented all three presidential candidates when discussing the charges, but only used sound when Carlos Salinas, the PRI candidate, was speaking. The anchorwoman spoke over the two opposition candidates. State-owned channels are not much better with regard to bias (Harvey 1993).

The 1988 election, however, marked a watershed for Mexico's electoral system. The PRI's candidate, Carlos Salinas Gotari, officially claimed just over 50 percent of the popular vote. Manuel Clothier, the National Action Party's (PAN) candidate, received 17 percent. Most startling to official and academic analysts, Cuauhtémoc Cárdenas, Party of Democratic Revolution (PRD) candidate, former PRI governor of the state of Michoacan, and son of Mexico's much-honored president Lazaro Cárdenas (1934–40), officially won 32 percent of total votes. Cárdenas claimed that PRI election officials were corrupt and distorted the true election results. Both PAN and PRD supporters protested the election after government computers compiling election results inexplicably shut down for hours as votes were being tabulated. Two years later, as if to confirm their suspicions of fraud, President Salinas (1988–94) destroyed the election records.

CAMARILLAS AND CLIENTALISM

The concept *clientalism* refers to the reliance by political parties and political interest groups on government patronage. These patron–client relationships are the lifeblood of Mexican politics. In Mexico, the entire political culture is organized through an institutionalized hierarchy of relations wherein *patrons* who have political power provide resources to their clients, those with less rank, in exchange for loyalty, deference, and services. In Latin America, clientalism pervades virtually all government social programs and education.

Functionalist sociology would view clientalism as the continued prevalence of particularistic values as opposed to universalistic values. Clientalism therefore serves to maintain social stability by incorporating threatening groups into an exchange network. **Conflict theory** would interpret this pattern as the competition among interest groups rooted in control of economic and political resources. It would emphasize the fact that these networks include only a fraction of the total population and that those on the outside lack a voice, lack influence, and are excluded from rewards.

These exchange networks form a complex web of power/resource relationships much like a pyramid, with the president and his *camarilla* at the top. *Camarillas* have their own deeply entrenched culture but are composed of personal alliances usually traceable back to neighborhood, club, and school-based relationships that have long histories and intensively intertwined legacies of honor, status, and debt. Rivalries between *camarillas* are intense, and this intensity becomes more strident toward the top of the pyramid, since Mexican presidents serve only one term. When presidents succeed each other, *camarillas* also change position, reflecting existing relationships of loyalty. Once in power for a limited term, the network of patron–client relationships must work to secure and distribute resources. When the presidency changes, they will be out.

CORPORATISM AND POLITICAL INTEREST GROUPS

Corporatism is a concept that describes a political system in which functional groups such as unions, business associations, and peasant organizations are formally linked to the government and party through a bureaucracy, budget, and public policy. These organizations are dependent on the party and government for financial support and, when challenged, political pressure against competitors. The government depends on these groups to integrate and co-opt elements of the civil society through clientalistic bonds, the highly personal exchanges of loyalty and resources that saturate the dominant institutions of economic and political life. Corporatism is "inclusionary," as it brings into the government's funding and policies those organized groups that dominate important sectors of civil society. In the following sections, we discuss aspects of Mexican corporatism, including institutions outside the corporatist umbrella.

Religion

The Roman Catholic church is a powerful and pervasive political influence throughout Latin America. Until the 1960s, **liberation theology** movements called for social and economic change in the name of social justice and equality, the Roman Catholic church was an almost uniformly conservative political force. Since 1950, its significance has declined, particularly as nonreligious political parties have gained ground. Mexican governments since the Revolution have viewed the Roman Catholic church as an opponent to secular change and a threat to the political elite's authority. Nevertheless, well over 90 percent of Mexicans are baptized Roman Catholics, and government hostility to the Roman Catholic church's political influence is tempered by its commitment to stability.

During Spanish colonial rule, church and state were closely entwined, but soon after independence Juárez established formal separation of religious and secular authority in Mexico. The Revolution brought a decade of anti–Roman Catholic political campaigns in the 1920s so intense that churches were closed for several years. Only in the late 1930s was a semblance of peace restored by President Camacho. Accommodation between church and state produced Roman Catholic acceptance of government social programs and government acceptance of parochial schools for children of Mexico's elite, but Catholic opposition to the socialist component of economic policies remained strong.

For 130 years, since Mexico's 1859 Laws of Reform a liberal code guaranteed freedom of religion, separation of church and state, and confiscation of land owned by the Roman Catholic church (Blancarte 1996). Catholic church opposition to the Revolution led to

Folk Catholicism unites traditional community practices with celebration of St. Sebastian, the village patron saint. (Courtesy of the Inter-American Foundation; photographer, Philip Decker)

restrictions on all religious political participation. The 1990s legal reforms remove prohibitions on religious involvement in education and allow churches to own real estate and capital if they are "indispensable for their purposes within the requirements and limitations established by regulatory law." Clergy now have the right to vote, and some limitations on religious speech and publications have been removed. However, political meetings may not take place on church property. Finally, religious organizations must be registered with the government.

While these reforms modify the government's exclusionary anticlerical and strongly secular stance, the climate of suspicion and hostility continues. The 1993 assassination of Cardinal Posadas, archbishop of Guadalajara, has led many Mexicans to question these new government relations with the Catholic church and fueled belief that the PRI will not tolerate opposition and dissent, even from the Catholic church.

Unions

By the late 1930s, the **Confederation of Mexican Workers (CTM),** representing thousands of affiliated unions, was formally integrated with the PRI. Union leaders became an integral part of the clientalistic system. Closely linked to government and PRI policies, the

CTM-affiliated unions comprise 90 percent of Mexican unions and union members. Alliance with the government and PRI is so close that some unions are awarded congressional seats and government appointments. A large portion of union funds come from the government budget. Government regulation of union organizing, wages, strikes, and grievances has served to produce a low wage and a docile labor force. Labor officials who challenged policies were quickly dispatched, and union leaders who wanted to retain their privileged positions learned that political loyalty was the price. Unionized workers in Mexico, however, became a relatively privileged labor elite in exchange for tranquillity in the workplace. As the principal mass-based organization within the PRI, unions have enjoyed slightly more autonomy than other groups, peasants, and white-collar sectors. As in the United States, continuity of union leadership has been associated with stability (Middlebrook 1995).

Under the leadership of one man, Fidel Velázques from 1939 until his death in the summer of 1997 at age 97, the CTM, with roughly 5 million members, built its identity on internal discipline. Stridently anticommunist, the CTM is closely linked with the U.S.-based federation of labor unions, the AFL–CIO. Close ties with the PRI and entrenched leadership produced corruption. Labor leaders repressed any threats to their authority and cut deals with business owners. Loyalty to the PRI during López Portillo's 1970s presidency meant accepting low wage increases during a period of high inflation. The CTM gained, however, from government repression of independent unions, creation of a new Workers' Bank, and CTM control of the state housing fund (Riding 1986, p. 121).

Through the 1980s and 1990s, CTM's iron control of its affiliated unions, despite severe loss of earnings linked to devaluation of the Mexican peso, made it an active and central partner in the economic stabilization programs. Nevertheless, 15 years of economic crisis have undermined the CTM's power. Employment declined in its traditionally strong industrial sectors. Employment expanded in the nonunion *maquila* border industries and informal sector. Criminal convictions against union leaders strained the CTM–PRI relationship. The future relationship remains a cipher, but Mexico's political culture of clientalism continues to produce loyalty between the PRI and CTM (Middlebrook 1995).

Business

The modern business community first developed after the 1917 Revolution, but it was rooted in Mexico's class of large landowners.

Beginning with World War II, however, an industrial business class emerged and forged an alliance with Mexico's political elite based on a model of **import substitution industrialization (ISI).** While the political elite maintained a tight corporatist control of other interest groups, its authority remained unchallenged by private sector business, which operated in a limited but protected and subsidized national market. The relationship has been a paradox, as business leaders who benefited from government policies also chafed as the PRI excluded them from policymaking processes and appropriated large sectors of the economy for itself. Government-owned industries and economic sectors limited business opportunity and drove business associations to seek fundamental political change. That goal was not tolerated by the PRI, and conflict between private sector business interests and the government was frequent (Valdés Ugalde 1996).

Since the oil boom of the 1970s and 1980s debt crisis, political activity of organized business has expanded and intensified. First, the PRI's authoritarian rule and unchallenged corporatism have been fractured. Independent political movements and new viability for opposition political parties have given the business community new opportunity to voice its interests and lobby for policies that benefit private property. Second, privatization of government-owned industry, a hallmark of the late 1980s and 1990s neoliberal economic policies, was in part influenced by the political mobilization of a Mexican business community strengthened by links to foreign corporations.

Business political organization occurs through a complex of regional and national organizations representing employers. **COPARMEX,** the employer group, is a broad-based association with membership cutting across specific industries and economic sectors. CCE, the Entrepreneurial Coordinating Council, has affiliates at the regional level. CMHN, the Mexican Businessmen's Council, is restricted to the industrial elite. This associational complex is roughly comparable to business associations in the United States—for example, COCUS (Chamber of Commerce of the United States) and NAM (National Association of Manufacturers). In the United States, additional employer groups—NAIFB (National Association of Independent Federated Businesses), COSMA (Council of State Manufacturing Associations), and hundreds of trade and industry associations—create a complex, well-funded web of lobbying and public relations activities representing business at every level of government. They may target legislation and policies pertaining to their own narrow interests, but they often form alliances.

The Mexican associations form a network with strong interorganizational links and coordinated policy strategies. COPARMEX's 1929 origin was rooted in opposition to government labor legislation. Confederations such as CONCAMIN and CONCANACO were founded right after the Revolution to guide and coordinate the redevelopment. While these associations continued to have a role influencing government policies, it was only the shift to neoliberal economic policies under President Salinas that brought Mexico a profile of business activism similar to that in the United States. Valdés Ugalde's (1996) research concludes that Mexico's recent political transition has insulated a new coalition of business and public officials from democratic influence. Business is more influential, but other sectors of Mexico's civil society have not been able to construct political organizations independent of the PRI. Thus, Mexico's political transition in the 1990s has opened the state to influence from the business community while remaining firmly corporatist. Business interests are represented through a hierarchy of associations that affect policy through established links to government agencies but limit independent action or influence through political parties.

Military

Until the recent wave of democratization and slashed military budgets in Latin America, Mexico's relatively weak and docile armed forces stood in marked contrast to the large, politically powerful, and often interventionist military in most of the region. When the military ruled, Latin American budgets ranked arms and ordinance over social needs and often over economic development investments. By 1994, however, widespread return to civilian rule saw regional military spending decline from 3.1 percent of **gross domestic product (GDP)** in 1985 to 1.7 percent in 1994. ("Latin American Arms" 1996, p. 43). Mexico's military were never as strong as elsewhere. Military officials holding political office declined from 27 percent in the 1935–40 Cárdenas government to a mere 5 percent in the mid-1980s under de la Madrid (Cornelius 1996, p. 86). Military spending in Mexico was only 1 percent of GDP, by far the lowest of any Latin American country. During the 1990s, Salinas- and Zedillo-led governments have pressed the military into service as a domestic police force. While always subservient to PRI rule, the Mexican military has received considerable attention from PRI leaders who seek to shore up their support in the face of opposition political challenge, popular uprisings in Chiapas and Guerrero, and widespread alienation linked to declining living standards under austerity.

Peasants *(campesinos)*

Since the 1930s, Mexican governments cultivated support from the rural poor. They traded on the PRI's links to the Mexican Revolution, a continual campaign through rural education, agricultural policies, and mass media control. Most central were government policies redistributing land to peasants. President Cárdenas's 1930s regime institutionalized this relationship through the *Confederacion Nacional Campesina* (**CNC**). Virtually all peasant organizations were thus formally linked to the PRI. Since 1982, however, neoliberal policies of structural adjustment aimed at paying off Mexico's massive foreign debt have struck hard at peasant farmers. Subsidies have gone to large-scale **export sector agribusiness.** The end to land redistribution and social policies subsidizing peasants has strained traditional support for the PRI. In Mexico's poorest and least-developed states such as Chiapas, Guerrero, and Oaxaca, lack of access to land, despite seven decades of promise, has helped motivate armed peasant rebellions (see Chapter 11, "Social Problems and Social Movements").

CONCLUSION

Since 1988, Mexican political reforms have begun to combine with the effects of a global economy, especially economic and demographic integration with the United States, to bring about dramatic steps toward democracy. The official political party, the Institutional Revolutionary Party (PRI), continues to dominate Mexico, but the foundations of democratic opposition are well established and bearing fruit in local, state, and congressional elections. Fraud and corruption remain part of the political process and central to government practice. News reports detailing scandals involving Mexico's high officials and their families dot the weekly international press. Nevertheless, the now-independent **Federal Electoral Institute (IFE)** and private watchdog groups confirm that the 1997 midterm local, state, and congressional elections were the least fraudulent in this century. As Sergio Aguayo from Civil Alliance noted, "The opportunity for democracy is coming to Mexico." ("Mexicans Hand Defeat" 1997, p. A14).

The roots of pluralist democratic electoral politics appear to be more solidly established. Other democratic institutions and the guarantee of civil and social rights, however, remain remote dreams for most Mexicans, especially the urban working class and rural peasantry. For them, social protest, insurrection, and migration remain viable and, for many, necessary survival strategies. Mexico remains a Third World nation whose economic profile reveals profound concentration of wealth and income in the hands of a small elite. Such inequality presents a continuing barrier to full political participation and stable democracy. The impact of Mexico's burgeoning drug economy also threatens to limit and derail whatever trends we currently see toward competitive political life and efficient, effective, and honest democratic government (see Chapter 11, "Social Problems and Social Movements").

The Mexican Economy

The British journal *The Economist* ("A Survey of Mexico" 1987) refers to "Amexica the beautiful" to capture in a phrase Mexico's integration with the much larger U.S. economy. In a "second Mexican revolution," growing exports, manufacturing, and gross domestic product (GDP) derive in part from government policies promoting private investment, free trade, and reduced regulation. Mexico, a market of nearly 100 million people, has become the third-largest trading partner of the United States. But Mexican economic growth has not meant well-being for Mexican workers, who constitute a vast pool of cheap labor. Mexico has a population with an average income of less than 25 percent of average income in the United States, with an average age of under 20 years. Many doubt that Mexico will ever close the gap in living standards. Millions of Mexicans seek the American dream by migrating, legally and illegally, to the United States. If Mexico's economy is to provide Mexicans with a living standard approaching that of the United States, perhaps the nearly 20 percent of Mexicans living north of the border will be a factor in that transformation.

Social scientists who study economic development in Latin America, Asia, and Africa fall into two major camps. We can characterize one group as **structural functionalist.** Known as **modernization theory** researchers, they assume that entrepreneurs increasingly will spread modern social values and expand market-based institutions resembling those in Europe and the United States. They believe higher incomes, greater literacy, and democracy will result from unregulated market activity under governments that support private property rights. A second group supports **world**

system theory, which begins with the history of colonial exploitation and institutions linking Third World nation-states to a global economy. In that global economy, a **division of labor** between wealthy economically powerful states and former colonies consigns the latter to be exploited for their raw materials and cheap labor. This camp views national governments and local capitalists as part of a chain that maintains this division of labor. Economic and social inequality, as well as antidemocratic political institutions, are seen as outcomes of dependency.

Modernization theory concludes that prior to the 1980s reforms (discussed in the next section), Mexican authoritarian governments limited private business and excluded entrepreneurs from politics. This theory blames government ownership of large sectors of the economy and limited democracy for Mexico's low standard of living and distorted economic development. It presumes that recent free market reforms and privatization will lead to rapid economic growth, higher standards of living, and increased democracy. World system analysts, on the other hand, emphasize Mexico's vulnerability to international trade and investment patterns that embed Mexico in an unequal exchange relationship. They conclude that deregulation and privatization will increase inequality, depress living standards, and undermine democratic institutions that would give the majority of Mexicans, who are poor, some political influence. Recent market deregulation and privatization open Mexico to the forces of the global economy. This leaves most Mexicans with three options—migration, revolution, or destitution. In the words of economist Albert Hirschman (1970), they must choose between "exit, voice, and loyalty."

STATE AND ECONOMY

From the moment of Spanish invasion, through centuries of colonial control and then independence, mineral and agricultural exports defined Mexico's relationship to the world economy. First, Mexico was looted and pillaged, then it was taxed. Finally, caught in a web of trading and investment relationships, Mexico sold cheap and bought dear as its leaders prospered and the rest of its population paid. In recent decades, exports of minerals, petroleum, and agricultural products were complemented by growth of industrial product exports. This modern export economy developed under the umbrella of treaties creating **export production zones (EPZs),** which exploited Mexico's cheap labor and lax regulations.

Most Mexicans, however, saw their standard of living decline. In sum, for over five centuries, value has flowed out of Mexico and into the **core** of the world system, although some Mexicans and the Mexican state have prospered.

In this century, Latin America's import–export economic structure made the region highly dependent on U.S. and European markets. Economic crises like the 1930s Depression hit the region hard at first. In response, governments sought to develop economic strategies that would reduce their dependence by building domestic industry and jobs for urban working-class populations. These policies promoted a political opening wherein labor organizations were courted as a political resource. In Mexico and Brazil, unions were viewed as a potentially important political base that would mobilize popular support for these nationalist industrialization policies and maintain social stability. Government subsidies for domestic industries produced products almost exclusively for the national market, not for export. High tariff barriers protected these industries from competition with foreign products. Social programs subsidized costs of food, utilities, and public transportation for urban workers. This strategy succeeded for three decades until the 1960s. Behind these barriers developed an industrial capitalist class. It did so not in a competitive market economy but rather in one subsidized and protected by an activist government.

Since the Revolution, Mexico's federal government has played a pivotal economic role. The post-Revolution decade saw little growth outside mining and oil production. Echoing the destruction wreaked during Mexico's independence wars, civil war destroyed the transportation infrastructure and the financial system and decimated agriculture. Foreign investment dried up. With the onset of a worldwide depression in 1929–30, Mexico embraced domestic policies that placed key economic sectors under government control. Railroads were nationalized and numerous large estates expropriated. High tariffs on consumer imports and currency devaluation provided protection for Mexico's manufacturing sector. Creation of rural development banks and nationalization of the oil industry further insulated Mexico from world markets, but government policies, including further cuts in the value of Mexico's peso, encouraged exports. Investment in roads encouraged expansion of national markets.

Following World War II, the government implemented policies guaranteeing advantages to Mexico's wealthiest industrial, banking, commercial, and landowning families. These policies were at the heart of Mexico's three "miracle decades." First, the government intervened to control and suppress widespread demands for programs that would improve wages, provide access to cheaper consumer goods, and redistribute wealth more equitably. During this period, much of Mexico's economy was directly owned by the state, making it the nation's largest employer, investor, and entrepreneur. Mexico's growth rates averaged over 6 percent and inflation was low. Able to produce and export oil even during the years following **OPEC**'s embargo, Mexico seemed, by the late 1970s, to have made an economic transition that was parallel to the "demographic transition" (see Chapter 10, "Population") taking place at the same time. Mexico's rapid pace of economic growth, however, was fragile and vulnerable. Aiming to limit popular protest and provide incentives to wealthy Mexican and foreign investors at the same time, Mexico kept taxes low and financed large-scale infrastructure development (roads, rail, communications, etc.) with loans from foreign banks and international agencies such as the International Monetary Fund and World Bank.

This "debt-led development" worked well when export markets grew fast, credit was cheap, and the economy, buoyed up by subsidies and cheap domestic oil, expanded yearly. The crunch came in 1979 when the U.S. Federal Reserve, its central bank, put the brakes on double-digit inflation by restricting the money supply. Private banks and international agencies responded to the resulting higher interest rates by cutting back loans and demanding strict financial accountability by debtor countries. Mexico was the first Third World government to crack, and in 1982 it threatened to default on its loans. Bankers and politicians worried that Mexico might set off a cascade of debtor government defaults and collapse the entire world financial system.

In response, organizations like the **International Monetary Fund (IMF)** and **World Bank,** sources of credit for short-term trade and long-term development, were joined by transnational banks and governments in the advanced capitalist nations. They cobbled together a flexible but coordinated policy of renegotiating and rescheduling loans, but imposed specific measures on borrower countries who sought to reschedule loans at the new higher rates. These national policies included: (1) devaluation of the national currency, (2) reduced public spending, (3) elimination of public subsidies, (4) wage restraint, (5) increased interest rates and taxes to force lower consumer demand, (6) elimination of state-owned or state-supported industries, (7) more open access to foreign investors, and

(8) application of savings to pay off the debt to foreign banks, governments, and lending agencies such as the IMF and World Bank (Canak 1989).

Mexico's government fulfilled all these demands. Mexico implemented a neoliberal economic model that "stresses the need to give much freer reign to market forces both domestic and international" (Cornelius 1996, p. 105). Mexico abandoned its long-established commitment to an import substitution industrialization (ISI) model that protected domestic industry and a national market that developed behind a wall of high tariffs and subsidies. The new neoliberal model has aimed to open Mexico to the global economy and expand exports, even at the expense of domestic consumption and standards of living. After decades of subsidies and strong government control of the economy, however, this transition was difficult for many in the political elite to fully accept. Thus, President Salinas (1988–94) mobilized the National Solidarity program to once again distribute resources through patronage and co-optation, but located under an umbrella of political rhetoric claiming the PRI's commitment to social justice. Despite the National Solidarity program, since the early 1980s Mexico's neoliberal policies have hit hard at wages and living standards for the poor and much of Mexico's middle class.

Faced with declining world prices for Mexico's exports, limits on industrial exports to the United States, and high interest rates, the government capitulated to demands by the World Bank, International Monetary Fund, and private investment bankers. Dramatic economic restructuring policies slashed employment for public employees, provided subsidies and incentives for those companies with export potential, and began the privatization of many state enterprises. Airlines, petrochemical companies, and mining began the process. In the 1990s, privatization included the national telephone company, TELMEX, steel companies, and banks. Out of 1,150 state corporations operating in 1983, only 200 remained in 1993 (Teichman 1996). Finally, in 1994, NAFTA opened Mexico's financial sector to foreign bank subsidiaries.

In 1995, Mexico's government once again faced financial collapse and the prospect of defaulting on loans. Forging a new export industrial economy required Mexico to import equipment and parts. Consumer imports increased rapidly as tariffs were removed. In sum, while imports grew 238 percent between 1985 and 1992, exports expanded 73 percent (Otero 1996, p. 7). In 1994, foreign investors who had flooded Mexican markets during the previous few years quickly withdrew their capital. Convinced that

Mexican collapse would reverberate through world financial markets, President Clinton lent $12.5 billion to shore up President Zedillo's new government. The loan, however, came with conditions that Mexico implement severe austerity policies.

The loan was repaid, three years early, in January 1997, when improved trade and government finances convinced international banks to let Mexico refinance its loan from the U.S. federal government. While the Mexican government was widely praised, Mexican workers paid a high price in lost jobs, bankrupt small businesses, and lost homes for thousands of Mexicans who could not pay mortgages. Skyrocketing crime rates and continued low wages remain the legacy of this bailout. Recession produced dramatic declines for Mexican imports, especially consumer goods, and thus Mexico now enjoys a trade surplus. The long-term outcome for the Mexican economy remains unclear. Industrial growth and trade surpluses may produce a more sound government audit and rising stock market, but they come at great cost to Mexico's average citizen.

INDUSTRY

Mexican industry rests on three pillars: petroleum, mining, and manufacturing.

Petroleum

Mexico's oil industry originated in the late 19th century when foreign oil exploration companies were encouraged by dictator Porfirio Díaz. Petroleum exports were just beginning in 1910 when the Mexican Revolution intervened. Despite the resulting chaos, by the 1920s Mexico was second only to the United States in oil production. Mexico's 1917 Constitution, consistent with a pattern in all Latin America, declared mineral resources to be property of the state. Private companies operated concessions that strictly regulated exploitation of Mexican oil reserves. While exploration and production continued at reduced levels, Mexican government insistence on strict controls and worldwide discoveries of vast oil resources elsewhere limited foreign interest in Mexico's reserves. Virtually all of Mexico's petroleum production was exported, and virtually all of that went to the United States.

In 1938, President Cárdenas, looking to the populist 1917 Constitution for legitimacy, nationalized the oil industry and created **PEMEX** (Mexican Petroleum Company). PEMEX soon became a vast and powerful state bureaucracy, absorbing much public investment and providing great opportunity for political corruption and economic malfeasance. Foreign oil companies whose property was nationalized retaliated by asking the U.S. government to boycott Mexican exports. Under pressure from the U.S. federal government, however, they eventually settled with the Mexican government, receiving compensation amounting to a fraction of their investment. Mexico's oil industry grew and was supplemented by the discovery of large natural gas fields near Texas. Thus, Mexico's manufacturing and transportation industries were able to develop with access to cheap domestic petroleum, an advantage enjoyed by very few Third World countries and one factor that aided rapid economic growth during the post–World War II decades.

The 1970s witnessed discovery of vast untapped oil and gas reserves in Mexico. This discovery coincided with the OPEC (Organization of Petroleum Exporting Countries) cartel's 1973 action to increase world oil prices. For Mexicans, the availability of new petroleum and gas reserves produced heated debate over whether to pump it out fast to get money for development needs or conserve it and solve Mexico's problems slowly but autonomously. Despite production quotas, escalating trade imports led officials to increase oil production, most of which was exported to the United States. But in the early 1980s, exports dropped by half, and the world market was awash in oil after OPEC's cartel lost control—some exporting countries, including Mexico, had taken advantage of artificially high prices and increased unofficial petroleum exports.

Mexico's 1980s economic restructuring—slashing federal budgets and public employment, devaluing the currency, eliminating high tariffs on imports, and privatizing public corporations—did not spare the petroleum sector. By 1992, these changes culminated in PEMEX's reorganization as a holding company over four subsidiaries. Transformation of Mexico's petroleum industry produced two important outcomes. First, the Petroleum Workers Union, long the wealthiest and most powerful labor union in Mexico, saw its membership decimated and political power undermined. Long a bulwark of Mexico's corporatist and patron–client relations, which stifled dissent, marginalization of petroleum workers signaled major political changes for the country. Second, contracts for exploration and development have drawn foreign investments into Mexico's oil industry for the first time in decades (Quintanilla and Bauer 1996). Now partially open to the global market, investors are rapidly integrating Mexico into their global corporate strategies.

Petroleum, however, has attained a symbolic status closely linked to Mexican sovereignty. Opening the industry to global markets threatens the Mexican state's image as defender of the nation.

Mining

Mexico's geology, rich with diverse minerals, allows Mexico to be a major exporter of numerous metal and nonmetal deposits. The lure of gold and silver drew Spaniards to colonial Mexico. While gold and silver remain important, over 40 different minerals are currently exploited in Mexico's three major mining zones, the northern region, the Gulf coast states, and the west coast states. Porfirio Díaz stimulated foreign investment in the late 1800s by granting concessions for mining operations, and until the 1970s, 95 percent was foreign owned and controlled (Osterling 1985, p. 199). By the mid-1980s, legislation radically altered the nature of ownership, until 90 percent of mining concessions were operated by Mexican corporations. Once again, wealthy Mexicans connected to the PRI reaped windfall gains. Benefits to the average Mexican have been minimal, but nationalist rhetoric legitimated the policies. In the 1990s, new legislation once again opened mining to foreign investments.

Agriculture

Structural dualism typifies Mexican and Latin American rural economies. A vast population of peasants work small subsistence plots or as landless agricultural workers. Most rural Mexicans are officially defined as poor by international agencies. Large-scale plantations, ranches (*haciendas* or *estancias*), and commercial farms comprise the other side of Latin America's rural profile. Large estates typically are owned by families who trace their social status back to the colonial period or by subsidiaries of multinational corporations exporting to the global economy.

The Mexican Revolution mobilized poor rural farmworkers behind banners proclaiming the goal of equitable land distribution. For landless peasants throughout Mexico, access to land, especially the great estates owned by a powerful rural elite, was a glorious and distant goal. During the Porfirio Díaz dictatorship (1876–1910), landowners successfully concentrated and centralized their control. One percent of the population owned 97 percent of the land. A mere 260 families owned 80 percent of Mexico ("Mexico: Survey" 1993). In contrast, 96 percent of rural families were landless workers on the estates (Osterling 1985, p. 119). It was a world of extremes—wealth and poverty, with little between.

Thus, land ownership and access to water became cornerstone articles of the Mexican Constitution. Land reform and land ownership, however, remain linchpins of rural social problems and political disputes. Nearly half of Mexico lacks well-documented property titles. The 1910 Mexican Revolution's rhetoric targeted huge land holdings accumulated by an elite closely tied to the government. The immediate aim was to expropriate land without payment and distribute it to the peasant communities. Mexican government leaders, however, sought to attract foreign investments and encourage wealthy Mexicans to invest in export agriculture. Land redistribution was very limited and economic policies did little to subsidize revitalization of peasant communal agriculture. Instead, commercial agriculture expanded and highly concentrated land ownership continued. The Revolution promised an end to poverty, access to land, universal education, and freedom from hunger. However, by the 1990s, the promises had not been fulfilled, and a lack of land, education, and sufficient food and income remained deeply entrenched in Mexico's **rural social structure.**

Most of Mexico's rural population subsists beyond the reach or interest of government agencies and policy. Those agencies and policies have been focused, instead, on the needs of agribusiness, especially the export sector. Large-scale commercial agribusiness has benefited from government subsidies to extend irrigation, build roads and communication, and provide credit and access to agricultural extension services. Much as in the United States, technocrats provide information vital to improving productivity and marketing strategies (Myhre 1996).

One uniquely Mexican agricultural institution is the *ejido. Ejidos* are communally owned lands that peasants may farm through various means, some individual and some collective. Peasants have use of the land *gratis* but cannot sell it, transfer title, or take mortgages, nor can they rent it out—they must farm it themselves. The *ejido* was originally legitimated as a policy that recognized Amerindian's inability to cope with markets and private property systems. Complex legislation regulated these collective peasant lands, and the Mexican Congress continued to revise statutes and governance into the 1970s. The *ejidatarios* (peasants living and working on *ejidos*) were a vulnerable population lacking education and political organization. Ironically, recent changes in the legal status of *ejidos* will allow the sale and privatization of *ejido* lands.

Ejidatarios, however, comprise the vast majority of rural Mexicans and farm nearly half the farmland in Mexico. Within the *ejido* sector one can find a great variety of farm size and type. Surveys of peasant farms found the majority were very small, less than the equivalent of 30 acres. While legislation provided for both individual and collective farming, more than 9 of 10 *ejidos* are individual. Despite a lack of access to credit and government help, this population of small illiterate farmers has survived. However, it has never prospered—in fact, it remains among the poorest sectors in Mexico. Low productivity and food prices artificially kept low by the government in order to subsidize urban consumers have forced much of Mexico's rural farming population to work for wages on large commercial farms. In a sense, the *ejido* sector subsidized and maintained a large low-wage rural working class, thus cutting costs for agribusiness.

Mexico's small and middle-sized "family farm" sectors together make up about 30 percent of farm plots. Small farmers working holdings under 13.5 acres (5 **hectares** in the metric system of measurement) are mostly oriented to subsistence production of corn, beans, and other legumes. They typically supplement farm production with income from craft activities conducted in the home and wages earned by working on large commercial farms. Implementing **family survival strategies,** individuals may migrate to the United States or work as maids in urban areas. Medium-sized farms comprise a very small percentage of Mexico's farm sector. They resemble North American family farms in their cultivation of commercial crops, although these vary greatly by region, ranging from grains and animal husbandry in the north to coffee and tropical foodstuffs in the south.

The large landowners with farms larger than 540 acres (200 hectares) are commonly estimated to comprise under 3 percent of farms but over 80 percent of private sector land holdings (not *ejido* or government owned). Despite constitutional provisions allowing the government to expropriate land holdings over 100 acres, Mexican administrations throughout this century have failed to take action against this powerful but small population. One reason has been Mexico's reliance on high-productivity agriculture exports to obtain foreign exchange. In recent decades, northern Mexican farmland, benefiting from heavy government infrastructure investments, became an important source of winter fruits and vegetables for the U.S. market, competing with California and Florida. With credit from the Mexican government, these large farms imported technology and became highly mechanized. Displaced Mexican workers faced one more limitation on their ability to sustain themselves, and pressure increased for migration to urban areas or the United States.

Mexico's agricultural economy was hit hard by the 1980s debt crisis and subsequent economic reforms. Twenty years earlier, Mexico's farm sector, balancing a vast but unproductive small farm and *ejido* population with a commercial export sector, failed to produce sufficient food crops to meet the **basic needs** of Mexico's urban working class. By the mid-1990s Mexico's agricultural gross domestic product (GDP) fell below that of 1965. Despite a favorable climate and sufficient arable land to support a population of 200 million, Mexico was importing corn and wheat and became the world's largest importer of milk ("Mexico: Survey" 1993). In response to mounting peasant protests, 1970s Mexican governments had increased farm sector spending. Highly politicized, however, the top-down highly bureaucratic policies undermined an efficient domestic farm sector. Corruption, lack of adequate credit, poor coordination of programs, and the concentration of small farmers on poor quality land resulted in a sequence of failed harvests.

Through the 1980s and 1990s, Mexico's agricultural economy became the focus of policies linked to the debt crisis and aimed at implementing World Bank and International Monetary Fund programs to diversify production and reduce taxes on trade. During the Salinas presidency (1988–94), reforms reduced government subsidies and withdrew government programs targeting the peasant sector. Legislation permitted collaboration between the *ejido* farms and large-scale commercial farms. In sum, the policies aimed to open the agricultural economy to market forces. Within 15 years, NAFTA will end all tariffs on corn, beans, and powdered milk.

Long-run prospects do not favor small farmers and the *ejido* sector, but social mobilization and political protest may well influence future outcomes, just as they have in the past (Gates 1996). Roughly 2.4 million farm families who produce corn, roughly half the entire rural population, face economic disaster. They and subsistence farmers will be driven into Mexico's factories, service sector, and U.S. labor markets as they migrate north.

MAQUILADORAS AND MEXICAN MANUFACTURING

In 1965, Mexico passed legislation allowing factories to be built on its northern border in order to spur industrial development and growth of manufacturing jobs for its rapidly growing population. *Maquiladora* is a Spanish word that refers to factories located on

Mexico's northern border. Almost entirely foreign owned, these factories import goods in order to assemble them or use them in manufacturing and then reexport them without tariff (import–export taxes). Prior to 1983, all *maquiladora* industry products were exported, but new legislation that year allowed 20 percent of *maquiladora* products to be sold in Mexico provided they contained a specified portion of Mexican components. Since passage of the North American Free Trade Agreement (NAFTA) in 1994, the proportion of new *maquiladoras* in regions away from the border has expanded rapidly. These companies were attracted by Mexico's relatively cheap and docile labor force, the lax enforcement of Mexican labor laws, and equally weak enforcement of environmental regulations.

Owned mostly by U.S.-based corporations, but with increasing investment by European and Asian companies too, Mexico's *maquiladora* industry has evolved through several stages since 1965. During the first decade, *maquiladoras* focused on a labor force of young single women with little or no industrial experience. Taking advantage of lower labor and manufacturing costs, U.S. companies rapidly expanded operations. In 1974, 455 factories employed 75,974 workers; by 1995, more than 600,000 Mexicans worked in *maquiladoras*. While the original legislation required foreign investors to have

Women's labor in factories at home provides essential income for most Mexican families. (Courtesy of the Inter-American Foundation; photographer, Miguel Sayago)

CHAPTER 3

Mexican partners, by the middle 1970s this restriction was lifted except for textile and garment industries (Kopinak 1996).

During the mid-1970s, a U.S. recession tied to the first OPEC oil embargo produced lower growth and some job losses, highlighting Mexico's increasing integration with the North American market. But rapid growth resumed quickly as Mexico's export-oriented growth strategy attracted more companies seeking to lower their production costs while remaining close to the U.S. market. Today, parts of northern Mexico, from Monterrey in the east to Tijuana just across the border from San Diego, are leading Mexico out of recession because their economies are so thoroughly enmeshed with the U.S. economy.

Uneven economic development reduces the impact of *maquiladoras* on Mexico as a whole. A mere 2 percent of parts and supplies originate in Mexico, so these jobs fail to spawn more jobs and business for other Mexicans. *Maquiladoras* have failed to produce an export industry for the rest of Mexico. Analysts attribute this failure to several sources. First, much of Mexico's entrepreneurial talent flees to the United States or seeks out jobs in the *maquiladora* industries themselves. Second, Mexico's banking and financial system fails to support fledgling and start-up industries. Third, government data fail to provide accurate information about costs, supplies, and markets. Fourth, transportation costs over Mexico's road system are so high that shipments to Los Angeles from Asia cost less than from Mexico City. Finally, the extreme centralization of government regulations and high levels of corruption slow down business and stifle innovation ("Mexico: Survey" 1995). In sum, *maquiladoras* will not act as a catalyst for more widespread Mexican development until fundamental cultural and political changes take place.

Subsequent to Mexico's 1982 debt crisis, a devalued peso and reduced regulation improved Mexico's capacity to compete with Asian countries as a low-cost producer. Employment in *maquiladoras* mushroomed. With a new factory opening every five days, some 34,658 jobs were created between 1984 and 1986. Rapid expansion produced changes in the labor force, as more males were hired overall. Nevertheless, this continued to be a predominantly female labor force, especially in factories located away from the border. The 1990s saw a strong formal commitment by the Mexican government to using *maquiladoras* as an instrument to redirect Mexico's economy from import-substitution to export-led growth. Dedicated to the proposition that foreign investors would save Mexico, the Salinas government pressed for expansion of an existing U.S.–Canadian treaty to include Mexico. The result was the North American Free Trade Agreement (NAFTA). NAFTA integrated Mexico's economy with those of the United States and Canada, creating a regional economy free of tariffs and restrictions on investment. Salinas hoped that by dropping trade barriers and fully integrating Mexico with the U.S. and Canadian economies, he could increase employment, attract investment, and build a more balanced Mexican economy.

As NAFTA is implemented over a period of years, this regional economy may restrict the operations of European and Japanese corporations that had taken advantage of tariff-free production in Mexico to process their goods for the U.S. market. No taxes will be required by Mexican-, U.S.-, or Canadian-owned companies that produce and distribute within the three-country market. In essence, the goal of Mexico's political elite has been to modernize its industry using NAFTA, then gradually reduce restrictions on selling goods in Mexico.

Along the U.S.–Mexico border, *maquiladoras* have become concentrated in four zones closely linked to counterpart industrial areas in the United States. First, the Pacific center, located between the northwest Mexican cities of Tijuana, Tecate, and Mexicali, has close organizational and market ties to the California economy. Second, just south of Arizona and New Mexico, a western center has developed around the cities of Nogales, Agua Prieta, and Hermosillo. A third center, about midway along the 2,000-mile border near Ciudad Juarez and Chihuahua, is closely linked to the U.S. midwest industrial heartland. Finally, along the Texas gulf coast region one finds *maquiladoras* integrated with Texas industries and economies extending north to Chicago. NAFTA develops a regional division of labor within the world system. With the United States as its core, this regional bloc integrates various industries and markets. Something very similar has developed in East Asia, as Japan's advanced economy has integrated with newly industrialized countries where raw materials and cheap labor are distributed across several **semiperipheral** (South Korea, Singapore, Taiwan) and **peripheral** (Philippines, Malaysia, Indonesia, and China) nation-states (Gereffi 1996).

Mexico's lack of tariffs, low wages, well-developed transportation and communications systems, and, until now, political stability makes it an attractive site for investments within the North American bloc. As this regional economic bloc expands to include the Caribbean and Latin America, Mexico will consolidate its status as a semiperipheral country with moderate wages and capital-intensive or high-technology industry. Service industries and intellectual property industries, such as publishing, music, and software, will also expand, taking advantage of Mexico's lower costs.

The impact of NAFTA and *maquiladoras* on the American economy is becoming clearer in 1997. A recent empirical analysis of plant closings and threats of plant closings uses data from more than 500 union-organizing campaigns between January 1993 and December 1995. Bronfenbrenner (1997) found that in 59 percent of U.S. factories, employers threatened to close the plant and move to Mexico. Where unions actually won elections to represent workers, 12 percent closed the plant, triple the rate prior to NAFTA. The study concludes that NAFTA, integrating high- and low-wage economies, creates a climate that allows coercion, threats, intimidation, and law violations to exist. Combatting this will require substantial reform of current U.S. labor laws and amendments to the North American Agreement on Labor Cooperation (Bronfenbrenner 1997). Thus, Mexico's economic transformation and the growth of *maquiladoras* reverberate through economic and political lives on both sides of the border.

Radical deregulation since 1989 transformed the structure of Mexico's industrial economy. Trucking, electricity, mining, and tourism were "cleaned" of rigid price controls and work rules. Privatization and general deregulation have followed. Yet many of Mexico's economic sectors remain monopolized by single companies. CEMEX controls over 60 percent of the cement industry. Ninety percent of Mexico's glass is produced by one firm, Vitro. Televisa's monopoly is no longer complete, but it owns 25 percent of its nearest competitor, which has about 20 percent of the audience. Vitro, Cemex, ICA, and Televisa are controlled by one family ("Mexico: Survey" 1993). While these large firms are demonstrating the capacity to increase productivity and some have expanded overseas, small and mid-sized Mexican companies face a bleak future. Bankruptcies have soared as NAFTA tariff reductions expose these companies to competition from U.S. firms with much higher productivity. Those small and mid-sized firms trying to compete face problems getting access to credit. Analysts predict many more Mexican companies will not survive the shock of open competition.

CONCLUSION

Mexico presents a paradox. Its stable government, vast mineral resources, arable land, and proximity to the United States should guarantee modern Mexico wealth and prosperity. Instead, since the

16th century defeat of Mexico's grand Amerindian indigenous civilization, demographic collapse, economic peonage, and chronic cycles of boom and bust have defined its economic history. Independence wars in the 19th century and Mexico's Revolution in this century produced human carnage and widespread destruction. Even as Mexican manufacturing and agricultural exports have grown, as they did in the 1990s under NAFTA, most Mexicans saw their economic status decline. As a result, millions of Mexicans exploited the one quality that distinguishes Mexico from all other Third World nations—the 2,000-mile border with the wealthiest economy in the world. Migrants commonly send a large portion of their wages to family members who remain in Mexico. Thus, foreign wages have become a key component of the Mexican economy.

Mexico's integration with the U.S. economy rests on its status as a low-wage manufacturer, its cheap agricultural products from large-scale subsidized agribusiness; its rich and diverse source of minerals, including petroleum; and its growing market for U.S. exports. In Mexico, the growth of *maquiladoras* first on the border and, after NAFTA, in other regions, has produced rapid expansion in such industries as automobiles, textiles, electronics, and pharmaceuticals. NAFTA has also opened Mexican markets to lower-priced, higher-quality consumer goods from the United States, displacing expensive and shoddy goods from local firms that previously operated without competition, protected by high taxes on imports.

Nevertheless, since 1982, millions of Mexicans have seen their real wages decline and a drastic drop in living standards. On the U.S. side of the border, NAFTA's impact has been the focus of debate and dispute. U.S. exports to Mexico and Canada increased rapidly, but imports from both countries grew even faster. Thus, the U.S. trade deficit under NAFTA grew 332 percent between 1993 and 1996. Declines in U.S. manufacturing employment have been linked to NAFTA, as firms relocate factories to Mexico to take advantage of lower wages and lax environmental regulations.

In 1997, Mexican's real hourly wages are more than 25 percent below where they were in 1994 and 37 percent under their 1990 levels. Two-thirds of Mexican workers lack any fringe benefits, and nearly one in five works for wages below Mexico's minimum wage. Rather than buoying up prosperity, economic growth and increased trade saw millions of Mexicans fall into poverty. The question remains whether Mexico can sustain its current development model while avoiding social chaos.

CHAPTER 4

Mexican Stratification and Mobility

To be poor in Mexico, and most Mexicans are poor, means a life where meeting basic needs is often a dream and no more. A few chickens, a single room of adobe (mud and straw bricks), a fiberglass roof, and a door made of scrap metal define home for millions of urban and rural Mexicans. Hard work and frugality bring no hope of prosperity or upward mobility despite widespread faith that education may one day help children. For Mexico's typical professional and middle-class families, home often means two cars, servants, multistory concrete dwellings with polished wood floors, running water, electricity, and sewage. For them, education and stable **formal sector** jobs usually mean some association with the state and politics. For the elite, Europe and the United States are familiar business and vacation stops. Multiple homes, servants, and conspicuous consumption define the norm. For almost all Mexico's elite, close association with the government and PRI (Institutional Revolutionary Party) has been typical, not rare.

For both extremes of Mexican society, **social mobility,** whether up or down, is overwhelmingly influenced by Mexico's relation with the United States. In the 1980s and early 1990s, while Mexico's poor faced extreme poverty and destitution, the middle class discovered its world collapsing as a devalued currency and restricted government budgets undercut their lives. Meanwhile, the lure of a booming U.S. economy and a wave of foreign investment and culture washing through Mexican life create intense contradictions. Profound wealth and opportunity for the Mexican economic and political elite cannot be separated from the everyday reality of children working the streets to feed their families.

Sociologists commonly categorize Mexican society into three classes: upper, middle, and lower. Those distinctions are only meaningful if we recognize the vast gulf separating regions, rural and urban economies, and the unique role of Mexico's corporatist culture. Nevertheless, we can use these concepts to describe Mexico's system of stratification and patterns of social mobility. Some Mexican families are among the world's wealthiest. At the other end of the spectrum, Mexico's poorest quintile (20 percent) is destitute even by the standards of the poorest developing countries.

THE UPPER CLASS

Sociological profiles of Mexican society estimate the upper class at between 5 and 6 percent of the total population. Mexico's Revolution transformed the nation, as a powerful authoritarian state imposed itself on a traditional social order. Yet Mexico's elite has sustained great continuity. In keeping with the highly institutionalized and segmented structure of Mexican society, individuals and families are linked to organizations in business, politics, labor, and the church. Upper-class status is always embedded in one of these principal components of **social structure.** In the post–World War II era, however, one can simplify these divisions into two domains—economics and politics—that define and identify Mexico's elite. And within the economic elite there is an important distinction between rural and urban groups, the one tied to land ownership and the other to manufacturing and commercial interests.

Mexico's elite always has been extremely cosmopolitan. Until recent years, its cultural orientation was distinctly European. French was a more typical second language than English. Today, however, Mexico's political elite is more likely to have pursued advanced studies in the United States. Racially, the economic and political elite is much more likely to be of pure European ancestry than are other Mexicans. This has been an active and class-conscious group, organizing to influence government regulations and laws that affect them. Their sense of national loyalty and identity, however, did not prevent them from engaging in "capital flight" by sending billions of dollars overseas when Mexico faced its 1980s economic crisis. Mexican investments in U.S. as well as European banks and real estate limited Mexico's capacity to cope with the crisis and intensified its negative impact on the rest of the nation.

The Economist ("Mexico: Survey" 1995) notes that despite economic growth, integration with the U.S. economy, and foreign investment, "power remains in remarkably few hands." A few families control entire economic sectors such as banking. A handful of companies dominate each industry and do so through strong connections to the PRI.

Mexico's upper class benefited from government import substitution industrialization policies after World War II. They monopolized national markets, protected from foreign competition and subsidized by policies that provided cheap energy and enforced low wages. Old traditions linking families through marriage led to the formation of **industry groups** that shared information and resources. These multibusiness alliances are somewhat akin to Asian industry groups, which also build on family relations and link businesses within and across economic sectors.

Perhaps the most famous industry group is Mexico's Monterrey Group. This group originated in the city of that name, an industrial center where the Garza Sada family began in brewing but developed a conglomerate of businesses in finance and manufacturing. Sociologists have identified dozens of industrial groups spanning Mexican society. Politically and economically diverse, they all are elaborations of family-based business organizations. As elsewhere in Mexican life, a hierarchy of power and status defines these groups. Thus, the Monterrey Group stands at the peak of a pyramid of industry and business groups that all have close subordinate relationships.

Alejo Peralta, who died in April 1997, epitomized the first generation of Mexican industrialists. His father ran a small sewing machine business. In 1939, Peralta began a small business making candles, then added one making buttons. By 1943, he owned companies making electrical goods, and by 1996 his conglomerate, *Industrias Unidas Sociedad Anónima,* covered dozens of companies making everything from pens to phones. *Forbes* magazine estimated Peralta's worth at U.S. $2.5 billion. As with other industrialists of his generation, Peralta's close relationship with the PRI paid off handsomely though government subsidies and contracts.

Mexico's rural landowning elite can be traced back to the early days of Spanish colonial control. Large landholdings convey a social status in Latin American society, and Mexico is no exception. In Mexico, large landowners, some of whom control extensive ranches or export-oriented fruit, vegetable, and grain holdings in the north, others of whom control plantations in the tropical southern states and Yucatan, typically have diversified business activities with investments in banking, manufacturing, and other sectors.

A political upper class emerged from the Mexican Revolution and uniquely authoritarian "official party" status of the *Partido Revolucionario Institucional* (PRI). Social mobility through the political party has been linked to widespread corruption. Thus, political office has been a path to material wealth for some Mexicans. In recent decades, Mexico's political elite has been associated with advanced education in technical fields. A few exclusive public and private universities and colleges produce virtually all of Mexico's political elite, but many have also pursued advanced degrees in the United States. The last two Mexican presidents, Salinas and Zedillo, have doctorates from Harvard and Yale, respectively. Mexico's academic elite also has become integrated with its counterpart in the United States as training, research, and academic exchanges link university cultures in the two nations.

THE MIDDLE CLASS

Twentieth-century industrialization, urbanization, and the growth of government and large business bureaucracies led to growth of the middle class. Comprising about one-quarter to one-third of the population, Mexico's middle class contains several important groups but lacks any coherent sense of identity or common purpose. White-collar workers in the public and private sectors are the traditional core of Latin American middle classes. They are joined by professionals. **Petit bourgeois** (self-employed) small business owners and managers are a third sector of the middle class.

Latin American elites conserved family property through inheritance norms. This meant that the eldest son typically inherited the family land and other forms of property. With large families, this often meant that many children inherited little or nothing. Families conferred access to education on these children. Thus, much of Latin America's middle class has the memory of downward mobility, if only through family stories, and carries with it aspirations to emulate elite language, behavior, and values. Upwardly mobile members of the middle class are no less conventional. Materialist values predominate. Middle-class values emphasize proper language, manners, and dress. Both the middle class and the elite avoid manual labor. In Mexico and Latin America, manual labor and practical skills are associated with lower-class status.

From the Mexican Revolution until the 1990s, **civil servants** and professionals made up the most important core of Mexico's middle class. Organized into unions and linked politically with the PRI, their economic and social status have been closely tied to the government and ruling party. While incomes were moderate, their status guaranteed job security, pensions, social security, and various subsidies, such as public housing and access to better schooling for their children. Since 1982, however, middle-class incomes have dropped, although the **cost of living** for an urban middle-class lifestyle in Mexico and Latin America remains very comparable to costs in the United States. When the debt crisis hit Mexico and the peso's value dropped fast, the wealthy already had their savings in U.S. dollars. Mexico's poor had nothing and so they lost nothing. The middle class has never recovered. In response, they have become an important resource for opposition political party support and protests against government human rights violations, environmental policies, and election fraud (see Chapter 11, "Social Problems and Social Movements").

THE LOWER CLASS

Mexico's lower class is far larger than the upper class and middle class combined. For lower-class Mexicans, life chances and standards of living vary greatly. Life in cities provides access to more resources and opportunity than rural Mexico. Those who work in the formal sector tend to have better pay and working conditions than those in the informal sector. Some poor Mexicans have relatives in the United States who send money. Lower-class Mexicans survive at extremely low wages by engaging in a wide variety of strategies to cut costs and use resources to the maximum (see Chapter 7, "The Mexican Family"). Although Mexico has an official minimum wage, a high percentage of Mexicans earn much less.

In urban areas, many lower-class Mexicans, and much of the middle class as well, work multiple jobs. Families will pool resources and incorporate multiple income earners into a mix of wage earning and other economic activities to support the family unit. Links to family members in rural areas and the United States may provide access to additional resources, with food from the former and cash transfers and commodities from the latter. Labor unions provide an important resource for slightly less than one worker in five, but for lower-class Mexicans, membership in a union provides much greater job security and fringe benefits, including subsidized housing and pensions unavailable to others.

Roughly one-third of Mexico's urban workers survive in the informal sector where government regulation over wages, hours, and working conditions is not enforced. Child labor, always pervasive among Mexico's rural poor, is also common in the urban informal economy. Their labor became a vital component of lower-class **family survival strategy** during the 1980s and 1990s. The Mexican debt crisis and general economic decline pushed millions of lower-class Mexicans below minimal subsistence levels just as government slashed basic needs programs directed at housing, nutrition, and health. With many lower-class families earning roughly one-fourth the income estimated to provide subsistence-level consumption, families cut back on food, overexploited themselves by taking on additional work at any price, and left formal sector housing to construct shacks in squatter settlements that ring Mexico's cities.

STRUCTURAL SOCIAL MOBILITY

Changes in role and status may be considered as characteristics of individuals, families, or social categories. Thus, when we evaluate social mobility in Mexico, our analysis must look at individual mobility and structural mobility. The latter type refers to broad changes in the occupational and class categories within which Mexicans live and work. Throughout Mexico's history we find a high degree of social mobility. Changing one's occupational or class position has usually involved geographic mobility—migration. For most Mexicans, that has meant movement from rural to urban environments. In recent decades, migration to the United States has influenced social mobility in Mexico. **Binational labor markets** have integrated the two nation-states as millions of working-class and middle-class Mexicans were drawn to higher wages across the border.

Poverty and highly concentrated wealth, income, status, and power typify Latin America. The region has one of the most inequitable distributions of wealth in the world system—core, semiperiphery, or periphery. The relative income of the top 20 percent of the Latin American population exceeds the income of the bottom 20 percent by almost 12 times (Lustig 1992). Economic and social inequality are historically embedded in Mexican society. The vast majority of Mexicans, 90 percent, are either **subsistence farmers** or low-wage urban workers, especially in the informal economy (Allensworth and De Wit Greene 1990). Patterns of **land tenure,** asset distribution, and differential access to services and opportunities for social mobility, especially education, have intensified inequality in Mexico and Latin America (Barkin 1990, Krooth 1995).

Since the 1988 election of President Carlos Salinas Gotari, a Harvard-trained economist, Mexico's commitment to market forces, **privatization,** and reduced government regulation has been unsurpassed. By shrinking the state and opening the economy to global competition, Mexico's leaders hoped to increase productivity and sweep away impediments to market growth embedded in old social institutions. The economy has grown and Mexico's exports increased rapidly when foreign corporations built factories whose products are flowing to the rest of North America. Leaders argued that **modernization** and economic growth would improve incomes and raise living standards for all Mexicans as the benefits of progress "trickled down" to the urban and rural working class.

In response to comments that economic policies would have effects "in the long run," British economist John Maynard Keynes replied, "In the long run, we are all dead." For most Mexicans, these words have hit home as their quality of life declined significantly. Family and individual incomes fell from levels common to "middle-income countries" of the world system and hit levels typical of the poorest nations in Asia and Africa. Many more Mexicans found themselves reduced to working in marginal jobs and multiple jobs in the informal sector. The impact was so profound that wages fell from 37 percent of the gross domestic product (GDP) in 1986 to 26.4 percent in 1994. Real income, the value of wages to purchase housing, clothes, food, and other necessities, was only 40 percent of its 1982 level. Thus, Mexicans have experienced widespread downward structural mobility for over a decade (Graizbord and Ruiz 1996).

Mexicans officially in poverty grew to nearly 15 percent of the population during the 1980s. Inequality, already severe, became even more dramatic as the poorest 40 percent of families saw their share of **national income** drop from 14.4 percent in 1984 to 12.7 percent in 1992. Mexico's wealthiest 20 percent had income growth, and their share of all income went up from 49.5 to 54.2 percent. The middle class saw its proportion of income drop from 36 to 33 percent. Thus, an open economy and rapid growth were purchased at great cost, and the price was paid by Mexico's poorest citizens. Meanwhile, Mexico's wealthiest population enjoyed spectacular financial gains. By the middle 1990s, the top 10 percent of Mexicans earned 37.9 percent of the nation's total income (Gollás 1994).

REGIONAL PATTERNS OF INEQUALITY

Regional stratification parallels inequality in other areas of Mexican life. In short, the southern states of Chiapas and Oaxaca, the central state of Hidalgo, and the Yucatan, states with large Amerindian populations and historically the most rural, poor, and politically marginal, have the most extreme levels of inequality and the deepest poverty. Wealth is geographically concentrated in a few states with the largest metropolitan populations and concentrations of banking and industry. The Federal District (Mexico City, Mexico's capital), Jalisco, Nuevo León, Tamaulipas, and Veracruz have 77 percent of savings accounts and 95 percent of investment banking activity (Graizbord and Ruiz 1996).

Urban Mobility

Mexico's economic elite enjoys a lifestyle similar to wealthy citizens of the United States and other developed nation-states. Mexico City's elite neighborhoods have architecture, amenities, and services similar to those in North American suburbs in Canada and the United States. The houses are large, often constructed of brick, and typically house one nuclear family. It is not unusual for the patriarch of a wealthy family to purchase a house for himself and at the same time purchase plots of land nearby for each of his children (Lomnitz 1984).

Urban planning in Mexico has reinforced unequal development patterns. Money dedicated to urban planning has been concentrated on developing **central business districts (CBDs)** and the elite residential neighborhoods nearby. Residential planning and low-cost housing for the poor are virtually nonexistent. In large part, Mexico's poor live in *barrios* (neighborhoods) without planned streets, potable water, sewage, utilities, or other services.

Most Mexicans live in poverty. Fifty percent of Mexico City's working population resides in shanty towns that developed as squatter settlements (Lomnitz 1984). A radical rural to urban population shift began in the 1930s. The Mexican government, however, did not respond to the shift with aggressive urban planning (Bennet 1992). Population increase and inadequate urban planning led to housing shortages, especially for the poor. The latter were often displaced from low-income communities when their neighborhoods were targeted by real estate developers. Without access to affordable housing, Mexico's urban poor were forced to become squatters.

Residents of these shantytowns typically construct one- to two-room houses in densely packed neighborhoods. Their tiny houses are constructed from an eclectic mix of materials, including wood, tin, cardboard, and stone. Often, two or three generations live together, sharing resources and collectively engaging in what social scientists term *family survival strategies.* When first formed, these shantytowns seldom have access to urban services such as sewers, electricity, and water. High levels of underemployment and unemployment in the formal sector are usually compounded by few welfare benefits.

Rural Stratification, Poverty, and Inequality

After the 1980s economic crisis, living conditions throughout Mexico became desperate for many poor and even middle-class Mexicans who saw the value of their savings and wages plummet. The rural population suffered the most. Poverty and economic inequality are present in both urban and rural areas. Overall, however, urban conditions tend to be much better than rural areas, where government social programs are only a rumor. In 1989, almost 70 percent of Mexico's poor were in rural areas (McKinley and Alarcón 1995). The eight poorest states, where two-thirds of the **Amerindian indigenous** population lives, had a mere 17 percent of the gross domestic product (GDP). Illiteracy in these states is over 20 percent (Lustig 1996, p. 163).

Rural income inequality reflects land-owning patterns. In Mexico, rural Amerindian indigenous populations consistently have been forced to forfeit their land to wealthy landowners whom the government felt would more productively use the land. Land reform to ease unequal ownership patterns is much discussed but rarely implemented. Today, productive land is concentrated in large plots close to 3,000 acres and typically owned by wealthy *mestizos.* The rest of the largely indigenous rural population is left to farm "microplots" of land that are typically too small, infertile, and lacking in resources to support a family. Lack of access to irrigation intensifies much of the small farm sector's problems with poor quality soils.

A large percentage of the rural and indigenous population is either self-employed small farmers or wage workers employed by large landowners. Poverty is most severe among these two groups. In the southern state of Chiapas, where most of the population is of pure Amerindian ancestry, few areas have access to basic services, and many areas even lack roads. According to the 1990 Mexican census, half of Chiapas's homes lack potable water, one-third lack electricity, and over half lack sewage connections. Illiteracy rates also greatly exceed the national average, and infant mortality rates are the highest in Mexico (Nash 1995). Other rural states in the south face similar conditions.

Infant mortality, unemployment, and poverty are all substantially higher in Mexico's rural areas. Government policies have used the agricultural economy to subsidize urban and industrial growth. When the government's debt to foreign banks and international agencies spawned a fiscal crisis in 1982, debt service took half the federal budget. Austerity policies enacted under demands by creditors cut hard into budgets for health, education, and the wide array of government subsidies that provided some cushion for Mexico's poor.

If the cost of government cutbacks hit hard at Mexico's rural and poor in the 1980s, it did not come as a surprise. Mexican governments from 1946 to the present were committed to **supply side** economic policies that aimed first to concentrate wealth. Government policies aimed at equity and redistribution would have to wait until Mexico achieved economic development. Thus, the majority of Mexicans never saw the fruits of the Mexican miracle. In the 30 years before the debt crisis produced plummeting real wages and lowered standards of living for Mexico, absolute poverty did decline. The middle class grew to nearly 30 percent. Yet measures of economic disparity increased. Income and wealth (capital in the form of land, stocks, bonds, and savings) became less equal (Felix 1982).

Social indicators document the full impact of this level of inequality. By 1989, more than 25 percent of rural children were malnourished, double the rate just one decade earlier; 78 percent of Mexicans began elementary education but only 54 percent completed elementary school; 57 percent of dwellings in 1990 had no sewage connections, 50 percent were without fresh water, and 13 percent lacked electricity. In a 1996 "Olympic Profile," U.S. television praised Mexico's premier marathon runner, whose village is located not far from Veracruz, for pressuring the state's governor into extending electrical service to his village.

CONCLUSION

Mexican stratification embraces a complex web of social, political, and economic relationships quite distinct from those found in the

United States. First, the impact of region and rural–urban location determines access to resources regardless of one's class status. Second, traditional bonds linking family relationships to extended networks of resources and loyalty, *compadrazgo*, extend throughout Mexican society. They influence access to jobs, education, housing, and most factors that comprise standard sociological measures of class and status.

Race and ethnicity importantly determine one's social status in Mexico, but with the vast majority of Mexicans identified as *mestizo*, racial identity and race relations play a very different role in Mexico than the United States. At the extremes, Amerindian indigenous Mexicans, especially in rural and southern states, are much more likely to be extremely poor and marginal to government programs. Mexico's political and economic elite often physically resemble northern Europeans more than they do Mexico's indigenous population. But the United States has no population whose social status compares with the racial identity of Mexico's *mestizo* "cosmic race."

Social mobility data for Mexico are very poor, but we can conclude that education and migration are central to upward mobility. Migration takes two forms, rural to urban migration and migration to the United States. Each type is linked closely to both individual and family mobility. Many Mexicans, however, have experienced downward structural mobility during the 1980s and 1990s as real wages declined in the face of government austerity policies and Mexico's integration with the global economy.

Gender Relations

All societies socialize men and women into distinct **gender** roles. Through gender role socialization women learn to be feminine and men to be masculine—and just what roles and responsibilities come with these identities. Gender roles determine, to a greater or lesser degree, women's and men's place in social institutions such as the family, economy, and polity.

Matthew Gutmann (1996) observes that what it means to be a man or a woman in Mexico today is less clear than ever before. The masculine ideal "is no longer the pistol-packing *charro* (cowboy) of yore, looking for a tranquil rancho where he can hang his sombrero" (p. 6). Recent research into female gender identity in Mexico also reflects change. Mexican women are no longer universally *las mujeres abnegadas* or self-sacrificing and docile women. They are less likely to accept a subordinate position in the household or community (Gutmann 1996; LeVine and Correa 1993).

Changes in gender roles and relationships in Mexico can largely be attributed to several recent economic and political transformations. First, economic necessity pushed vast numbers of women into the wage labor force. In Mexico over the last 20 years, the rate of women's economic participation has increased 67 percent (Inter-American Development Bank [IDB] 1995, p. 57). Second, women's educational attainment increased. Currently, approximately as many girls as boys complete primary school (though girls less often advance to secondary school). Third, between 1970 and 1989, the average number of children born to a Mexican woman dropped from 6.7 to 3.4 (LeVine and Correa

1993). Finally, all of these factors, combined with a special concern for family welfare, persuaded women to increase political involvement, personally and collectively.

Gender roles in any society reflect both continuity and change (Gutmann 1996). A gender analysis of Mexican society reveals several consistent patterns of gender inequality. First, Mexican **social norms** continue to relegate women to certain "feminine" tasks and men to certain "masculine" tasks. While a **gender division of labor** is common to most nations in the world, it has a unique patriarchal justification in Mexico. Second, while women have made significant gains and have achieved some equality in economic and political spheres, men continue to dominate the formal economy and polity. In addition, domestic violence, which hinders women's ability to fully participate as citizens, is widespread (see Chapter 11, "Social Problems and Social Movements"). Third, the social costs associated with **structural adjustment programs** in the 1980s have been unequally shouldered by women, who in Latin America typically have less power and fewer bargaining resources than men (IDB 1995). Export-led growth in the 1980s, which accompanied structural adjustment programs, altered the gender division of labor. A mostly male-dominated workforce was made "flexible" and "feminized" (Moghadam 1995). A redistribution of women's traditional domestic responsibilities, however, has not paralleled increased economic responsibilities for most women.

Finally, previous research indicates that men and women in developing nations do not benefit in the same manner from development programs (IDB 1995). It is necessary to understand the relations between men and women and the position of each gender in the broader society to understand their variable ability to obtain and control the resources that result from economic, political, and social change.

To focus our review, the following definition of gender and gender analysis will be used in this chapter:

> The concept of gender is a system of socially ascribed roles and relations between men and women, which are determined not by biology but by the social, political, and economic context. Gender roles are learned, they can change over time. It is the analysis of these roles and relations which shows the imbalances of power, wealth, and workload between women and men, and it is this analysis which may then lead to the possibility and necessity of change (GENESYS 1994, p. 60).

PATRIARCHY AND SEX ROLE STEREOTYPES IN MEXICO'S GENDERED PAST

Patriarchy's historical role in Mexican society defines the nature of gender roles in modern Mexico. In patriarchal societies, male authority is the rule. In Mexico's past, male authority was supreme in virtually all relations: family, sexual, social, economic, and political. Patriarchy provided normative legitimation for a gendered double standard of sexual and social behavioral norms.

The *cult of machismo* has shaped Mexican men's behavioral norms since the colonial era. *Macho* men are expected to demonstrate strength, aggressiveness, and fearlessness in their relations with other men and patriarchal control over their spouses and children. *Macho* men have uncontrollable sexual appetites and engage in sexually aggressive relationships with their spouses as well as numerous sexual affairs. Personal and family pride are the historical foundation of masculinity. Thus, "honorable" men are the primary breadwinners for their families (*jefe de familia*) (MacLachlan and Rodriquez O. 1980).

Machismo is an internationally familiar concept, now part of popular vocabularies outside of Latin America, including in the United States. The less popularized corresponding behavioral ideal for women is the cult of *marianismo*. *Marianismo* also dates to the colonial era and links behavioral characteristics associated with the Virgin Mary, such as patience, spiritual strength, and moral superiority, to "real" and "good" women (Stevens 1994). *Mariana* women are expected to be *abnegada* (self-sacrificing), *ahorradora* (frugal), *dócil* (obedient), and *aguantadora* (capable of almost infinite emotional and physical endurance) (LeVine and Correa 1993). In contrast to men's fervent sexual desire, *marianismo* requires virginity for unmarried women, fidelity for wives, and abstinence for widows (Stevens 1994).

Unlike colonial men, women could not possess honor, but they could damage family honor, and thus family social and economic status, by not conforming to the established codes of behavior. Instead of honor, *mariana* women developed a proper sense of shame (*vergüenza*) and respect for the moral order of society. *Vergüenza* is a moral characteristic similar to innocence—once lost, it is gone forever. Thus, the fear of losing one's sense of shame and facing public sanction provided women with the motivation to conform to accepted behavioral norms. Women without shame (*sin vergüenza*),

Traditional handicraft and artisan labor maintain Mexican culture and provide access to cash for Amerindians who often live and work in the unregulated informal economy. (Courtesy of the Inter-American Foundation)

"bad women," faced banishment from proper society and the loss of legal protection (MacLachlan and Rodriquez O. 1980).

In colonial Mexico, *machismo* and *marianismo* were universal to all social classes, but everyone clearly did not conform to these exaggerated codes of behavior. Individual behavior often deviated from the norm, as it does in most societies. Traditional indigenous communities, for example, did not conform to *machismo/marianismo*, although their cultures were patriarchal in nature. These behavioral norms predominantly existed in the *mestizo* communities in Mexico (Stevens 1994).

The "honor/shame complex" associated with the normative orders of *machismo* and *marianismo* produced distinct gender divisions in Mexican society. Women are considered the moral superiors of men, but they must yield to men's unquestioned dominance. Though great change has certainly occurred in gender relations, remnants of colonial era patriarchy and the norms of behavior that accompany it can be seen in modern Mexico. Field researchers in Mexico in the 1980s and 1990s observed gender relations that "broke the stereotypical mold" and gender relations that remarkably paralleled historical stereotypes (Gutmann 1996; LeVine and Correa 1993). *Machismo* in Mexico today is described by researchers in two different ways: the traditional view, where men are dominant, violent, promiscuous, heavy drinkers; and the less traditional, where men are "proud but not arrogant, reflective, authoritative, and hardworking" (LeVine and Correa 1993, p. 80). It is probably most accurate to conclude that both of these types of *machismo* exist in modern Mexico. As Gutmann (1996) concludes:

> there exists no stable set of determining and essential gender quali-
> ties that can adequately capture the situation for the region as a
> whole . . . Whenever I was in doubt, for persuasive evidence, I had
> only to walk through my section of Colonia Santa Domingo, begin-
> ning with the agnostic printer who bragged about his vasectomy a
> week after I met him, who worked in front of the house with a single
> mother and her five young children, who lived a block over from the
> woman who resided openly with her children and a series of male
> lovers, who was next door to a woman who could not leave home
> without her husband's permission, who was across the street from
> the cobbler who ridiculed state- and church-sponsored marriages in
> the same breath as he rebuked unfaithful husbands, whose shop was
> below the home of a notorious and belligerent wife beater and his al-
> coholic sons, one of whom was the boyfriend of a young mother of
> two small children who lived in a home in which all the males were
> waited upon by all the females in the household, all of whom were
> surrounded in the *colonia* by young women who would be the first
> people in their families to graduate from high school (pp. 9–10).

PATRIARCHY AND REVOLUTIONARY PROGRESS

The Revolutionary period in Mexico is often credited with the first significant gains in equality for Mexican women. However, prior to the Revolution, changes in colonial family law subtly altered the nature of gender relations. The colonial Civil Codes modified patriarchal authority (*patria potestad*) over children and weakened patriarchal control over women by granting female-headed households the same authority over children as male-headed households. Divorce was also legalized on the grounds of "mutual consent" (Arrom 1994).

Progressive efforts toward change, however, including the Civil Codes and the establishment of public education for both sexes, often were not implemented. Patriarchy remained firmly intact throughout the early decades of the 20th century. Although the *patria potestad* was altered legally by the Civil Codes, men continued to exert exclusive and often total control over their spouses and children. Most importantly, progress that occurred prior to the Revolution was achieved under the late colonial premise that progress might lead women to become more interested in the establishment of an "enlightened patriarchal society" (Stern 1995).

During the Porfirian era (1876–1910), significant modernization and economic progress occurred and, as a result, education and urban services grew. Women's roles subsequently began to reflect modest change, with women frequently assuming public roles in education, as wage workers, and as revolutionary activists. Middle- and upper-class women attended schools and universities in greater numbers than ever before. They also entered the workplace in unprecedented numbers as nurses, teachers, and office workers.

During the Mexican Revolution, many women followed their husbands or male companions onto the revolutionary battlefields as *soldaderas*. A *soldadera* performed various services, from gathering and preparing food and washing clothes to sexual relations. These women endured deplorable living conditions, often giving birth "in the field" with little or no assistance, then returning immediately to work. *Soldaderas* also took up arms and fought alongside men with such distinction that a few women even became officers in the revolutionary armies. *Soldaderas* who were poor and often Amerindian, however, received little formal (in the way of rank or military pensions) or informal recognition after the Revolution ended (Stern 1995; Soto 1990).

Most Mexican women (those who were poor) did not benefit from pre- or postrevolutionary social change. The Revolution did weaken patriarchal ideology, but despite their central role, women did not immediately benefit from reforms (Stern 1995; Soto 1990). The interests of women and children were seldom considered. Policymakers were most concerned with improving employment opportunities for men. They sought to strengthen and preserve social cohesion within the family in order to preserve social order (Monteon 1995). Women did gain a limited number of legal rights, but they still had few political rights. Women's exclusion from formal politics was justified by politicians' reference to women's traditional support for the Roman Catholic church (Miller 1994; Soto 1990). Revolutionary leaders claimed the Church's political role had to be weakened to ensure the success of revolutionary principles. They distrusted women's dedication to the revolutionary cause.

A first-wave **feminist** movement emerged in Mexico toward the end of the Revolution, around the same time the suffragist movement was making significant gains in the United States. Two feminist congresses were held just prior to the drafting of the 1917 Constitution in January and November 1916, but the ideas discussed in the congresses had little impact on the all-male drafters of the Constitution (Soto 1990). Like the first-wave feminist movement in the United States, the first wave of **feminism** in Mexico was largely confined to middle-class women. Despite minor gains by middle-class women, however, **sex discrimination** and inequality continued.

INEQUALITY AND THE MODERN MEXICAN WOMAN

Gender divisions and inequality continue in contemporary Mexico, just as they continue in the United States and other nations around the world. Some progress toward equality has occurred in politics, economics, and the family, but not without resistance. Women's situation in Mexico is similar to that of women across Latin America. Sex discrimination and the legacy of patriarchy endure to some degree in every institution.

It is still considered ideal for men to have as their priority the family's financial well-being, and for women to have as their priority the home (children, husband, and housework). This is true in most Mexican communities and for most men and women. Nonetheless, gender-based social change has occurred. Economic reality leads many women into wage labor, and most men accept their wife's employment in the case of family survival or when it is *por necesidad* (Gutmann 1996; LeVine and Correa 1993). Economics has forced change in gender roles, but women also have been active agents in their social, economic, and political progress. Women's efforts for equality since midcentury and women's current position in Mexican society will be the focus of the remainder of this chapter.

POLITICAL RIGHTS, PARTICIPATION, AND THE LEGACY OF SUFFRAGE

Prior to the 1940s, feminism was a distinctly middle-class movement. The initial movement gave way to a second wave of organized women's activity that encompassed a broader spectrum of women. After 1940, as women increased their educational levels and became more economically active, they also joined unions and other organized interest groups.

Mexican women achieved suffrage in 1953, but women's struggle for political rights began years earlier. Women actively rallied for the right to vote during the first wave of the feminist movement. Men resisted. It was not until Lazaro Cárdenas assumed the presidency in 1934 that women achieved any real progress in their quest for suffrage. Cárdenas argued that revolutionary rhetoric called for the incorporation of peasants (*campesinos/as*), Amerindians (*indígenas*), workers (*obreros/as*) and women (*mujeres*) into the national plan for progress. Cárdenas vocally and practically supported women's rights, appointing Mexico's first woman to a high political office, Palma Guillen, minister to Colombia (Miller 1994).

In 1936, women gained the right to vote in party primaries for the official party, the PNR (later the PRI), and in several states. Cárdenas drafted the first constitutional amendment for women's suffrage in 1938. By 1939, all 28 states had confirmed the amendment. The confirmation process, however, was not completed by Congress before adjournment. With the onset of World War II, the passage of women's suffrage was effectively delayed until 1953. Women's first opportunity to exercise their new civil right did not arrive until the 1958 elections (Miller 1994; Soto 1990). Compared with the United States and many other Latin American nations, Mexico was quite tardy in passing women's suffrage (see Table 5–1).

The right to vote is not necessarily a path to liberation. An **Equal Rights Amendment** still eludes U.S. feminists. After women gained the right to vote in Mexico, organizations dedicated to women's rights often dissolved or were incorporated into a branch of the official party (PRI), instead of continuing their drive for gender-specific political and economic rights. Independent female leaders were removed as women's groups were incorporated into

TABLE 5–1

Female Suffrage in the Americas
Year in Which National Women's Suffrage Was Received

United States	1920	Chile	1949
Ecuador	1929	Costa Rica	1949
Brazil	1932	Haiti	1950
Uruguay	1932	Bolivia	1952
Cuba	1934	Mexico	1953
El Salvador	1939	Honduras	1955
Dominican Republic	1942	Nicaragua	1955
Guatemala	1945	Peru	1955
Panama	1945	Colombia	1957
Argentina	1947	Paraguay	1961
Venezuela	1947		

Source: Thomas F. Skidmore and Pete H. Smith. 1992. *Modern Latin America* (New York: Oxford University Press), p. 64.

CHAPTER 5

the PRI (Monteon 1995). Thus, the drive for equal rights after suffrage often became subordinated to official party concerns.

Throughout Latin America, advocates of women's suffrage campaigned on the premise that suffrage would lead to a more "moral" society, rather than advocating women's right to vote as a path to gender equity (Miller 1994). Few economic and political benefits followed suffrage. Divorce was not made more accessible or equitable. Women continued to lack reproductive autonomy. Sex discrimination persisted, with women excluded from most male-dominated occupations and professions. Men continue to dominate the formal avenues of power in Latin America, including political parties, labor unions, and professional associations (see Table 5–2). These organizations rarely consider women and women's place in the nation's development. Although to a lesser degree, men in the United States also dominate the formal avenues of power, particularly politics. Currently, U.S. women comprise only 11 percent of the House of Representatives and 10 percent of the Senate (Janofsky 1996, p. B2).

Mexican women confront many obstacles on the path to political power. For example, Irma Serrano, a Mexican actress, initiated a political career in the 1990s. Her successful campaign drew thousands of supporters as well as the attention of the PRI. A massive campaign of harassment followed, with loud music interrupting her rallies and an alleged kidnapping. Although she failed to win her first electoral bid, she is still politically active (Dubois 1993).

Greater numbers of women than ever before are facing the obstacles and entering political races. Many are associated with the coalition *Mujeres en Lucha por la Democracia*. This group's central aim is to encourage women to enter politics (Dubois 1993). In 1991, 50 women ran for state and federal offices—the largest number of women in Mexico's history. This is partly due to the success of female political activists in the 1970s and 1980s elected to the federal Senate, chamber of deputies, and various state-level positions. In 1982, Rosario Ibarra de Piedra, a human rights and antigovernment activist, accepted the PRT's (Revolutionary Workers Party) invitation to become their presidential candidate. According to the official count, she garnered only 1.8 percent of the vote. The PRT claims the actual percentage was closer to 8 percent. Regardless, as the first female presidential candidate, she sent a powerful symbolic message to Mexican women. According to Ibarra, "We live in a country of 'machos' . . . but men are changing" (Epstein 1988, p. 68).

TABLE 5–2

Women in Politics in Latin America

	Congress (%)	Government*
Antigua and Barbuda	23	—
Argentina	25	NA
Bolivia	8	—
Brazil	8	1
British/ Virgin Islands	15	1
Chile	7	3
Colombia	10	2
Costa Rica	17	9
Cuba	23	3
Dominica	16	NA
Dominican Republic	10	1
Ecuador	5	1
El Salvador	10	2
Grenada	27	1
Guatemala	7	3
Haiti	NA	2
Honduras	5	1
Mexico	8	2
Nicaragua	16	2
Panama	8	NA
Paraguay	5	—
Peru	10	2
Surinam	6	—
Trinidad and Tobago	21	4
Uruguay	12	1

*Cabinet members.

Source: "Women—The Invisible Victims of the '90s." 1995 (June 22). *Latin America Press* 27(23): 4.

WOMEN'S COLLECTIVE STRUGGLE

Mexican women have played an "initiating role" in changing gender roles and conventions (Gutmann 1996). Women initiate this change individually, in their own households, and collectively, in their communities. Since the economic crisis of the 1980s, government resources have failed to meet basic social needs. When the economy declines, as it so often does in the "boom and bust" cycles of Latin America's economy, state budgets are slashed and rearranged to offset losses. Women tend to bear a greater burden than men. Social expenditure cuts led to an increase in unpaid labor by women (including domestic and community work), constraining both women's time and choices. According to the IDB (1995), since the economic crisis of the 1980s, "women have played a crucial role in contributing to household income, not only in terms of salary but also in terms of the rationalization of expenditures (at the cost of their own time) and through their efforts to resolve community problems via local support networks" (p. 37).

Women from all economic backgrounds join a variety of social movements to improve their community, their family situation, and their own lives. These include human rights organizations, community affairs associations, feminist groups, domestic violence organizations, unions, and rural and urban popular movements. One of the most prominent figures in the indigenous popular movement, *Ejército Zapatista Liberación Nacional* (EZLN), is a female Tzotzil Indian known as Ramona (see Chapter 11, "Social Problems and Social Movements," for a complete description of indigenous movements).

Women's heightened sense of responsibility for family survival leads them to mobilize collectively. The decision to become involved in community activities for both women and men, however, must be weighed against the benefits to be received by spending time in other activities (i.e., a second or third job). For example, Hellman (1994) describes the community activities of a woman interviewed during field studies in Mexico and the rationale behind her involvement. Conchita Gómez volunteers at the *Mujeres en Lucha* or the Women in Struggle food cooperative. This program feeds hundreds of poor Mexico City children. This is not the only local organization to which she belongs—she also belongs to several block committees, popular assemblies, and women's commissions. She describes her involvement in these groups in both practical and personal terms. Her volunteer status allows her to bring home two meals per day to her children, food on which her family depends. However, she also very much enjoys working with the other women in the organizations, whom she describes as *compañeras* (friends). In addition to her volunteer work, Conchita runs a home-based business in ladies underwear and is solely responsible for the household (since her husband migrated to the United States several years earlier and no longer sends regular checks). This example illustrates not only women's participation in the community but also the balancing act Mexican women must perfect to survive what is often called women's "triple burden."

Moser (1993) identifies the three facets of women's employment in Latin America: productive (wage labor), reproductive (household labor), and community-management (described above). Together, these three roles comprise women's triple burden. The concept is similar to the double burden concept in the United States, which describes the unequal division of household and child care tasks between working parents. Latin American women increasingly participate in wage labor, yet they are still primarily responsible for the household. In addition, as described above, Mexican women comprise large percentages of rural and urban social movements. It is not surprising, therefore, that many women report they spend little or no time on leisure activities (IDB 1995).

WOMEN AND THE HOUSEHOLD

Reproductive or household work is not commonly measured in any country's national surveys. Thus, this important aspect of women's work lives remains invisible. In Latin America, household work can be a time-consuming effort. In addition to child bearing and rearing, women's daily domestic routine often includes housework, laundry, and shopping for, preparing, and preserving food. Mexican men have relied on women for food preparation, particularly the labor-intensive preparation of tortillas (a dietary staple), since the colonial era (Stern 1995). Today, Mexican men are involved in child care and help with other household responsibilities more than ever before. Household responsibilities are rarely split equally, however, even if the woman brings home an equal wage (Gutmann 1996).

ECONOMIC PROGRESS AND WOMEN'S LABOR

Since the 1950s, Latin American women have steadily increased their participation in the labor market, for reasons that are unique to each nation's development. In Mexico, paternalistic labor laws that "protected" women from performing dangerous, unhealthy, or "abnormal" work were eventually modified, increasing economic opportunities for women (Vasquez 1994; Soto 1990).

Global restructuring has led to a fast and steady rise in the proportion of women workers throughout the world. This trend altered the nature of and rate of women's productive labor in Mexico. In the **formal sector,** women predominately work in EPZs such as the *maquiladora* (or *maquila*) industries that are located along the U.S.–Mexico border (see Chapter Three, "The Mexican Economy" for a fuller description of EPZs). Wages are not necessarily higher in the *maquilas* than they are in the **informal sector,** but benefits such as social security and medical insurance are often offered. This is particularly important to women with children (Fernandez-Kelly 1983).

Maquiladora employers prefer young, single, childless women with at least a primary school education. The work is repetitive; hours are long; unions are rare. The number of males hired for *maquila* work has increased in recent years, especially in high-wage jobs. Nevertheless, 80 percent of the *maquiladora* employees are female (Dubois 1993, p. 48). According to Raul Garcia Perez, president of the *Maquila* Industry Association in Baja, California (quoted in Dubois 1993): "Women are still more conscientious, more punctual, more interested. Men don't like this kind of manual labor. They're more restless" (p. 49). Women do not appear to enjoy the work, either—close to 35 percent of *maquila* workers leave their jobs each year (Dubois 1993, p. 50). Fernandez-Kelly (1983), who conducted a **participant observation** study in the *maquiladoras,* lists several common reasons for women's exit from the factories: marriage or increased household responsibility, desire for a "rest" period, and health problems. In addition, *maquila* workers are not usually encouraged to develop into a permanent workforce. Factories frequently hire employees on a temporary basis or encourage them to leave voluntarily during slow periods.

Employers hire women for *maquila* work partly because common stereotypes about women's passivity and docility and men's rebelliousness still prevail. Employers presume women are more suitable for work that requires small hands and quick fingers. In addition, because women feel a greater burden for their family's well-being, they will often accept lower wages. Women, then, are seen as the ideal worker . . . quick, docile, cheap, and dependable.

Despite women's active economic role, Mexico's labor statistics fail to include the entire working population. Female workers across the world work for wages in the informal sector. Thus, they are often excluded from formal sector labor statistics (Baud 1992). The number of women employed in wage labor is estimated to have increased from 28 percent in 1980 to 34 percent in 1989, but these figures underestimate the actual percentage, due to underreporting of employment in the informal economy (Chant 1994).

Mexico's formal sector employs many young, single, and childless women, while most older, married women with multiple domestic responsibilities find jobs in the informal economy. Women comprise between 52 and 62 percent of Mexico's informal workers

(IDB 1995, p. 66). Approximately 40 percent of Mexican women are employed in domestic services (Hall 1987, p. 53). The advantages of domestic work include flexibility; permission to use household resources (such as the shower), leftover food, and used clothing; and the opportunity to bring small children to work. Domestic workers sometimes earn higher wages, particularly if they work in several different households. The disadvantages are poor benefits and grueling work schedules (as long as 14 hours a day/6 days a week). Mexican law requires employers to register domestic workers with a government agency and follow the same regulations as factories, including salary, social security pay, and safe working conditions (Baud 1992). These laws, however, are rarely enforced.

Middle-class women have benefited from greater access to education (see Chapter 9, "Mexican Education"). Throughout Latin America, they occupy white-collar jobs as teachers, nurses, trained midwives, and government workers. The majority of working women in Mexico and Latin America, however, are still segregated into the poorest paid, lowest skill jobs. This includes women in white-collar occupations who typically work in low-paid positions. In addition, women's increasing wage labor participation has occurred in the context of a general decline in the social power of labor. Mexican women face an economic climate in which workers, male and female, are disadvantaged (Chant 1994). It has been estimated that women in Mexico earn 86 percent of men's wages, but since men and women both lack bargaining power in the market, women earn 86 percent of an already depressed wage (IDB 1995, p. 59).

CONCLUSION

There is no question that the lives of Mexican women differ from the lives of their mothers. Gender roles in Mexico reflect both continuity and transformation. Economic and political transformations that altered women's lives also significantly affected men's lives.

Macroeconomic policies of the 1980s led to increasing economic activity for women. Women's wage labor is increasingly central to the family economy (see Chapter 7, "The Mexican Family"). The burden of responsibility outside of paid labor, however, often leads women in Latin America and across the world to take a more flexible (but lower paid) job in order to maintain domestic and community activities (Moser 1993). Thus, Mexican women still concentrate in low-wage, low-productivity jobs. The support needed by Latin American women is similar to that needed by women in the United States: adequate and affordable child care, more spousal assistance with domestic responsibilities, and economic support from negligent fathers (IDB 1995). Progressive policy making to address these needs has not occurred.

Women are still largely excluded from formal policy decisions. The few female politicians in Latin America often adhere to stereotypical notions of women's "proper place" and do not vote for programs to benefit the majority of women ("Women—The Invisible Victims of the '90s" 1995). Policy initiatives seldom recognize the diversified roles of both men and women in modern Mexico. In a society where progress in economic and social policies for one group means losses for another, less powerful groups such as women have difficulty institutionalizing their gains.

Race and Ethnic Relations

Latin America's **race** and **ethnic** divisions are less dramatic than in the United States, where racial awareness emphasizes distinct categories such as white, black, Asian, and Hispanic. Mexico's history, in great contrast, has produced a racially mixed majority group that resists distinct classification (Davis 1995; Knight 1990).

Three racial types predominate in Latin America and the Caribbean: whites of European ancestry (*criollos*), **indigenous** groups or **Amerindians,** and mixed race categories, most commonly white/Amerindian mixtures (*mestizos*) and white/African mixtures (*mulattos*). Mexico, Guatemala, Bolivia, Ecuador, Paraguay, and Peru have strong cultures and significant numbers of Amerindians and *mestizos.* They also have a *criollo* or white population. Race relations in these nations are the most complex in Latin America. By the end of the 19th century, most Latin American and Caribbean nations were either majority *mestizo* or *mulatto.* In Latin American and Caribbean nations where large Amerindian civilizations once existed, *mestizos* are the majority race. Where indigenous populations were few and African slave imports numerous, *mulattos* became the majority race (Davis 1995).

Mestizos have comprised Mexico's majority population since the 19th century (Knight 1990; Vigil 1980). While it is true that the majority of Mexicans are mixed race (*mestizos*), today at least 7 million indigenous Amerindians inhabit Mexico. Mexico, like the United States, has a long history of racial and ethnic inequality. From the earliest days of the Spanish conquest, race has been closely associated with class, status, and power.

THE COSMIC RACE

Spanish and other European whites, Africans, Asians, and the indigenous population (Amerindians) contribute to the genetic composition of modern Mexico (MacLachlan and Rodriquez O. 1980). Colonial Mexico imposed a distinct social separation of Spanish and other whites, Amerindians, and Africans. Racial distinctions evolved into a "caste" system where power and privilege ran parallel with racial divisions (Knight 1990). *Peninsulares* (those born in Spain) and *criollos* (those of Spanish descent born in Mexico) ruled the early social hierarchy. The *mestizo* population ranked beneath pure Europeans. The *mestizo* category initially included only those of white/Amerindian descent. A small group initially, *mestizos* numbered fewer than blacks or *mulattos* because wealthy mixed white/Amerindian individuals were often considered *criollo*, while less fortunate *mestizos* were considered Amerindian. Amerindians and Africans were considered inferior. Whether they worked as slaves or for wages, violence and legal regulations restricted their freedom (MacLachlan and Rodriquez O. 1980; Vigil 1980). Although intermarriage between Amerindians and Europeans or Africans was legally prohibited during the colonial era, by the 19th century few Mexicans were of pure European descent (Knight 1990).

The African impact continues most importantly in Latin American societies where the indigenous population is small. Afro-Creoles form an important and distinct cultural presence in Brazil and the Caribbean. They significantly contribute to those nations' music, food, and religious cultures. African impact in nations with large indigenous populations, such as Mexico, is mostly confined to the genetic **assimilation** of African ancestry with indigenous and white ancestry during the colonial period (Davis 1995). The black population blended into Mexico's *mestizo* race by the 19th century (MacLachlan and Rodriquez O. 1980).

Several other immigrant groups contributed to Mexico's racial and ethnic composition. For a period in the 17th century, the third largest European group in Mexico was Jewish. In addition, approximately 6 thousand Asians arrived in Mexico per year in the 17th century, many as slaves. Asians, however, were not recognized in colonial Mexico as a separate race. Both of these groups intermarried and blended into the dominant culture by the end of the colonial era (MacLachlan and Rodriquez O. 1980).

Racial mixing since the 16th century resulted in the creation of a unique Mexican people, *mestizos,* who are not European or Amerindian but distinctly Mexican (Knight 1990). In the 1920s,

Mexican historian José Vasconcelos coined the term *cosmic race* to describe the unique identity resulting from mass **amalgamation** in Mexico's past. Since the Porfirian era (1876–1910), Mexico has formally declared itself a *mestizo* nation with *La Raza* (the *mestizo* "race") at the center of Mexican nationalism. The majority of political and social elites are *mestizo*. The only Mexican citizens claiming pure white European ancestry today are descendants of old, aristocratic families who have often "forgotten an Indian ancestor" in their family's heritage (Beals 1969). Estimates of indigenous peoples in Mexico range from a low of 7 million to a high of 10 million. In Mexico, a person is classified Amerindian if he or she speaks a native language. However, at least 9 of 10 Mexicans today have enough Amerindian blood to be considered indigenous by U.S. standards (Payne 1996).

The apparent indistinctiveness of racial lines in Latin America has led people to assume that the region is "racially democratic," with limited racial conflict. To the contrary, racial and ethnic prejudice and structural inequality have existed in Latin America since the first days of the Spanish conquest and continue today between those populations considered superior (usually with fair skin) and those considered inferior (usually with dark skin) (Toplin 1974). In Mexico, since the 19th century, racial discord and inequality have continued most strikingly between the dominant *mestizo* and marginalized Amerindian populations.

ANCIENT AMERINDIAN CULTURES

Today, 56 different Mexican Indian languages and cultures live through the descendants of ancient Nahua and Mayan Indians. Two hundred years before Christ, a Náhuatl-speaking civilization existed in the highland areas of Mexico and a Mayan civilization in the Yucatán Peninsula. The first and last great Indian civilizations were Náhuatl-speaking, the Olmecs and the Aztecs. In between, the Mayas developed perhaps the most magnificent ancient Amerindian civilization.

Long before the Europeans, ancient Mayas developed one of the first written languages (with over 500 symbols) and possessed advanced mathematics, solar calendar-making, and medicinal skills. In addition, Mayan architects and engineers constructed amazing buildings, temples, and roadways. Many of these structures were destroyed by the Spanish, but those remaining today testify to this ancient society's grandeur. The Toltecs (a Náhuatl-speaking culture) conquered the Mayas and passed their language and culture to the Aztecs—the last great Amerindian civilization (Salloum 1996; Dubois 1993). The Spanish eventually defeated all Amerindian cultures and assigned them to the lowest realms of the colonial social, economic, and political hierarchy (see Chapter 1, "The Place, The People, and the Past").

ASSIMILATION: AMERINDIANS IN A *MESTIZO* NATION

Spanish colonial rule dealt with Amerindian groups in three distinct ways. From the earliest contact, Spaniards viewed indigenous peoples as intellectually, culturally, and physically inferior. In Argentina and Brazil, tribes were annihilated through genocide; in Costa Rica and Colombia, Amerindians were restricted to certain land areas such as reservations; and in Mexico, integration or assimilation of Amerindians into the dominant culture proceeded through encouragement or force (Van Cott 1994).

The Spanish desired to integrate Amerindians into the dominant culture in Mexico because their continuing independence after conquest was a threat to colonists' economic objectives. Organized Amerindians controlled their labor power and controlled natural resources on communal property (Tresierra 1994). The Spanish saw Mexico's indigenous population as a cheap labor source, and the integration of Amerindians into the dominant culture facilitated their availability. In addition, Amerindians were eventually needed to strengthen Mexican armies in the Independence and Revolutionary wars.

The Porfirian era (1876–1910) was a time of intense oppression. Amerindian communities were assimilated by force when necessary. These campaigns resembled assimilation policies imposed on Native Americans during the United States' frontier expansion. Those Amerindian cultures that did not cooperate were "hunted down, deported and enslaved" (Knight 1990). Assimilation policies conformed with Díaz's nation-building project and perceived or actual threats to Mexican sovereignty. First, several states had nearly seceded during the Revolutionary period. Lessons of the U.S. Civil War were not lost on Mexico. Second, conflict between local, state, and national governments led Mexico's political elite to see the importance of breeding a nationalist ideology. Finally, loss of national territory during the Mexican–American War (1846–48) led Mexico's leaders to fear the potential for greater loss if they were "a house divided." Those Amerindians who did not assimilate into the dominant culture were thought to be standing in the way of a consistent national project necessary to defend national territory and the Mexican state (Knight 1990).

Throughout Latin America, ethnic blending has proceeded through *mestizaje* or the integration of cultures. This acculturation process resembles ethnic blending in the United States after years of immigration. Today, a large part of the dominant *mestizo* group in Mexico is similar in appearance to the Amerindian. Though Amerindians do have physically distinct traits (i.e., smaller body frames, darker skin), in general *mestizos* and Amerindians are separated only through cultural characteristics such as dress, language, community organization, and/or economic status. Amerindians who attain educational, social, and economic status may "whiten" their racial classification. In other words: "when an Indian can speak Spanish reasonably well, wears store-bought clothes and has [blank] number of pesos, he ceases to be an Indian" (Beals 1969, quoting from an interview with an unidentified Mexican man, p. 249). The process of *mestizaje* in Mexico is both racial and social. Amerindians are ascribed a "whiter" status when they culturally blend with the *mestizo* race (Knight 1990). However, many Amerindians who speak Spanish and have abandoned traditional dress choose to maintain their indigenous identity. The objective of the Mexican government since the Revolution has been (in the words of José Vasconcelos) to make the Indian "a civilized member of a modern community," but Indian culture is resilient (Riding 1984, p. 201).

ASSIMILATION AS ETHNIC POLICY

The Revolutionary era (1910–20) defined a turning point for Mexican race relations, as Amerindians' prominent role in the wars compelled change. The revolutionaries sought an end to the forced assimilation policies of the Porfirian era. They sought new acculturation methods that would recognize and preserve the Amerindian culture within the *mestizo* culture. Amerindian status, however, changed little.

The revolutionary regime claimed that Amerindian assimilation was desirable because it would emancipate Amerindians from historic exploitation and integrate them into *La Raza*. This was all to be accomplished through an official policy of *indigenismo*. *Indigenismo* "combined an idealized view of the Indian past with the pursuit of the material advantages of modern Spanish civilization" (Payne 1996, p. 63). *Indigenistas* held that Amerindian assimilation was possible without "de-indianization" (Knight 1990). The theory was that Amerindians could, through *indigenismo,* acquire the education, language, and political skills necessary to succeed in *mestizo* society while maintaining their traditional cultures.

A series of *indigenismo* state policies were advocated to foster Amerindian integration, including rural educational development, "folklorization" of Amerindian customs, transformation of Amerindian revolutionaries such as Zapata into heroes of the *indigenista* approach, and agrarian reform through land redistribution (Knight 1990). The National Indigenous Institute (INI) was created to achieve *indigenismo* goals such as teaching Indians Spanish to "civilize" them into *mestizo* culture. The INI treated Indians as ignorant and backward, reinforcing negative stereotypes in the greater *mestizo* society. This led to increasing discrimination, including a greater loss of communal lands and continued exploitation of Indians as a cheap labor source (Payne 1996).

Land redistribution, *tierra y libertad* (land and liberty), was a revolutionary goal. The Land Reform Act required that Amerindians be paid for communal lands taken during the liberal period (1855–72) and that national land be vacated to make room for *ejidos,* or the communal land system that establishes the right of *campesinos* to a piece of land (Nash 1995a). Land reform was not a success. In many rural areas, Amerindian groups gained access to small, nonarable plots, while agricultural elites purchased the largest, most desirable land. In the area of education, a number of rural schools were established. Publicly funded education, however, was not consistently provided to Amerindian communities. When available, schools functioned to propagandize nationalist sentiment and legitimate agrarian reform (see Chapter 9, "Mexican Education"). Resources associated with *indigenista* policy were provided to Amerindian communities when it suited the political interests of the elite, not necessarily when it benefited the communities (Tresierra 1994).

Amerindian cultural preservation did succeed to a certain degree. Mexico's Amerindian past is honored in museums, folk tales, and public heroes. The Spanish conquistador Cortés is a villain, while Indian warrior Cuauhtémoc is a hero. Traditional Indian arts and crafts are popularized today, selling in both Mexican and U.S. markets. Romantically revered since the 1920s, Amerindian traditions have been transformed into national traditions that every citizen is encouraged to respect or celebrate (Knight 1990). For example, the Mexican National Dance Theater performs the Yacqui Indian tribe's traditional "deer dance" as part of its program (Hill 1991).

Official policy endorses Amerindian culture, but in reality it is ridiculed by many. Amerindians are viewed as one homogenous group, rather than many distinct cultures. Stereotypes characterize Amerindian identity and link it to negative characteristics. It is not uncommon to hear even dark-skinned *mestizos* refer to Indians as *feo,* ugly (Payne 1996; Knight 1990).

Indigenista ideology and policy, whether liberal, supporting measures for government assistance to Amerindian groups, or racist, supporting negative stereotypes about Amerindian culture, express the views of Mexico's elite (Bartra 1977). The integrationist/ *indigenista* approach continues to enjoy acceptance by the majority of *mestizos. Indigenismo* is not, however, accepted by most Amerindian cultures in contemporary Mexico. In recent years, indigenous groups have protested for political rights and autonomy, as well as an end to the sociopolitical circumstances that foster prejudice and discrimination (see Chapter 11, "Social Problems and Social Movements") (Nash 1995a).

PREJUDICE AND DISCRIMINATION

By the 19th century, equal political rights were extended to include all citizens. Legal equality, however, was rarely practiced. The postrevolutionary *indigenista* policies reformed the openly racist rhetoric of the Porfirian regime (1876–1910), but they still expressed the logic of racism. Revolutionaries attempted to combat overt racism by striving for a nationalist incorporation of the Amerindian, but in the process sometimes practiced "reverse racism," claiming the cultural superiority of Amerindians and *mestizos.* Non-*mestizos* and non-Indians, particularly Chinese immigrants, were persecuted during and after the Revolution. Chinese immigrants were recruited as a cheap labor source for railroad construction but were stereotyped by Mexican leaders as dirty, drug-addicted, greedy, and sexually threatening to Mexican women. In 1931, they were expelled from Mexico. Many Mexicans saw the Chinese as a potential threat to the *mestizo* race (Knight 1990).

Mexico's 1910 Revolution is often credited with ending **racial stratification** and moving toward class-based stratification. In reality, the two remain intertwined. In modern Mexico, discrimination is based on a combination of ethnic and class status. The exception to this is the treatment of Amerindians who have not assimilated into the dominant culture. Amerindians are often discriminated against solely based on their status as Indians. Bartra (1977), in his study of the Valley of Mezquital and the Otomis tribe, reveals this persistent prejudice toward Amerindians and the lingering desire for assimilation in Mexico. A millionaire farmer (one of the wealthiest in the region) in an interview with Bartra (1977) responded to the question of why the Otomis (Indians) are so poor:

> Well, you've read some history, haven't you? The Otomis have always been shiftless and apathetic right from the time they were first heard of . . . They are a different people, a stubborn race. I have lived among them a good deal in a remote place. You have seen from history how the Otomis exchanged families, daughters, wives. They have no idea what they're doing: they are a different race, but this doesn't mean to say that they can't be integrated into our society . . . through education, young people and children could be integrated, but you won't be able to change the older generation now (pp. 423–24).

Even though the Latin American indigenous population remains large (see Table 6–1), Amerindians are still concentrated in the lowest social, political, and economic ranks.

Salary discrimination data illustrate the economic status of Amerindians. According to the World Bank, a 48 percent salary gap remains between indigenous people and their *mestizo* peers in

Carolina Mericrano repots coffee plants at the nursery of Asociación Agricola Local de Huatla, which she will eventually transplant to her family's cafetal on a thickly canopied hillside outside her village. The Asociación is an affiliate of CEPCU. (Courtesy of the Inter-American Foundation; photographer, Stella Johnson)

CHAPTER 6

TABLE 6–1

Latin America's Indigenous Population

Country	National Population	Estimated Percent of Indigenous
Argentina	33,000,000	1%
Belize	250,000	1
Bolivia	7,500,000	54
Brazil	155,000,000	1
Chile	13,000,000	6
Colombia	34,000,000	2
Costa Rica	3,000,000	1
Ecuador	11,000,000	25
El Salvador	6,000,000	17
Guatemala	10,000,000	65
Honduras	6,000,000	7
Mexico	86,000,000	19
Nicaragua	4,000,000	4
Panama	3,000,000	8
Paraguay	4,500,000	3
Peru	23,000,000	50
Venezuela	21,000,000	2

Source: "This Land Is Our Land." 1995 (October 5). *LatinAmerica Press* 27(36): 3.

Mexico ("This Is Our Land" 1995, p. 3). Across Latin America, Amerindians usually work as subsistence farmers, as migrant agricultural laborers in commercial agriculture, or in the production of traditional crafts, which are sold in regional or national markets (Cornelius 1996). Labor market discrimination between *mestizos* and Amerindians produces an overwhelming representation of indigenous people among those classified as poor: 17.9 percent of Mexico's nonindigenous population is poor, while 80.6 percent of the indigenous population is poor (Psacharopoulos and Patrinos 1994, p. 41).

AMERINDIAN CULTURES: SURVIVAL IN A *MESTIZO* NATION

Despite forced assimilation, land seizures, and incorporation into the modern capitalist system, Amerindian communities and customs persist. Some traditional indigenous practices were lost over the years, but many continue. In the state of Oaxaca alone, at least 12 different indigenous languages are spoken. The Zapotecs speak

42 different dialects within their single ethnic group (Lumsden 1991). Every individual Amerindian community recognizes distinct fiestas, language, art, and ancient worship and ritual.

According to Riding (1984), however, "[the] need to survive physically inevitably threatens the survival of [Indian] culture" (p. 209). Without traditional lands to cultivate, an increasing number of Indians migrate to cities today in search of wage labor. Amerindian enclaves have emerged in and around many Mexican cities. Amerindian communities with traditional lands close to city borders also seek work in city environments. Although many of these Amerindian city dwellers continue to identify with their indigenous culture, they also adopt *mestizo* customs. Indians returning to their rural communities often bring *mestizo* culture with them.

Rural indigenous villages, however, retain many ancestral traditions. The Yucatán Mayans, for example, continue to construct their hutlike homes (*palapas*) in the same manner as their ancient ancestors. The huts have two entrances, front and back, to facilitate cool breezes. The walls of the hut have tiny holes to allow for air flow, and the roof is thatch-style to keep out rain and keep in cool air (Salloum 1996). Mayan women also wear traditional *huipils* or dresses with ornate and colorful stitching.

Indigenous societies also have sustained cultural integrity through what Nash (1995a) terms "selective response" to modern practices. In her **ethnographic study** of indigenous groups in the highland Maya village of Amatenango del Valle, Nash (1995a) found that the groups "selectively responded" to modern practices by adopting those that fit their needs, while at the same time maintaining traditional practices in other areas. For example, the chief *u'uletik*'s (curer–diviner) son was a paramedic in Amatenango del Valle, and father and son shared patients. The son cared for individuals in situations where modern medicine has been effective, such as immunizations against contagious diseases, while the father cared for individuals with illnesses caused by witchcraft.

Good health is still considered a gift of the gods in Amerindian communities. Medicine, magic, and religion remain intertwined in modern Mexico. Thus, *curanderos* or folk healers, continue to provide medical care for many ailments. They combine their rich knowledge of herbal medicine with magic and ritual (Riding 1984). Both rural and urban Mexicans seek folk healers for certain illnesses and modern treatment for others. Illnesses such as *mal de ojo* (evil eye), *rabia* (rage), and *susto* (shock), which may be attributed to supernatural or magical power, require the assistance of a *curandero.* Folk healers also treat those suffering from indigestion, bronchitis, and rashes. Home remedies are often prescribed consisting of ingredients such as herbs, leaves, tree bark, animal fat, and oils (LeVine and Correa 1993).

ETHNICITY, RURAL SEPARATISM, AND POVERTY

Mexican Amerindians were not relocated to government-assigned reservations, as in the United States. Nevertheless, Amerindians generally inhabit the most economically depressed and resource-starved rural areas (Cornelius 1996). All Latin American indigenous cultures and most indigenous cultures in the world are intimately tied to their land for economic and cultural survival as well as social well-being. Land reform, however, was largely ignored in most rural areas.

In the southern state of Chiapas, home to 14 different indigenous cultures, political leaders ignored the Land Reform Act of 1917: 2.9 percent of Chiapas's landowners own farms larger than 2,700 acres (1,000 hectares), equal to 42 percent of the land available; 40.6 percent of the landowners own small farms of 27 acres (fewer than 10 hectares) (Nash 1995b, p. 179). Through the years, communal lands were stolen by *caciques.* Indians were allowed to rent small plots of land by large landowners only to have the landowner repossess the land after it had been cleared. Often, access to land was denied altogether (Riding 1984). With few choices, Indians sold their labor to wealthy *mestizo* landowners. Land is the backbone of indigenous culture. The high concentration of land in the hands of a wealthy minority thus provokes the major demand of native people in Mexico today—access to land (Van Cott 1994).

In 1992, Mexico removed subsidies for subsistence crops such as corn that small-plot cultivators (mostly Amerindians) sold for profit. Instead, American farmers were permitted to bring their subsidized corn to the Mexican market (this occurred prior to **NAFTA**). This policy made Mexico more dependent on food imports and forced many Mexican farmers from their land. In addition, PROSONAL, the program Salinas created to aid the poor, bypassed most rural Amerindian villages (Nash 1995b).

SOCIAL CHANGE AND AMERINDIAN SOCIAL MOVEMENTS

Indigenous people inhabited communities lacking even the most basic resources prior to the 1980s economic crisis and subsequent social cuts. The dispossession of Amerindian land undermined these communities' ability to survive without government assistance. Recent neoliberal economic policies withdraw much of this assistance. Rural indigenous peasants began organizing in the 1970s to protest their marginalization from the Mexican social structure and their lack of access to necessary resources, including land. Indigenous groups condemn both neoliberal economic policies and NAFTA, realizing that they are unlikely to benefit from either. The new economic structure is designed to produce enormous dividends for the wealthy (and largely *mestizo*) elite. The rebels argue that an elite-controlled Mexican state has for centuries made decisions without considering the costs to Amerindians (Nash 1995a; b). Payne (1996) quotes one Indian *campesino*'s explanation of the Amerindian position: "I am not an educated man. But I know this: government after government, we have been betrayed. Now they are selling Mexican land to foreigners to enrich themselves and who knows what these foreigners will do with us" (p. 65).

For many years, Mexico's Amerindian groups fought their battles against assimilation, repression, and land seizures separately. In the 1980s, they began a collective movement. Diverse Amerindian cultures such as Tzeltales, Tzotles, Choles, and Mayas have united to form "rebel armies" and have declared war on Mexico's political and economic elite (see Chapter 11, "Social Problems and Social Movements," for a complete discussion of rural social movements). The official response to Indian unrest in Mexico has largely consisted of increased militarization in states with large Indian populations. The largely indigenous states of Oaxaca and Guerrero are two of only four states in Mexico with two military bases (Payne 1996). Military repression is most severe in Chiapas where the *Ejército Zapatista Liberación Nacional* (EZLN) is headquartered—one of Mexico's most noted indigenous rebel movements. Although the government claims they have strengthened military forces to combat the drug trade in these areas, Amerindians believe the military is there to intimidate and repress.

CONCLUSION

Mass blending of different races in Mexico's past created a unique majority population, *mestizos*. Many races contribute to *La Raza* (the *mestizo* "race"), but Mexico's Spanish and Amerindian heritage most complicate race and ethnic relations. Since the 16th century, racial discord and inequality have continued most prominently between the dominant *mestizo* and marginalized Amerindian populations.

Despite years of forced assimilation, land seizures, and incorporation into the modern capitalist state, at least 7 million Amerindians with 56 different cultures and languages populate Mexico today. *Indigenismo,* the official government position toward Amerindians for over 50 years, stresses the preservation of traditional indigenous practices as long as indigenous communities acquire the education, language, and political skills necessary to succeed in *mestizo* society. This ideology is supported by most *mestizos* in Mexico today. *Mestizos* often view Amerindians as one homogenous group, rather than many distinct and separate cultures. *Indigenismo* is rejected by Amerindians, however, who often continue ancestral traditions. Each separate Amerindian community celebrates its own culturally distinct fiestas, language, and art. Though some Amerindian traditions are celebrated in greater Mexican society (e.g., arts and crafts), prejudice and discrimination against Amerindians continue.

Labor market discrimination between *mestizos* and Amerindians increases the incidence of Amerindian poverty. A high concentration of land in the hands of wealthy elites worsens the economic situation of Amerindians (often small farmers), as do neoliberal economic policies, including NAFTA.

As global restructuring and the logic of privatization become reality in the rural agrarian sectors where indigenous people are concentrated, these policies threaten to further impoverish their communities and thus further weaken their cultural foundations (Tresierra 1994). In response, Amerindians have organized one of the most significant antigovernment movements in recent years, capturing the attention of the United States and other nations around the world (see Chapter 11, "Social Problems and Social Movements").

The Mexican Family

The Mexican family and its ability to survive in an unstable state have fascinated social scientists for a half century. Since the famous field studies of Oscar Lewis in the 1950s, researchers have visited Latin America to study family life and the poor. Their work today, however, often contradicts the "culture of poverty" thesis developed by Lewis. Lewis concluded that poor Mexican families passed a "design for living" from one generation to the next. It was this lifestyle design, along with particular personality traits (apathy, lack of control) that impeded lower-class families' **social mobility** (LeVine and Correa 1993).

Lewis described poor families as marginal to the economy and society. Current research, in contrast, describes the family as central to economic and social stability in Mexico. In the United States and other advanced industrial nations, typical families have become smaller and less cohesive. The family's economic unity in these nations has also declined. The Mexican family defies this pattern. Though Mexican families must adapt to the changing social and economic conditions that accompany industrialization, the family survives as one of Mexico's most important institutions.

The family has maintained its institutional status in part because of the historic and continuing significance of personal relationships. Food, housing, jobs, political appointments, and so on are secured through personal relationships rather than through the exchange of money or personal achievement. Latin America's economic crisis in the 1980s placed a great strain on all families, rich and poor. Mexican families, however, flexibly adapted (in size and structure) to the new economic demands. Mexico's unstable economy increases the importance of kin groups with flexible structures able to adapt frequently to changing economic circumstances. Mexican family size and structure are not fixed. Families alter their size and structure to best meet their *current* domestic and economic needs (Economic Commission for Latin America and the Caribbean [ECLAC] 1995).

Ingenious family planning and *hard* work (by all family members) allow Mexican families to survive frequent economic bust periods. Often this involves family separation, with fathers and older children migrating to cities or the United States to work. Other times, family survival demands that an entire **nuclear family** relocate temporarily or permanently to a distant family member's home in another region. It is not unusual for several related nuclear families to live in a two-room house in order to save housing expense and increase the **family economy.** Nor is it unusual for every family member (from children to the elderly) to engage in some type of wage-earning activity. Hall (1987) describes a Mexican family in which a grandmother, mother, and her five children share a residence. The mother works as a maid; the grandmother contributes by begging; the older children work a variety of odd jobs to contribute what they can. There is simply no end to the strategies undertaken by Mexicans to ensure economic survival. Because social welfare provided by the state is inadequate, an individual's survival in Mexican society depends upon the maintenance of an intricate personal network, including both kin and nonkin relations.

"NUCLEARIZATION" OF THE MEXICAN FAMILY

Prior to the Mexican Revolution, family organization typically resembled the **patrilineal extended family** structure. The typical **extended family** household performs both production and consumption activities, much as one sees on a family farm. All members of the extended family—men, women, and children—contribute to the family economy. In patrilineal extended families, the first son usually remains at home after marriage to assist his parents. Other sons marry and establish their own households. Daughters generally settle with their husband's family.

Unique to the Mexican extended family, however, the youngest son traditionally returned to his parents' home after marriage and inherited the responsibility of assisting his parents with the family farm or other business. He was responsible for caring for his mother and younger siblings when his father died, and he inherited the family property. If there were no sons, this responsibility could be transferred to the youngest daughter (Lomnitz 1984).

In contemporary Mexico, however, married children (whether male or female) live in their parents' home for shorter periods of time. The reason is primarily economic. As societies become less dependent on subsistence agriculture and more dependent on wage labor activities, the structure of the family changes. Mexicans increasingly search for wage work, rather than depending on family agricultural plots (Olivera 1976). Children, particularly sons, still frequently build homes either on their parents' property or in close proximity—often in the same neighborhood or *barrio*. Many working-class or poor Mexicans acquire plots of land from their family or pool their resources with family members to purchase a small plot of land.

During the boom cycle of the 1940s to the early 1980s, a "nuclearization" of the Mexican family occurred (ECLAC 1995). **Nuclear families** are typically smaller than extended families, consisting of a married couple and their children. As the children in nuclear families marry, they move from their parents' household and establish their own nuclear family unit. The Mexican nuclear family, however, functions in a significantly different manner than nuclear families in the United States and other industrialized nations. The line between nuclear and extended families is often blurred in Mexico. When nuclear families reside and seemingly function independently, they often routinely interact with members of related nuclear or **extended family networks.**

THE EXTENDED FAMILY NETWORK IN MEXICO

During economic booms, nuclear family units can function independently and draw resources from government programs. During economic crisis, however, greater reliance is placed on extended family networks. Nuclear families in Mexico form the core family unit, but they do not function in isolation from one another. Extended family networks typically link several related nuclear families who live in the same neighborhood or *barrio*. The families do not share a common budget, but they do exchange goods and services on a regular basis. A variety of goods and services can be acquired without money in Mexico through exchange (*tequio* or *guelaguetza*). Child care, laundry, food, tools, clothing, and other necessary items are exchanged, in addition to information, job assistance, help with home construction or with agricultural plots, and monetary loans (Winter 1991; Selby, Murphy, and Lorenzen 1990). This type of extended family network has functioned throughout Mexico's history (MacLachlan and Rodriquez O. 1980).

Most Mexican families remain poor despite rapid economic expansion from the 1940s to the 1980s. Life became an even more complex struggle for survival when the economic crisis began. Rather than turning to individualistic strategies, however, Mexican families held steadfast to the "Mexican solution" to **poverty.** They adopted **family survival strategies** that strengthened extended kinship networks to collectively offset their shared risks and coordinate resources (Selby, Murphy, and Lorenzen 1990).

Extended family networks unite groups of nuclear families into **"reciprocity networks."** Reciprocity networks are found throughout all social classes. The goods and services exchanged, however, differ. Poor households exchange goods and services that they would otherwise have to purchase but cannot afford, such as child care, food, and transportation. Middle- and upper-class families exchange bureaucratic job associations and political connections with members of their extended family (Winter 1991). Extended family or kinship networks include both real **(consanguine)** and **"fictive" kin.** Godparenthood is a significant nonkin affiliation in all social classes, which serves a religious as well as economic function. Godparents (*compadres*) are required for Catholic baptism and confirmation, but being a godparent in Mexico requires much more than a religious commitment. *Compadrazgo* relationships supplement kin networks to provide individuals with economic and emotional support. These relations are sometimes referred to as fictive kinship because the godparents, although not blood relations of the parent or godchild (*ahijado*), are often included in their extended family network (LeVine and Correa 1993; Carlos and Sellers 1972).

Two types of kinship networks exist in contemporary Mexico, vertical and horizontal. **Horizontal kinship networks** are mutual assistance networks between people of similar socioeconomic levels (ECLAC 1995). Horizontal kinship networks include both real and fictive kin. **Vertical kinship networks** join families of different socioeconomic status in **patron–client relationships.** Vertical kinship networks are usually formalized through *compadrazgo* (godparenthood). *Compadres* are often selected from wealthier families, and the *compadres* act as patrons to the family, helping them with important expenses for the child (such as baptismal clothing or religious wedding expenses). Patrons and clients are expected to behave like kin, with patrons loaning money and attending important family events (LeVine and Correa 1993; Selby, Murphy, and Lorenzen 1990).

Clients are sometimes employees in the patron's service. Young women commonly migrate to patrons' homes under clientage networks. The woman provides domestic service to wealthy patrons connected to her family, and the patron takes responsibility for supervising the young woman. Hellman (1994) describes a patron–client relationship between a wealthy patron she interviewed and his male driver. Although the driver is becoming too old to drive (his eyesight is failing) and can no longer repair the car, the wealthy patron will not dismiss the driver. The patron explains that he is "personally responsible" for the driver, who his father hired over 30 years ago. At the same time, however, the patron has no personal conflict with laying off hundreds of his factory workers. He is an employer but not a patron (*padrino*) to the factory workers, and thus he is not "personally responsible" for them.

Patron–client relations are common to both middle-class and poor families. All Mexicans sometimes need a well-connected patron to intervene on their behalf. The political powerlessness of most Mexicans leads them to seek a more powerful relation to influence the political decisions of the minority political elite (Hellman 1994).

Vertical kinship networks help middle- and upper-class patrons to manipulate their clients for "favors" such as political support (ECLAC 1995). Early in Mexico's history, certain elite family networks dominated political and economic activity and monopolized the best employment and educational opportunities. These powerful elite families are often labeled "grand-families" because they consist of three generations of extended family and function as the basic unit of elite solidarity in Mexico. In contemporary Latin America, grand-families play a more modest role. Many of their family businesses were financially hurt by the move to privatization and the increase in multinational corporations (Kuznesof 1989).

The strength and cohesiveness of upper-class family networks is partially responsible for the concentration of certain groups in politics and in the private and public sectors of business—families stick up for their own. Individuals who obtain and maintain power and status in Latin America, regardless of class or locale, do so with the help of their family, whether nuclear, extended, or fictive (Carlos and Sellers 1972). Family ties directly affect political appointment and also affect political participation by increasing children's opportunities to attend certain universities where political recruitment is highest (see Chapter 9, "Mexican Education"). According to Camp (1982), there is a "consistently high level of political leaders with kinship ties to other politicians" (p. 853). More than one in eight Mexican national politicians from 1970 to 1988 were the children of nationally prominent political figures. When extended family ties are considered, between one-fifth and one-third of all politicians were related to national political figures during the same period (Camp 1993, p. 101). The ideological orientations of political leaders are affected by their elite family connections.

RURAL FAMILIES

Rural and Amerindian families often continue traditional extended family organization. These families operate small-scale family farms in which every family member is needed to contribute to farming activities, including women and children. Indigenous families in small-farming communities are generally organized through individual descendant status, through common ancestors or multiple kinship ties between members. Amerindian groups that share cultural traits maintain extensive ties. These communities intermarry and trade labor and goods. With the growing scarcity of land available for small and subsistence farmers, most rural families combine both family farming and nonagricultural income from temporary wage work on other farms or in cities. The sense of identity that indigenous people get from family membership and their culture, however, often continues when individuals migrate to urban areas or the United States (ECLAC 1995).

SURVIVAL AND THE FAMILY ECONOMY

After the 1980s economic crisis began, Mexican families, especially working-class and poor families, adopted *estrategias de supervivencia*, or survival strategies. Middle-class families also have adopted strategies to offset their losses as they struggle to maintain their economic position. Specific strategies vary by family, but they typically include pooling economic resources across extended family networks (discussed above), increasing the number of family members in the workforce so they do not depend on a single income source, changing the family structure (i.e., single-parent families), and reducing fertility.

Urban families offset economic losses by sending more members into the workforce. Women entered the workforce in unprecedented numbers in the 1980s and 1990s, mostly in the informal economy (see Chapter 5, "Gender Relations"). The increasing importance of women's wages has produced a significant transformation within the Mexican family. Traditional culture defines Mexican husbands as primary breadwinners and wives as homemakers. The ideal is for a husband to earn enough money so that his wife does not have to take a job outside of the home and work a *doble jornada* (double day). Mexican women, however, now regularly supplement their husband's earnings with a variety of activities—from baby-sitting to homework to *maquila* (export zone factory) work (LeVine and Correa 1993). In the northern border areas where *maquila* production is located, female household members are a significant economic asset, since women are the preferred labor source (Staudt 1993).

Home-based productive activities (homework) have become an important income supplement for the urban population. Women typically make garments using material supplied by local factories. Four or five sewing machines often are set up in the front room of the house to establish a family workshop (*talleres familiares*). Sometimes other female family members or neighbors will be hired to assist with the sewing. The hours, wages, and working arrangements of homeworkers vary considerably. Most homeworkers are paid a piece rate (a certain amount for each piece they complete), typically much less than the minimum wage (Miraftab 1994).

When men's job opportunities declined in the 1980s, Mexican men lost economic and family status. *Maquiladora* factories and **informal economy** employers often prefer to hire women (see Chapter 3, "The Mexican Economy," and Chapter 5, "Gender Relations"). Even when the male head of household earns higher wages, the family's economic position may not improve. Men often keep a portion of their income for personal needs, while women tend to contribute a greater portion of their income (generally, all of it) to the family budget (Miraftab 1994; Selby, Murphy, and Lorenzen 1990).

Mexican children have always offset their expense to the household. Their assistance with household responsibilities frees parents and older family members for wage labor outside the home. After the economic crisis, however, an increasing number of children became active in wage activities. Although it is illegal for children under 15 to work, children as young as 5 or 6 contribute to household income, with most working regularly by age 12. By age 12, children contribute substantial paid and unpaid resources to the family economy (Selby, Murphy, and Lorenzen 1990).

Urban children, particularly in Mexico City, work the streets washing car windows, selling candy, and dressing in elaborate costumes to perform for money. *Street waifs* (as they are sometimes termed) usually position themselves at major intersections. These children earn only a few pesos a day. According to a government census, more than 13,000 children work the Mexico City streets, many full-time (Moore 1996). In rural areas, children are socialized into the family labor process early in life. Rural children are expected to contribute to the family farm at a young age and have no defined childhood free of responsibility.

Mexican families devise many other survival strategies in addition to those described above. One of the most interesting economic strategies is the *tanda*. The *tanda* is a savings strategy or a "revolving credit association," described by LeVine and Correa (1993) as:

> organized by an individual who is respected in his [her] home community or place of work, where he [she] approaches between 10 and 20 people, all of whom he [she] is confident will abide by the rules. To be accepted into an already existing *tanda*, an applicant must come highly recommended by someone whom the organizer knows and trusts. Having drawn a number, each member contributes a fixed sum at, for example, weekly intervals. Disbursement, too, occurs weekly. Thus, in a group of 10, the member who draws number four will receive the pool in the fourth week of a 10-week cycle. Peer pressure forces members to save while reducing the risk of being robbed, as might happen were they to keep large sums of money in their homes (pp. 115, 119).

Women, in particular, rely on this savings strategy. They contribute either a portion of their wages or a portion of the household allowance received from their husbands. These savings are used to start small businesses or for school uniforms/supplies, home-building materials, and land purchases.

A shortage of affordable housing plagued Mexico before the 1980s economic crisis. The economic crisis and the 1985 earthquake (in Mexico City) worsened the housing crisis. Mexican families respond to the housing shortage in much the same way they respond to other problems—through their own hard work and extended family support. Poor and working-class families construct homes by hand, bit by bit, in their spare time. Home construction is chiefly the responsibility of males in the household. Often homes begin as cardboard and tin shacks, eventually developing into brick or stone structures with several rooms and an asbestos roof. González (1994) describes the process of home construction for one Mexican family ("Modesto" and "Chuy"):

> Modesto's mother had a plot of land in *Lomas del Paraíso* and she gave it to Modesto on the condition that he build a room for her as well. Modesto and Chuy were in the middle of the construction of the house [when interviewed by González]. It had two rooms; they were all living in one room (Modesto, Chuy and the four children) which had brick walls, an earth floor, and a cardboard roof (through which lots of rainwater came in); the other room had only the walls (without roof, and with an earth floor). They were waiting for a free period (a Sunday) to install the cardboard roof. Modesto has built the whole house (what exists as a house). Because the cardboard was inadequate roofing, there is plastic on the roof, some walls and doors. During the rainy season they were getting wet every evening in spite of the plastic. Everything and everybody was wet: the beds, blankets, furniture, babies, and young children. At the end of the rainy season the asbestos roof was finally installed (in the room where there was no roof at all) and they were putting some bricks on the floor. Chuy said: "we are so comfortable now, the house is now twice as big because we can use the two rooms. I can't believe it . . . to sleep in a room without getting wet with the rain" (p. 239).

Poor Mexicans who cannot afford to purchase land sometimes "invade" unused *ejido* land. Often referred to as "squatters," they construct temporary cardboard rooms until they can afford to purchase or locate discarded building materials. Over time, they construct more substantial housing. Most of these houses have no electricity, running water, or indoor toilets. (See Chapter 11, "Social Problems and Social Movements")

Mexico's economic crises have strengthened the family as a social institution. Families (nuclear and extended) survive by depending on their own hard work and the assistance of other family members. Kinship ties (real or fictive) have been more reliable than government programs. Family structures, however, have changed. In recent years, in addition to growing reliance on extended family networks, Latin American nations have experienced higher divorce and separation rates, growth in the number of single-parent families (usually headed by women), an increase in premarital sexual relations, and growth of consensual unions in which the relationship is not formal by legal or religious standards (ECLAC 1995).

CHANGING FAMILY STRUCTURES

Religious and legal marriage is the norm in Mexico. In contemporary Mexico, however, the definition of what constitutes a "family" is changing. Mexican couples are more likely now than in the past to establish a household without legally or religiously "tying the knot." Families are also increasingly headed by women.

Female-headed households are common in Mexico today. Most are headed by widows, divorced women, or abandoned women, but "never married" mothers (*madres solteras*) are on the rise (LeVine and Correa 1993). Teenage girls who become pregnant by young men are more likely to marry than older women. Older women are more likely to become pregnant by married men who then desert them. Urban, female-headed households are not always poorer than other family types. Budgets are tight for these families, but smaller size compensates for the household head's lower earning capacity. Contributions from children or other household members also supplement reduced incomes (Selby, Murphy, and Lorenzen 1990). For example, González (1994) describes "Chabela," a female head of household and her family economy. Chabela takes in homework from the *maquilas* so she is able to manage housework and child care responsibilities. She lives with her 21-year-old daughter, Angeline, and three sons, Arturo (17), Santos (14), and Israel (12). Angeline works as a cashier and is the primary breadwinner of the family. Chabela's sons also contribute to the family economy but to a lesser degree. Chabela worries about Angeline marrying and moving away because it will be difficult to support the family without her contribution. The oldest son, Antonio, works as a bricklayer and contributes the least to the family economy. According to Chabela, he spends most of his earnings on drinking and his girlfriend. Santos is also a bricklayer and contributes approximately half of his earnings to family expenses. Israel is a part-time casual fitter's assistant (assistant to a plumber) and also works occasionally as a bus cleaner (a common job for boys his age). Both Santos and Israel work during the day and attend primary school in the evening.

Consensual unions (*unión libre*) are those in which couples agree to live together and sometimes have children but do not marry. The practice of consensual unions dates to Mexico's colonial era. Married men often would enter into a consensual union with a woman (*casa chica*) other than their spouse, thus establishing a second household. Any type of consensual union was ideologically unacceptable to the Catholic church and "decent society," but in reality, consensual unions were accepted throughout colonial society (MacLachlan and Rodriquez O. 1980).

Married men in Mexico generally are not shamed by their community for being unfaithful to their wives. Marital infidelity is still common, but **informal polygamous relationships** where a man maintains two households are less common in contemporary Mexico. It is more common for a man to be separated from his first wife *formally* but not *legally*. This occurs because divorce or legal separation is still difficult to obtain (financially and religiously), especially for poor couples. Divorce has become more socially acceptable in Mexico, but it is still not as accepted as it is in the United States. According to Riding (1984), only 2 percent of Mexican couples formally divorce. The term *casa chica* is typically used today to describe a second or later marriage and household (i.e., **serial monogamy**) (Gutmann 1996; LeVine and Correa 1993). Consensual unions in contemporary Mexico are most common among the lower classes, who often commit to this type of arrangement long term.

MARRIAGE AND MARRIAGE RITES

In colonial history, marriage was often used to form alliances between important families. Social and economic considerations prevailed. Family endogamy helped maintain equal distribution of wealth among family members. The most common **endogamous marriages** were between second cousins. Marriage between cousins also occurred in the United States and Europe at this time. Families sometimes arranged **exogamous marriages,** however, marrying their daughters to important bureaucrats or entrepreneurs to strengthen the family's wealth and power. Amerindian women and European men also entered into racially exogamous marriages during the settlement period (MacLachlan and Rodriquez O. 1980).

Contemporary Mexican families seldom control children's marriage decisions. Marriage partners, however, are usually from the same class background. Upper-class endogamous marriages further strengthen the close social network of this class (Carlos and Sellers 1972). Lower-class marriage is often endogamous to the neighborhood or *barrio*, but marriage between kin is not accepted. Increasingly, however, marriage partners originate in other communities or even other cities. The increase in migration has contributed to this trend. In rural and indigenous communities, marriage within the community is traditional. Marriage serves the greater purpose of strengthening formal alliances between families. Nevertheless, rural and indigenous people also increasingly marry individuals outside of their community due to an increase in associations external to the community (ECLAC 1995).

Traditional Mexican **patrineolocal residence** requires that a son bring his bride to live with his family. Today, both sons and daughters move into their parents' household. Young married couples live with their parents initially but move into a separate residence after the birth of their first child or when the next sibling gets married. Coresidence inevitably results in conflict, particularly for daughters-in-law who must subordinate themselves to mothers-in-law. Most Mexican newlyweds, like those around the world, prefer to establish a separate household (Selby, Murphy, and Lorenzen 1990).

Traditional marriage rites have remained somewhat intact in Mexico. Typically, the future groom goes to his prospective wife's home. Accompanied by his father and/or grandfather, he formally asks her parents' permission. The ideal is still for a woman to be a virgin on her wedding day, even though there is considerable evidence (i.e., increases in teenage pregnancy) that virginity on the wedding day is not widespread in Mexico. Two wedding ceremonies are traditional, one civil and one religious. Families that cannot afford both opt for the civil ceremony. The church and religious rites are not expensive, but a celebration is expected following a religious ceremony. Lower-class families often find the celebration too expensive (LeVine and Correa 1993).

SOCIALIZATION AND THE MODERN MEXICAN FAMILY

Mexico's contemporary economic crisis produced changes in the family's socialization function. Poor families have inadequate housing and are less able to provide the nutritional needs children require for emotional and cognitive functioning. Parents have less time to supplement children's formal schooling because they are working more hours to keep the family afloat. Ironically, the poor depend most heavily on the family's ability to socialize children because they lack adequate access to social services such as schools or health care. In addition, the number of female-headed households and consensual unions, which are generally thought to have weaker socialization potential, have increased in recent years (ECLAC 1995).

Traditionally, older siblings acted as the primary socializers for small children. This was particularly the case before the recent decline in Mexico's birthrate. In rural areas where families remain quite large and in urban families where women work a *doble jornada*, this practice continues. Mothers stress that they have no time for "play." Urban mothers, however, particularly from middle-class families, have fewer children and are more socially interactive with them. Relationships between a mother and her children are becoming more considerate and egalitarian. In traditional Mexican culture, expressions of honor and respect were emphasized over overt emotional affection. Daughters and sons are more "emotionally close" to their mothers today (LeVine and Correa 1993).

Families often have little time to spend with their children, but children still occupy a central place in Mexican society. Women work *por necesidad*, but most express great regret about being away from their children. With women's increasing economic role, some fathers have assumed a greater role in child rearing. A man's success at fathering is a source of personal pride. Further, a child's happiness and success are often perceived as a Mexican parent's most significant accomplishment (Gutmann 1996).

REPRODUCTION AND THE MODERN MEXICAN FAMILY

The changes in sexual **norms** evident in nations around the world are also evident in Latin America. Sexual restrictions and **taboos** have declined. Young people in Mexico are becoming sexually active at earlier ages. With the increase in divorce, consensual unions, unmarried mothers, and the liberalization of sexual behavior, the family is no longer considered the only legitimate place for sexuality and reproduction (ECLAC 1995).

Mexico's birthrate is declining. Birth control was made a national priority in 1973, with family planning publicized on television and other media (LeVine and Correa 1993). Men, however, take little responsibility for birth control. A 1990 governmental survey by the health department showed that less than 2 percent of men over 35 had vasectomies. Men actively used birth control only a quarter of the time (including withdrawal and rhythm methods). Condoms were used by only 5 to 6 percent of the men. Condoms are regularly dismissed by men and health professionals as only for promiscuous women. One government doctor surveyed even stated that condoms were "painful" for men (Gutmann 1996). Birth control is largely the responsibility of Mexican women. Today, more than half of Mexican women of childbearing age report using some type of contraception (Dubois 1993).

CONCLUSION

Mexican families devise a myriad of strategies to survive unstable social and economic circumstances. This chapter lists only a few. Undoubtedly, one of the most important strategies is the maintenance of extended family networks. Through reciprocity networks, Mexicans of all social classes acquire the goods (food, home-building supplies) and services (jobs, political appointments) that would otherwise be out of reach.

Mexicans also work *hard* to ensure economic well-being. People from industrialized countries may view the incidence of child and elderly labor as unseemly, but for Mexicans it is just one of many harsh economic realities. It is common for the elite in industrialized countries, especially the United States, to dismiss poverty as resulting from individual laziness or lack of work ethic. Most upper- and middle-class Mexicans, in contrast, recognize the hard work and sacrifices poor families must endure on a daily basis (Hellman 1994).

Over the years, the structure of the Mexican family has changed. Households headed by women and consensual unions are on the rise. The birthrate is declining. Women are leaving the household and earning an increasing share of the family economy. Young Mexicans have become sexually active outside marriage and at earlier ages. Nevertheless, the significance of family remains the same. Kinship relations (real and fictive) are still crucial to survival in Mexican society.

CHAPTER 8

Religion in Mexico

Religious institutions powerfully shape modern societies' normative order. Individual identity may be shaped by religious socialization. Intergroup relations often have a religious component, and religion influences social, economic, and political development. Religious values structure our perceptions and define the legitimacy of our activities. In turn, social change compels formal religions to adapt. For these reasons, Emile Durkheim, Max Weber, and Karl Marx all included religion in their analyses of modern society (McGuire 1992).

Religion can encourage social unity and societal integration, but it can also encourage social conflict. In Mexico, Spanish invaders often brutally imposed conversion to the Catholic religion on the indigenous population to accelerate assimilation and thus societal integration. Catholicism became rooted in Mexico's national identity. Catholic religious symbols such as *la Virgen de Guadalupe* are directly tied to nationalist sentiment and foster national unity (Floyd 1996). Modern Mexico's patron saint, the Virgin of Guadalupe, was first identified with invading Spaniards' efforts to promote Roman Catholicism nearly 500 years ago. Today, however, "Lupe" is a symbol of poor Mexicans' claims for economic, political, and social justice. And Internet surfers may find the "Interlupe home page" greeting them with the "Guadalupe Hymn" (see "Webliography").

Religious diversity abounds in modern societies. Latin America, however, experienced 500 years of dominant religious influence by the Roman Catholic church. It earned the label "Catholic continent," as 45 percent of the world's Catholic population resides in Latin America (Stewart-Gambino 1994, p. 130). Today, 90 percent of the Mexican population claim to be Catholic (Metz 1994, p. 72). In the past 30 years, however, widespread and rapid growth of Protestantism has occurred in Latin America and Mexico.

Religious conflict punctuates Mexican history. Church–state conflict marked both colonial and post-Independence eras. Conflict within the Catholic church and most recently tension between the Catholic church and emerging Protestant **denominations** also characterize religion in Mexico. The Mexican state and Catholicism have developed, fought, and cooperated together for 500 years. For most of the colonial period, church and state (under Spanish rule) functioned codependently. After independence, however, Mexico experienced cycles of conflict and compromise. Nineteenth-century liberals fought for access to church lands and Amerindian labor, which was protected by the Catholic church. In the 1960s, tension became particularly intense as the Catholic church mobilized Mexico's poor behind demands for social justice. Within the Catholic church conservatives resisted the new profile of a popular "people's church." Finally, the "Protestant explosion" in Latin America in recent years has led to a more religiously plural Mexican society, but it has also led to new conflicts between Catholics and Protestants.

The Catholic church's virtual monopoly of religious authority in Mexico has given it considerable social influence. Any institution in Latin America, however, must face the difficult task of adapting to a rapidly changing social and political environment (Cleary 1985). The Catholic church in Mexico has adapted, but today it risks losing its preeminent role as Latin America's and Mexico's dominant religious institution.

THE ROMAN CATHOLIC CHURCH IN MEXICO

McGuire (1992) defines a **church** as:

> a type of organization that is essentially conservative of the social order and is accommodated to the secular world. Its membership is not exclusive but incorporates the masses . . . The church is an integral part of the social order . . . The church tends to be associated with the interests of the dominant classes . . . The church has an institutional character. One is born into it, and it mediates the divine to its members (p. 134).

Mexico's Roman Catholic church closely fits this definition. First, the Catholic church has enjoyed a monopoly of religious authority, including almost 90 percent of the population until recent years. Second, Catholic authorities have maintained a close relationship with authorities in the Mexican state. Despite periodic conflicts between church and state, Catholic hierarchy and parish clergy have conserved and supported the existing social order, except for a brief period in the 1960s and 1970s.

THE CATHOLIC CHURCH AND MEXICAN STATE: A HISTORY OF CONFLICT AND COMPROMISE

During the early colonial period, the Catholic church served the Spanish monarchy but exercised great autonomy and influence. A schism between the two was almost unimaginable. By the eighteenth century, however, church–state relations were changed significantly. The Spanish elite increasingly viewed the church as an "obstacle" to state-building and in need of reform (MacLachlan and Rodriquez O. 1980). Legal and economic privileges were sheared from the church during the eighteenth century. From the 1800s to the 1960s, the Catholic church and Mexican state became embroiled in a cycle of conflict and compromise focused on the economic power and political influence of the church.

Mexico's Independence War epitomizes this issue. A number of Mexican-born clergy were active in the wars (Renato 1970). A Catholic priest, Father Miguel Hidalgo y Costilla, is credited with the initial call for independence in 1810. Hidalgo gathered parishioners and appealed to *la Virgen de Guadalupe.* He asked, "Will you free yourselves?" (Floyd 1996, p. 143). The newly independent Mexican state lacked financial resources. The Catholic church, however, continued to possess both wealth and power. It was the largest landed estate owner in Mexico, controlled education, and was responsible for its own legal and patronage system. The Independence War, however, weakened the church. Liberal reformers sought to create a republican government with a separation of church and state like that adopted in the United States. Mexican liberals felt the concentration of wealth and status in the Catholic church undermined prosperity and progress. Liberals filled with positivist ideals attacked the church's influence. They aimed to transform religion from a social to an individual practice (Floyd 1996).

During the period of liberal control from 1855 to 1872, reform legislation weakened the Catholic church's political and economic power forcing it to sell all property that was not used in daily operations. Religious registration for all births, deaths, and marriages was replaced with mandatory civil registration. The state limited the amount of money the church could collect when performing baptisms and marriage and death rites (Floyd 1996).

Although reform laws remained intact, the dictator Porfirio Díaz (1876–1910) felt that church support could be helpful to his regime, and he closely cooperated with the Catholic hierarchy. This compromise, however, was short-lived. During the 1910 rebellion, the church again lost power. This time, liberal leaders decided the Catholic church's power needed to be permanently limited. The Mexican Constitution of 1917 formalized state regulation over religion (Floyd 1996). It prohibited religious instruction in public schools, prevented the establishment of religious orders, prohibited the church from owning property, stripped the Catholic church (and any other religious groups) of legal recognition, denied the clergy political rights, and prevented participation by any church in political matters (Blancarte 1993).

These legal limitations prompted Catholic clergy to defend their interests. The Cristero Rebellion (1926–29) included both religious leaders and angry peasants fighting for land redistribution promised by the Revolutionary government but never delivered. At the end of the rebellion, conflict was again replaced by compromise. From the 1930s until Salinas's administration (1988–94), the constitutional provisions limiting church activity remained intact. The government did not enforce the laws, however, provided the Catholic church did not speak out against the authority of the Mexican state. From the 1930s to the late 1950s, the church limited social and political involvement, instead focusing on education (both religious and agricultural) (Floyd 1996). The Catholic church supported Mexico's political elite in return for financial support and institutional privileges.

The Catholic hierarchy and the majority of Catholic clergy traditionally supported the dominant social order. During periods of compromise, the church's role in state decisions was powerful. It was consulted frequently by the political elite. The late 1950s and 1960s, however, marked an important and transformative period for Latin America's Roman Catholic church. Many parish priests vocally criticized Latin American governments. In Mexico, the church still cooperated with the state in most matters, but the two were no longer "unquestioned allies" (Blancarte 1993; Levine 1986). Two events signified the Catholic church's transformation: first, the 1962–65 Second Vatican Council (**Vatican II**), and second, the Latin American Bishop's Conference at Medellin, Colombia, in 1968.

THE MODERN CATHOLIC CHURCH

Catholic theologians began to modernize religious traditions during Vatican II. Innovations in religious practice were introduced and had a profound impact on every Catholic church in the world. The relationship between priests, bishops, and higher level officials changed. Bishops and priests became more interactive. The Catholic mass and Bible were changed from Latin to the local language (Stewart-Gambino 1994). This lessened the laity's dependence on clergy for interpretation and led to broader participation. This was an especially important change for Latin American churches where priest shortages are widespread. The **Vatican** encouraged priests and nuns to live and work among the people, share in their everyday experiences, and gain deeper insight into their lives. In Latin America, it produced greater day-to-day interaction between clergy and poor parishioners (Levine 1986).

Latin America's 1968 Bishop's Conference in Medellin, Colombia, was convened to discuss what Vatican II meant for the Catholic church in Latin America. Vatican II changed the church's commitment to the poor. In turn, Medellin focused the Latin American church on the plight of the poor. The Catholic church had always declared its commitment to the poor and their needs, but prior to Vatican II poverty was seen either as God's will or the result of individual failure. After Vatican II and Medellin, the church began to attribute poverty to inequalities embedded in the structure of society rather than individual failure. The search for remedies switched from charity to demands for general social structural change (Levine 1986; 1980). Eventually, the Catholic hierarchy, including the Pope, began to speak out against the extreme inequality in Latin American society.

SOCIAL CHANGE, THE THEOLOGY OF LIBERATION, AND BASIC ECCLESIAL COMMUNITIES

Both Vatican II and the Latin American Bishop's Conference at Medellin committed the Catholic church to the poor and their needs. The church termed this "the preferential option for the poor" (Berryman 1994). It produced new pastoral approaches toward poverty. Vatican II and Medellin also spurred the growth of a new Catholic theology, **liberation theology.** Liberation theology links church doctrine to actions combating economic and social oppression. Originally confined to a small group of intellectuals, clergy adapted it and produced a significant religious movement.

As liberal clergy spread their progressive message, grassroots movements emerged. One of the most important practical applications of the preferential option for the poor and liberation theology in Latin America was the formation of *Comunidades Eclesial de Base* (Ecclesial Base Communities, or CEBs). CEBs are small (usually less than 30 members) grassroots organizations that begin when a layperson or sometimes a priest or nun organizes the members of a community, *barrio,* or workplace (MacNabb and Rees 1993). The groups are ecclesial because they are in communion with the church. They are base or basic because they are organized by and of the people who work in the parish context and lowest levels of the social hierarchy (Levine 1986).

CEBs are politically significant. By 1978, over 100,000 CEBs existed in Latin America. In Mexico, 70 percent of CEBs are concentrated in rural areas, which are less likely than urban areas to have access to a priest or other religious service (MacNabb and Rees 1993, pp. 728, 730). In addition to reading and discussing the Bible, the groups discuss local and national elections and their social and economic problems. CEBs unite individuals and help them discover their collective voice. The Catholic hierarchy has offered tentative support for CEBs, aware that base communities keep individuals active in the Catholic community and thus combat the growing threat of Protestantism. Priests and bishops involved with the groups, however, are closely supervised (MacNabb and Rees 1993).

Although CEBs and some members of the clergy continue to support the theology of liberation, the innovative period that began in the late 1950s has all but ended. Catholic leaders in the Vatican, including Pope John Paul II, have made increasingly conservative decisions since the late 1970s (Mainwaring 1990). The Catholic hierarchy also has become increasingly hostile to liberation theology and efforts to organize the poor (Drogus 1995).

Catholic conservatives favor backing away from political activity in Latin America and returning to the traditional structure and goals of the church. Liberal Catholics favor maintaining a focus on the poor and continuing activism. Liberal Catholic clergy usually have direct experience with the poor; emphasize grassroots organizations within the church, such as CEBs; and adhere to the tenets of liberation theology. Conservative members of the Catholic clergy tend to have more experience with church hierarchy and upper-class and political elites. They defend the traditional position and authority of the church. Liberals, always a minority in the

Catholic church, today face increasing isolation (Mainwaring 1990; Berryman 1980).

THE CATHOLIC CHURCH IN CONTEMPORARY MEXICO

A conflict may be brewing within the Catholic church, but the church and Mexican state are on their way to another period of compromise. The Mexican Catholic leadership condemned electoral fraud in the northern, southern, and western regions during the 1988 elections (Camp 1994). Following the elections, Salinas wanted to restore his political reputation and diminish the allegations of fraud. He did this through reestablishing relations with the Catholic church as part of his modernization project (Floyd 1996). The Mexican Constitution was revised in January 1992 to grant legal recognition to religions. In addition, the state now permits religious instruction in private schools; the church may establish religious orders and churches may now own property. Clergy now are allowed to vote but may not run for political office. Mexico also reinstated full diplomatic ties with the Vatican during Salinas's tenure (Blancarte 1993).

In Mexico, the Catholic hierarchy has removed itself and called for the removal of all clergy from political and social activities, particularly rebel activities. Latin American bishops appointed by Pope John Paul II are predominantly conservative. Some members of the clergy, however, continue to preach the theology of liberation and work closely with the poor. The depth of clergy participation in Amerindian rebel activities is less clear (for a discussion of rebel activities, see Chapter 6, "Race and Ethnic Relations," and Chapter 11, "Social Problems and Social Movements"). A few Catholic clergy are among a small minority of individuals willing to confront officials about the unjust treatment of Amerindians. A Mexican Catholic bishop, Samuel Ruiz Garcia, and a small group of peers still embrace liberation theology and continue to work with the poor in liberation efforts. Anyone speaking out against government repression, however, is immediately labeled a radical leftist by the government. The Catholic hierarchy is also increasingly critical of bishops and priests thought to be collaborating with peasants and urban poor in their political and social struggles. The hierarchy has even begun removing liberal bishops and priests from their Latin American posts (Stewart-Gambino 1994). The future official Catholic stance will most likely be conservative and traditional in nature—not necessarily less political but perhaps less politically influential (Mainwaring 1990).

THE CATHOLIC CHURCH AND THE MEXICAN PEOPLE

The Catholic church's spiritual or pastoral control over the Mexican population is not as clear as its position in state matters (Camp 1994). According to the 1990 Mexican census, 90 percent of Mexicans consider themselves Catholic (Metz 1994, p. 72), yet only 15 percent regularly attend religious services (Stewart-Gambino 1994, p. 133). Thus, the Catholic church may be embedded in Mexico's national identity, but its actual influence with the Mexican people remains weak and disjointed.

Mexico and Latin America face a chronic shortage of priests, particularly in rural areas. At times, one priest has served as many as 50,000 people (MacNabb and Rees 1993, p. 730). The official church is often absent from rural and marginalized areas of Mexico. Most Mexicans are baptized Catholic but do not practice in the traditional manner. They do not attend regular mass, receive communion regularly, send children to parochial schools, or participate in parish activities.

Rural Mexicans, in particular, practice a variation of Catholicism often referred to as "**folk Catholicism.**" Folk Catholicism combines Amerindian beliefs and myths with traditional Roman Catholic beliefs (Ingham 1986). This religious fusion began early in Mexico's history. The Spanish colonial administration encouraged the Catholic church to actively convert Amerindian populations, believing that conversion would facilitate Indian assimilation into Hispanic society. Missionary friars found Amerindian conversion easier when they incorporated indigenous belief systems and culture into their teaching of the Catholic faith. Thus, they did not destroy indigenous religious temples or culture. Amerindian conversion was also facilitated by the similarity of indigenous religious structures and Catholicism. Both were hierarchical. Catholics worship many saints but recognize only one supreme deity. Indigenous faiths recognized many gods but only one supreme deity. The adoration of saints (or tribal and clan gods) and belief in life after death were already a part of most tribal rites (Renato 1970).

Indians replaced their tribal and clan gods with Catholic saints. The saints became associated with weather and agricultural conditions, fertility, healing, and so on, just as tribal and clan gods were associated with these phenomena (Ingham 1986). For example, the all-powerful creator (supreme deity) of the universe for many Amerindian cultures was Teotl (or Ometeotl). Amerindians continued to worship the deity, simply under the name of God. The evil spirit, Tlacatecolotl, remained the evil spirit for Amerindians under the name of the devil (Braden 1966). Every god or goddess in pre-Hispanic Mexico was represented by a material image or idol (and usually a hieroglyph and mathematical-astrological-scientific symbol for priests). Catholic saints, similarly, are revered as an image of "humanity striving for union with the divine" (Nicholson 1967). Amerindians (particularly Aztecs), after converting to Catholicism, replaced their tradition of making sacrifices or offerings to the gods with offerings to the saints (flowers, animals, etc.).

The legend of *la Virgen de Guadalupe* was a key element in the acceptance of Catholicism by Amerindian cultures. *La Virgen* is said to have appeared to the Amerindian Juan Diego in 1531, 10 years after the Conquest. She told Diego she was the mother of Christ and asked him to deliver a message to the local bishop—build a church devoted to her on the hill where she appeared. The priest, although interested, doubted the validity of the story and asked Juan Diego to bring proof of this apparition. Thus, Diego returned to the hill. *La Virgen* reappeared and told him to collect the roses that were growing on top of the hill. To Juan Diego's amazement, in the middle of winter, a large patch of roses appeared. He collected them, wrapped them in his cloak, and returned to the bishop. When Juan Diego opened his cloak to free the roses, his cloak was embossed with the image of the *dark-skinned* Virgin just as she appeared on the hill (DePalma 1996; Dubois 1993). The Vatican, which is now considering the **cannonization** of Juan Diego as a saint, reportedly claims that the legend of Diego and the Virgin of Guadalupe was the most important factor in the Catholic conversion of the Amerindian population. As mentioned in the introduction, the significance of the legend endures. The image of *la Virgen* has been adopted as the symbol of many causes over the years, including Mexican nationalism and independence.

Another important example of the synthesis of native religious traditions and Catholicism is the practice of religious pilgrimages and festivals. Amerindian customs (dances, etc.) were blended with traditional Catholic elements in many religious ceremonies. For example, the festival dedicated to *la Virgen de los Remedios* is argued to be an Indian corn dance (to thank "God" for healthy crops) within a Catholic setting. In addition, a number of traditional Amerindian festivals were continued as "Christian" festivals (Braden 1966).

Traditional Amerindian religious beliefs and myths thrive in rural Amerindian communities today—they are simply clothed in Christianity. A few Amerindian cultures avoided Christian conversion altogether and continue to practice ancient religious rites. The Catholicism practiced by the majority of Mexicans today more closely resembles folk Catholicism than traditional Roman Catholicism (Drogus 1995). Mexico's upper classes, however, particularly those located in urban areas, usually attend formal churches and practice a traditional Roman Catholicism. Official Catholicism is predominantly confined to urban areas where the clergy maintain secure links with the Catholic hierarchy in Rome and the political elite in Mexico.

PROTESTANTISM IN MEXICO

In the last 30 years, Protestantism has become a significant social force in Latin America. Some Protestant missionaries were in the region as early as the 1800s, but few Protestant settlers from Europe and North America followed. Early Protestant migration flowed to North America, Asia, Africa, and the Pacific (Montgomery 1980). Protestants faced obstacles in Mexico. First, Catholicism was the official religion of the Mexican state until 1859 and freedom of worship was not protected until the 1857 Constitution. Second, legal obstacles implemented to limit the Catholic church also limited Protestant activity.

By 1930, Protestant denominations began to increase. From 1940 to 1950, Mexican Protestant membership grew 86 percent while overall population growth was 31 percent. By 1970, 1 million Mexican Protestants had established bookstores, hostels, and radio ministries (Metz 1994, p. 63). Religious services that emphasized emotional and participatory activities found widespread social support. "Mainline" Protestant denominations (i.e., Baptist, Lutheran, Methodist, and Presbyterian) and the evangelical denominations (i.e., Pentecostal) now claim approximately 15 percent of the Latin American population (Berryman 1994, p. 6).

Evangelical and charismatic denominations have experienced the most rapid growth. Pentecostals, a small religious **sect** in the United States, are one of the fastest growing Protestant denominations in Mexico (Metz 1994). In recent years, Pentecostal churches have attracted 75 to 90 percent of new non-Catholic membership across Latin America (Stewart-Gambino 1994, p. 132). Rather than emphasizing religious doctrine and formal liturgy, Pentecostal sects focus on "the emotional experience of the spirit." Evangelical Christians tend to interpret the Bible literally. In contrast, the mainline Protestant churches and the Catholic church interpret the Bible more critically. Their Latin American and Mexican practices closely conform to what one would see in the United States or Europe.

Within Pentecostalism, congregations emphasize different emotional experiences: some emphasize healing; others seek charismatic participation by the congregation such as speaking in tongues (Berryman 1994). In recent years, the emotional character of Pentecostalism has become so popular with Latin Americans that mainline Protestant and even some Catholic churches (termed Charismatic Catholicism) have begun to adopt emotional Pentecostal practices.

The Catholic Mexican Episcopal Conference (1988) found that the Catholic church does not meet the Mexican people's desire for a "live and participatory liturgy" in which they can feel their experience with God (Metz 1994, p. 71). Through greater participation by the congregation and more flexible styles, Pentecostal churches adapt to the needs of poor Mexicans and Amerindians. Often, such groups speak a native language and have low literacy levels. Pentecostals and other Protestant denominations are less bureaucratic and formal. Protestant clergy are often from the same cultural and class background as their congregations. Most Catholic clergy, on the other hand, are imported to the region and have a higher class and educational background than the population they serve (Berryman 1994).

Protestant growth was limited to the *mestizo* population in Mexico until the 1960s, but since then Amerindians adopting the Protestant faith have outpaced *mestizo* growth. Protestant growth has also shifted from northern states to southern states with largely Amerindian (indigenous) populations (Metz 1994). Protestantism, particularly evangelism, is concentrated in the lower classes and has greater female participation rates. Researchers link the growth in Protestantism and the emergence of new forms of Catholicism (e.g., Charismatic Catholicism and liberation theology) to the desire of marginalized groups, such as the poor and women, to create new cultural and political spaces for themselves. New forms of religious expression help marginalized groups create these spaces (Dixon 1995).

CATHOLICS VERSUS PROTESTANTS: A MODERN RELIGIOUS CONFLICT

The historic shortage of priests in Latin America has left the Catholic church unable to provide personal attention to its members. The region has the lowest ratio of Catholic priests to population in the world. For every Catholic priest in Mexico, there are two Protestant ministers (MacNabb and Rees 1993, p. 731). Furthermore, famous evangelicals make regular visits to the region, increasing the visibility of evangelism. The result is that now 15 percent of Mexico's population are estimated to attend Catholic mass or regularly practice the faith—roughly the same percentage of the population that are active Protestants (Stewart-Gambino 1994, p. 133).

The Catholic hierarchy initially ignored Protestant conversion, but over the years Catholic leaders have become concerned with the "Protestant explosion." Catholics view Protestantism, particularly evangelism, as an "alienating religion" (Berryman 1994). At the 1992 Latin American Bishop's Conference, Pope John Paul II encouraged bishops to defend their flock against the "rapacious wolves" of Protestant sects (Stewart-Gambino 1994, p. 132). Catholic leaders, both liberal and conservative, frequently have taken to adopting the stance that Protestantism is a conspiracy by the United States to weaken the Mexican culture and "uniqueness" (Metz 1994).

While millions of dollars have flowed into Protestant efforts in Latin America, U.S. financial aid is not the sole reason for increases in Protestant affiliation. Evangelical churches are almost completely dependent on donations from their Latin American members. Most request a tithe equal to 10 percent of church members' income. Even in the most impoverished regions, evangelical churches receive tithes from their members. Latin America's Catholic church depends more on outside financing (Berryman 1994).

Concern from the Catholic hierarchy has turned to hostility by some of the Catholic population in Mexico. According to Mexican polls, 33 percent of the population believe that Catholicism should be the only religion in the nation (Metz 1994, p. 68). Five evangelicals were killed in 1989, a number were injured, hundreds were forced to leave their homes or communities, and a number of Protestant churches were closed or destroyed. In February 1990, a Protestant interdenominational prayer meeting in Mexico City, attended by 160 evangelicals, was violently interrupted by approximately 4,000 Catholics. No deaths occurred, but almost everyone at the meeting was injured (Metz 1994).

CONCLUSION

The Catholic church has enjoyed a virtual religious monopoly in Mexico. Ninety percent of the population are baptized Catholic. Religious symbols, such as the Virgin of Guadalupe, represent both religious and secular events. Yet Mexican Catholicism for the majority is a Catholicism infused with Amerindian religious traditions. Roman Catholicism and the European-based religious hierarchy have a considerable degree of influence with the political and wealthy elite in Mexico but much less on the masses who practice a folk Catholicism.

The relationship between the Mexican state and the Catholic hierarchy dates to the Conquest when it was decided that Indian religious conversion would facilitate nation-building. Conflict, however, has defined the church–state relationship. The economic power and political influence of the Catholic church has frequently alienated the church from the Mexican state. Liberation theology and the role of priests and other clergy in combating economic and social oppression sparked the most recent church–state debate.

The church's position in state matters, however, is much more certain than its spiritual control over the masses. A consistent Catholic clergy shortage persists in Mexico and other parts of Latin America, particularly rural areas. In recent years, a "Protestant explosion" has occurred in Mexico, with 15 percent of the population attending Protestant and evangelical services—approximately the same percent that regularly attend Catholic mass. Protestant growth concerns the Catholic hierarchy and angers the devout Catholic population. This anger inspired the most recent religious conflict in Mexico—between Catholics and Protestants.

CHAPTER 9

Mexican Education

Aña Franco Ortuno is 18 and lives in one of the wealthiest communities in Mexico City, San Angel. Although Aña is currently employed as a waitress, she plans to leave her job soon to pursue university studies in history and literature. She dreams of having "a lot of money" one day and is confident she will achieve her career goals.

Osvaldo Bautista Romero is 16 and lives 15 miles outside Mexico City in the rural farming community of San Pedro Nexapa. He dropped out of school last year due to illness. He suffers from a ruptured hernia, but his family cannot afford the medical treatment. He hopes to attend vocational agricultural college someday, but cannot continue his studies until his health and family income permit.

—Scholastic Update 1988

The two teens described above have educational experiences not unlike other Mexican children in similar regions and of similar socioeconomic backgrounds. Children from wealthy families in urban areas typically complete both primary and secondary school. They attend well-equipped public (and often private) schools and encounter few obstacles to school completion. Like Aña, most middle- and upper-class children plan to attend the university. Their educational experience resembles that of many children in the United States.

Children from rural areas and low-income families, like Osvaldo, often drop out before finishing primary school. They seldom complete secondary school, and the schools to which they have access do not have sufficient resources or trained teachers. Schools in some rural and poor communities lack even the most basic tools: desks, paper, or pencils. The university, for most poor and working-class Mexican children, is a pipe dream. Low-income children face numerous barriers to school completion, including lack of money for school uniforms and supplies, health problems, and the need to work and contribute to the **family economy**.

President Ernesto Zedillo (1994–2000) has promised to make sure that all Mexican children complete secondary school by the end of his term. This rhetoric is old news for Mexicans. For 100 years, Mexican politicians have promoted free and mass education. Yet most Mexicans have only basic reading and writing skills. Access to schools without resources remains the fate of many Mexican children.

Mexican culture honors education, but formal schooling has rarely lived up to its reputation. After the Independence Wars (1855–76), education became firmly established as the path to nation-building. Government leaders began to promote formal primary education as a method to sustain political stability and economic progress (Vaughn 1990). In time, they also promoted education as a path for upward **social mobility.** Mexicans began to perceive free education as the right of every citizen. Article three of the 1917 Mexican Constitution guarantees free, secular, and universal education. Although the law is generally interpreted to establish a citizen's right to education through the primary and secondary levels, over time, the Mexican public has interpreted the Constitution to include university education as well (Lorey 1995).

The modern Mexican state increased the number of schools as a means of gaining mass public support. The quality of education and the equal distribution of quality schools, however, remain poor. Half of Mexico's children fail to complete the basic six years of education. Although most of the Mexican population are functionally literate (can read and write), higher literacy skills are mostly restricted to the middle and upper classes (Lorey 1995). Nevertheless, progress has occurred in Mexico's educational system, as it has in other social institutions. Mexico's rate of literacy compares favorably with other Latin American nations. Eighty-three percent of Mexicans are literate. Literacy in Costa Rica is 93 percent; in Venezuela, 86 percent; in Nicaragua, 60 to 75 percent; and in Guatemala, 60 percent (Arnove and Torres 1995; Reimers 1991).

FORMAL EDUCATION

Primary and Secondary Education

Mexico's educational structure resembles the U.S. system with six years of elementary school (*primaria*), three years of secondary school (*secundaria*), and three years of preparatory (*preparatoria*) or postsecondary school (Osborn II 1976). All children between the ages of 6 and 14 should receive the free and mandatory six years of primary education. Primary school enrollment rates for girls and boys are essentially equal in most Latin American nations, including Mexico, but girls less often advance to secondary education (Arizpe 1993). The goals and subjects of primary education in Mexico parallel elementary education in the United States, with the focus on reading and writing (in Spanish) and basic math skills. Unlike the United States, however, Mexico has a nationally standardized curriculum. The government distributes without charge approved standardized textbooks (*libros de texto gratuitos*).

Secondary schools either prepare students for preparatory school and the university or focus on vocational training. Preparatory or postsecondary school is roughly equivalent to senior high school in the United States and prepares students for the university. Although private schools have been part of the Mexican educational system since the colonial era, public education administered by the state accounts for 95 percent of total enrollment at the primary level (Izquierdo and Schmelkes 1992, p. 67).

School populations increased from 3 million in 1950 to 24 million in 1990 (Lorey 1995, p. 52). This increase can partially be attributed to overall population growth during the period (see Chapter 10, "Population"). Policy changes from the 1960s to the early 1980s that emphasized access to basic education also contributed to the dramatic increase. These policies, however, did not adequately address the problems of poor quality and educational inequality (Izquierdo and Schmelkes 1992).

Mexico's government leaders typically emphasize universal education (quantity) with a limited focus on quality. Typical primary and secondary schools lack equipment and face severe overcrowding. Mexican teachers often have limited education, lack specific training, and are overworked and underpaid (Izquierdo and Schmelkes 1992). Teachers at the primary level are not required to have a university education. Instead, teacher training for primary school teachers (*escuelas normal*) occurs at the secondary level. Educational quality varies with location (rural or urban) and economic class (see section below, "Stratification in Schools").

Educational inequality and the poor quality of education became more acute after the 1980s economic crisis. **Structural adjustment policies,** including attempts to decentralize and privatize education, reduced funding for primary and secondary schools. In 1987, almost 300,000 school-age children across Mexico lacked any access to primary education. Approximately 15,000 communities out of 95,000 with at least one primary school teacher in 1982 had no teacher at all at the beginning of the 1987–88 school year (Izquierdo and Schmelkes 1992).

Few students who complete primary education eventually complete secondary school. High student drop-out rates prevail across Latin America. In Mexico, 75.6 percent of children ages 6 to 14 enroll in primary school. However, only 40.1 percent of children ages 12 to 16 enroll at the secondary level; at the preparatory level, 21.3 percent of the population between 16 and 19 years old enroll; and at the university level, only 14.9 percent of 20- to 24-year-olds enroll. In 1990, the estimated population of 15-year-olds in Mexico was 15 million, but out of this number 35 percent had not completed primary school. Thirteen percent never attended primary school, 7 percent had two years of education, and 15 percent had three to five years of education (Lorey 1995, pp. 51–52). The number of students repeating primary grades each year has declined over the last 20 years to just under 10 percent in 1985 (Reimers 1991, p. 326).

University Education

The oldest university in the New World, Mexico City's *Universidad Nacional Autónoma de México* (UNAM), was founded in 1521. Most Mexican universities, however, were founded after 1940. Despite an early start, Mexico's and Latin America's university education lagged behind that of Europe and the United States due to periodic economic and political chaos. Although 12 universities were operating across Latin America in the 1700s, by the 1940s only 9 public universities and 1 private university had been founded in Mexico. After 1940, however, higher education rapidly expanded. By 1971, Mexico had 125 universities (Osborn II 1976).

University systems across Latin America exhibit a number of similarities. First, many universities were founded after 1945.

Second, most universities in the region teach in the nation's "mother tongue," either Spanish or Portuguese. Third, the Latin American university curriculum focuses on training individuals for professions or technical jobs and places little emphasis on the general liberal arts. Fourth, most universities are self-contained or restricted to national boundaries, with limited emphasis on international learning. Fifth, universities often operate in isolation, with little sense of a national academic community. Finally, universities tend to be intimately connected to politics (Albornoz 1993).

University education in Latin America follows the European model. The curriculum is organized by professional school or *carrera* (career), rather than major department as in the United States. Most professional programs are five years. A *carrera* is chosen by the student prior to entering the university; the student attends the university and then is licensed (*licenciatura*) to practice the profession. Individuals who graduate from Mexican universities, whether public or private, receive a *licenciado* degree. The *licenciado* is somewhat comparable to a U.S. bachelor of arts or sciences degree, but it is more vocationally oriented. Those graduating with the *licenciado* degree must register with the Mexican state to receive a license that allows them to work as a professional. Students who complete the coursework but do not complete the required thesis or project are termed *egresados*. *Licenciados* and those with higher education work as professionals in Mexico. *Egresados* and those who attend technical or vocational school work as technicians (Lorey 1994).

Public universities may officially register as **autonomous,** selecting their own president and board, or **nonautonomous,** where the government is active in university administrative decisions. All public universities have close ties with government officials, as they are financed by the government except for small tuition fees and donations. It is common for public universities in Mexico to have an affiliated preparatory school (*prepas*). Until Salinas (1988–94) introduced university reform, students enrolled in *prepas* often received an automatic admittance (referred to as the *automático pase*) to the university linked to their *prepa* (Lorey 1995).

In Latin America, enrollment is concentrated in public universities. Over the last 20 years, however, private universities in Mexico have significantly increased their enrollments. Prior to 1929, there were no private universities in Mexico; by 1982, 148 private universities were operating. In 1992, private universities accounted for 22.6 percent of all university graduates (Lorey 1995, p. 53). The increase in private university (and private primary and secondary) enrollment is partially the result of the elite's desire to escape large, bureaucratic, and often poorly staffed public schools (see below, "Stratification in Schools" and "Educational Stratification and the 'Myth of Mobility' "). The private university system in Mexico has enjoyed increasing prestige in recent years, with private universities regarded as the "best" quality universities since the 1980s. Private universities also tend to be more selective in their admittance procedures (Levy 1980).

Technical/Vocational Education

Mexican technical or vocational institutes have emerged as an important type of formal education in the last 30 years. Technical schools primarily function to train engineers and business managers. The government controls technical schools more rigorously than universities, regulating both curriculum and personnel decisions. Technical institutions comprise only 15 percent of the enrollment in higher education but perform an especially important role in regions with no university (Kent 1993).

NONFORMAL EDUCATION

Nonformal and popular education programs are important alternatives to formal education in areas where high illiteracy rates persist. The programs generally focus on adult education and serve the most impoverished and powerless social groups. They successfully reach communities where the standard, formal program does not fit the community's needs, as is the case in many rural and largely **Amerindian** areas. Arnove and Torres (1995) define nonformal education as "any organized and systematic educational activity conducted outside the framework of the formal system and having the objective of imparting selected types of knowledge and skills to particular subgroups of the population" (p. 313). These voluntary, short courses usually grant a special certificate.

Nonformal education is typically a low-budget priority. The programs serve poor and marginalized populations that lack political power to demand more public funding (Arnove and Torres 1995). Although the government under Salinas (1988–94) targeted adult education as a priority, public expenditures were cut for all social welfare and nonessential services (including adult education).

As of 1994, only 2 percent of Mexico's education budget was spent on both adult education and municipal public libraries (Palafox, Prawda, and Velez 1994). Most adults involved in nonformal programs drop out before completing their basic education. Adult students must weigh the long-term benefits of education with the short-term realities of family economics.

Grassroots educational programs in Latin America, particularly in indigenous communities, are labeled "popular education." Popular education is separated from nonformal education by its class-consciousness nature and its emphasis on the creation of social movements to promote a more equitable society. Often overtly political, it meets the needs of marginalized sectors such as women or indigenous groups. Instruction is less hierarchical than in nonformal education, with more emphasis on dialogue between teacher and student (Arnove et al. 1996).

THE NATIONALIST FUNCTION OF MEXICAN EDUCATION

The Mexican government has attempted to integrate Amerindian cultures into the dominant *mestizo* culture since the end of the colonial era. Government leaders consider education a key institution for mobilizing collective nationalist sentiment. Thus, schools became a primary channel for disseminating official state policy and national identity (Epstein 1985) (see Chapter 6, "Race and Ethnic Relations").

The educational system fosters ideological harmony by encouraging Amerindian and other culturally distinct groups to assimilate into the dominant society. A common curriculum and free textbooks channel this policy to students in all regions (Izquierdo and Schmelkes 1992). Integrationist and nationalist education, however, has not been an overall success in indigenous communities. Although bilingual educational programs include around 400,000 students, language barriers, high drop-out rates, and poor support by parents and students make educational attainment in rural and largely indigenous areas problematic (Epstein 1985).

STRATIFICATION IN SCHOOLS

Social class, ethnicity, and locale (rural or urban) determine Mexican students' access to quality schools. The education system performs the **latent function** of preserving the class structure. Children of the elite in all Latin American countries attend well-equipped schools, but for the masses schools often lack resources or there is no school at all. Mexico's primary education quality varies from state to state. Wealthy states in the north and near Mexico City have the best quality public primary schools and a number of private primary schools. Middle- and upper-class students typically attend the best public and private schools and usually complete secondary, preparatory, and university education.

Students in rural areas, with large Amerindian cultures, have higher drop-out and repeat rates than the urban population and are less likely to have access to a secondary school or higher education (Gimeno 1983). High drop-out rates for children in rural and impoverished areas partly express their obligation to work in the family economy (see Chapter 7, "The Mexican Family"). In poor areas, students are also undernourished, which makes it difficult for them to concentrate or stay awake in class. Free milk or lunch programs that could combat this problem are rarely available (Riding 1984).

While primary education is free and secondary school fees are minimal, poor families must pay for required uniforms and supplies. In addition, standardized educational content and teaching methods are often viewed by rural students and their families (particularly indigenous people) as irrelevant to their needs. The content in the *libros de texto gratuitos* rarely represents the reality of rural and Amerindian students' lives. The content of the free and compulsory standardized texts frequently provokes parental and student protests.

Mexican educational priorities and educational resources "trickle down" from the wealthiest and most developed regions (such as Mexico City) to the poorest and least developed. Schools in wealthy urban areas have well-trained teachers, good equipment, and adequate educational materials. Rural and marginalized areas, conversely, often face widespread teacher shortages, poorly trained teachers, poor buildings, and inadequate educational materials (Izquierdo and Schmelkes 1992). In rural areas, average class size is large and often resembles the one-room schoolhouse of U.S. rural history. It is not unusual for rural schools to go years without a teacher or for one teacher to teach all six primary grades (Riding 1984).

Structural differences also exist between urban and rural schools. Rural primary schools often offer coursework lasting two to four years rather than five to seven years (Gimeno 1983). In Mexico City, 3 percent of primary schools are incomplete (do not offer the full six years of study), whereas in largely indigenous Chiapas, 43 percent of primary schools are incomplete (Izquierdo and Schmelke 1992). The states with the largest indigenous populations have the highest rates of illiteracy. While Mexico's national illiteracy rate is 17 percent, the illiteracy rate among the indigenous population is almost 40 percent (Arnove and Torres 1995, p. 312).

EDUCATIONAL STRATIFICATION AND THE "MYTH OF MOBILITY"

The Constitution of 1917 mandates universal and free basic education for all citizens. Over time, however, the Mexican population, particularly the middle class, has viewed free university education as a government obligation as well. The government promotes the university as a means for social mobility. Thus, the social demand for free access to higher education has expanded.

Since the 1940s, demand for higher education has overwhelmed the universities' capacity to absorb new students and also has outpaced the Mexican economy's needs. Public and private universities have worked together for a number of years to supply students to different labor markets. Elite public and private universities are predominantly filled with upper- and middle-class students, while the regional public universities are filled with lower-class students. Elite public and private university graduates staff most corporate and government jobs. Students from regional universities find employment in technical or other nonprofessional jobs (Lorey 1994).

Many public universities, particularly those serving local and regional areas, provide their graduates with **social status** without **social mobility.** The university does produce social mobility for the middle and upper classes, but for the poor the university is often only a symbol of mobility. The Mexican public has recently become aware of this "myth of mobility," and there now exists a widespread feeling of betrayal by "the university, the government, the system" (Lorey 1994).

Since the 1950s, access to Mexican universities has increased. In 1988, 1,244,888 students were enrolled in Mexican universities, with 151,131 graduating in 1987 (Lorey 1992, p. 65). The National Autonomous University of Mexico (UNAM), one of the largest universities in the world, has an enrollment of almost 400,000 (Albornoz 1993, p. 23). This university expansion occurred due to "nonselective" admission processes. Most public universities followed an "open-door" policy for admission until very recently, with limited screening of applicants through previous academic records or national test requirements. Low tuition fees also contributed to high enrollments.

Although Mexican students are not formally tracked into educational paths, children of the middle and upper classes disproportionately take advantage of university education. They are more likely to complete primary, secondary, and preparatory school. Thus, they are more likely to be adequately prepared to pass college-level coursework. While admission standards and tuition fees have not limited enrollment, socioeconomic conditions and access to primary and secondary schooling limit the population prepared to attend the university (Levy 1980).

THE INTERRELATIONSHIP OF THE MEXICAN EDUCATIONAL AND ECONOMIC SYSTEMS

Beginning in 1950, professional and technical job growth increased as the population expanded. Job growth in technical positions, however, has far outweighed growth in professional jobs. The Mexican economy does not produce professional opportunities as rapidly as, for example, the United States. Rather, Mexico creates an increasing number of technical jobs. A fundamental mismatch exists, therefore, between the number of university graduates and the number of professional jobs. By the end of the 1980s, university graduates exceeded professional jobs by 1 million (Lorey 1995, p. 53). The mismatch intensified as the result of three economic strategies: the highly protected nature of the Mexican economy allowed outdated equipment and practices to continue and limited the need for research and development; the Mexican economy depended on imported capital goods and technology for expansion; and the government hired university graduates and university-trained professionals in industries that really did not require this skill level. This distorted the real demand for educated professionals (Lorey 1992). Further, university students are rarely encouraged to pursue university studies in technical or vocational areas (areas of job growth). Instead, they concentrate in professional studies such as law, economics, and medicine.

THE INTERRELATIONSHIP OF EDUCATIONAL AND POLITICAL SYSTEMS

The current educational system is largely the result of government policies to build national loyalty through the promise of social mobility and social benefits, such as access to education, land, and electricity. Mexico's political elite manipulate education as a "political resource" to satisfy the public's most pressing demands rather than as "an instrument to foster any visions of society they may hold" (Levy 1980, p. 56). According to Torres (1991), political leaders have promoted education not as a path to ensure greater human capital in Mexico but as a way to obtain political capital for the state.

A number of educational conflicts can be traced to **corporatist** relations between political leaders and educational leaders. An unspoken agreement exists between the university and the government. As long as the university (students and teachers) does not join or provoke antigovernment hostility, the government limits its interference in university matters. The relationship is mutually dependent. The government controls university funding, but at the same time the government is dependent upon the university for political legitimation, middle-class political support, a steady supply of professionals to fill government positions, and scientific research (Levy 1980). This relationship sometimes turns sour.

In 1968, a student movement, including students from both UNAM and IPN, began as a peaceful protest against federal cuts in education. After violent police attacks on student marches, the protest evolved to include more students as well as workers groups, peasants, and unions demanding official party reform and an end to government repression. It all ended abruptly on October 2, when hundreds of participants were killed by federal police during the group's last organized demonstration (see Chapter 11, "Social Problems and Social Movements").

University personnel also have their rebellious moments. Some university teachers and administrators belong to the SUNTU coalition of leftist unions. At times, the group has "paralyzed institutions" during struggles for higher wages (Riding 1984). The typical government response is to cut federal and state funding to their universities. Numerous government attempts to increase tuition, however, failed as politicians yielded to the demands of students and their families rather than risk social disruption.

Corporatist politics has produced a static primary and secondary educational system. The teachers' union in Mexico, the *Sindicato Nacional de Trabajadores de la Educación* (SNTE), successfully blocked government attempts for educational reform from 1982 to 1988. One of the largest and most powerful unions in Mexico with over 1 million members, the union readily mobilizes for higher pay (which is seriously low) but resists teacher retraining and innovative teaching techniques. Further, the union adamantly resisted government attempts to decentralize education during the 1980s. Decentralization would have weakened the union by forcing it to negotiate with state-level authorities (Lorey 1992; 1995; Torres 1991).

The university is also linked to the political system through the formation of political cliques (*camarillas*). In order to receive a political appointment, one must first gain admission to a *camarilla*, and to gain admission to a *camarilla*, one must complete a university education. The political elite in Mexico are selected from the narrow pool of those university graduates who excel and establish a name for themselves at the university. Most *camarilla* recruitment is concentrated in certain universities—historically UNAM, but increasingly also in elite private universities such as *Colegio de México*. The *camarilla* system is also connected to the university through professors who dually serve as faculty members and important political leaders (*jefes*). Professors direct the formation of student groups from which political *camarillas* often emerge. This political/education link is particularly important to educational funding because the institutions where political recruitment is highest receive a larger amount of government funding (Epstein 1985; Camp 1980).

Because of the interconnectedness of politics and the university in Mexico, the political elite shape educational policy to suit their class needs while limiting public unrest. According to Arnove et al. (1996), "[elite] offspring are able to obtain essentially a free university education. The state often spends 15 to 20 times as much on a college student as on a primary school child who may have to sit on a mud floor in a rural classroom without electricity, running water, books or supplies" (p. 144).

SCIENCE AND TECHNOLOGY

In the global economy, scientific progress is fundamental to economic and social progress. According to Albornoz (1993), scientific and technical development in higher education is essential for Latin America's future, because "economic growth in the next century will depend upon the ability of nations to trade in super-computers, industrial robots and bio-technology, as well as to be able to tackle the problems of the environment, pollution, transit, social security, and efficient management of the growing areas of services" (p. 4).

Yet economic and cultural dependency limit scientific achievement in Latin America. Latin American universities spend very little time on science and technology research and often have inadequate libraries and labs. According to the Inter-American Development Bank (1995), Latin America's total contributions to the "world total of scientific quotations" is less than 1 percent. Mexico is one of the four countries in Latin America responsible for this contribution, along with Brazil, Argentina, and Chile.

Most Latin American universities, particularly public universities, are unlike U.S. or European universities, which strive for scientific and technical excellence through faculty research. Exceptions to this rule, UNAM, *Colegio de México,* and *Universidad de Sao Paulo* in Brazil, grant at least 50 doctorates per year. Small private and public universities are almost always teaching institutions with little focus on research.

Latin American universities have not achieved the scientific and technical development necessary to advance in today's global economy. In the United States, hundreds of higher education institutions compete vigorously for the best students, faculty, and staff in order to achieve a high level of academic distinction. Most U.S. universities are autonomous, with their own boards, although state university systems may have a board of regents overseeing policy at multiple universities. In Latin America, faculty traditionally have not been encouraged to compete or engage in research activities, and they have not been rewarded based on performance (Albornoz 1993).

In the 1990s, Mexico's government leaders began to emphasize the importance of science and technology. Greater emphasis is now assigned to university research. Faculty research activities are regularly rewarded with salary bonuses. In part, NAFTA has led to the promotion of educational standards in Mexico to bring the nation on par with the United States and Canada.

CONCLUSION

Mexico's educational system developed to serve several social and political objectives: transmission of nationalist values, the desire for social mobility, and as a way of sustaining political stability and economic progress. Mexico's educational system, though improving in recent years, is still imperfect. The relentless focus on mass access to education without an equal focus on quality of education has led to uneven educational development by region and economic class.

Unplanned population increases since the 1940s have strained the state's ability to provide good quality education to the masses. Educational stratification resulted. Upper- and middle-class urban students attend well-equipped schools with capable teachers, while lower-class, rural students attend poorly equipped schools with few resources and deficient teachers. Corporatist politics between political and education leaders inhibit innovative solutions to Mexico's educational problems.

Government reform in the 1980s attempted to solve some problems but intensified others. Decentralization placed greater responsibility on individual states, increasing state responsibility in designing basic educational programs to fit the needs of regional students. Unfortunately, structural adjustment programs in the 1980s also reduced overall basic educational expenditures, and teacher and supply shortages increased in many regions.

Federal officials began to address the long-term shortcomings of the public university system in the late 1980s, including obsolete curriculum, inadequate facilities (labs, computers), poorly trained faculty (only 25 percent had doctorates), poor secondary school preparation, and school overcrowding. During Salinas's administration (1988–94), university reforms were proposed in response to widespread social questioning and loss of faith in the educational system. The proposed changes include: an increase in financial independence of public universities, tuition reform, the establishment of national entrance exams, and the end of the automatic pass for *prepa* students (Lorey 1994).

Mexico's future educational challenge is to draw a balance between funding quality, mass basic education to increase the number and quality of secondary school graduates, and funding higher education to train students for employment in the growth industries of the future. Mexico's inadequate educational system should concern the United States. Mexicans immigrating to the United States often come from rural areas where literacy is lowest. In addition, with the implementation of NAFTA, the United States must be more sensitive to economic issues in Mexico that are affected by Mexico's educational development.

CHAPTER 10

Population

Latin America is young, far younger than Europe, the United States, and Japan. The United States has a **median age** of 34. For Europe, the median age is 35, and in Japan, the median age is 36. Latin America's overall median age is only 21. However, some Latin American countries have extremely young populations while others have profiles that look more like that of the United States. The average citizen in Uruguay, for example, is 30, but in some Central American countries 50 percent of the population is under 17 (Oxford Analytica 1991, p. 12). Mexico's median age in 1980 was 17.6 years, according to the Mexican census, and in 1995 it was 20 years. Thus, very young **age cohorts** dominate Mexico's age profile.

This young population creates pressures on the economy and government. A large proportion of the population enters the job market every year, and **dependency–support ratios**—the ratio of economically active to inactive populations—are high. Mexico's economy must produce 900,000 new jobs each year just to keep up with young workers flooding into the workforce. That translates to a breakneck growth rate of 5 percent every year just to stay even.

Low wages throughout the economy are kept low by this constant supply of new workers. The pressure on government programs is evident in the need for schools, housing, and transportation. Mexican leaders have focused on two solutions. *The Economist* ("Mexico Survey" 1995) summarizes the first in three words: "growth, growth, growth." The second solution rests on opportunities for Mexicans to migrate north across the border. Millions do so. A third solution is emerging, but more from the actions of individual Mexicans than the

141

policies of leaders: Mexicans are reducing the birthrate. While Mexico and many Latin American countries have high birthrates and young populations, they are experiencing trends toward lower **fertility rates** and **mortality rates,** rising median age, and an increasing proportion of elderly. Thus, they are experiencing what demographers call a **demographic transition.**

Latin American countries can be identified at different stages of demographic transition (see Table 10–1). Each nation-state, however, exhibits sharp regional and social group differences. The poorest countries, Bolivia and Haiti, have high birthrates, but their growth is slowed by high mortality rates and relatively short life expectancies. A number of countries in Central America have managed to decrease mortality rates. Their high fertility rates are producing very rapid population growth. In countries such as Argentina, Chile, Cuba, and Uruguay demographic transition is advanced and we find low birthrates combined with mortality rates that result in low growth rates.

Demographic transition closely follows social and economic development. We can group Latin American countries according to social indicators of modernization—for example, education, urbanization, and proportion of service sector workers. Countries such as Mexico, which have fully entered the process of demographic transition, tend to be highly urbanized, with an above average per capita gross domestic product (see Table 10–2). Mexico's 2.4 percent annual population growth rate will continue to challenge the economy and the government's capacity to meet demands for jobs and services. Its population, which was 70.69 million in 1982, is 92.33 million in 1997 and is projected to reach 106.48 million in 2005 (Siembieda and Rodríguez M. 1996).

The U.S. population is nearly three times that of Mexico. However, as Mexico's growth rate is three times higher, by 2020 Mexico's population will have grown to 163 million while that of the United States will have grown only from 249 to 299 million. Mexico's overall demographic profile and trends are typical of developing countries experiencing a dynamic transition from rural to urban, agricultural to industrial, and traditional to modern social relations. Rapid population growth in the 1950s and 1960s was followed by a falling birthrate and much reduced rate of growth during the past two decades. Basic demographic processes, fertility (birthrates), mortality (death rates), and migration (internal and international) have made a significant impact on Mexico's social structure. High fertility, declining mortality, and high migration

TABLE 10–1

Latin America and the Caribbean: Country Situation
According to Stage of Demographic Transition, 1985–90

Birthrate*	Mortality Rate†		
	Low	**Moderate**	**High**
High			
		Nicaragua 3.5	
		Guatemala 3.2	
		Honduras 3.2	
			Bolivia 2.6
			Haiti 2.3
Moderate			
	Dominican Republic 2.5	Ecuador 2.5	
	Mexico 2.4	Peru 2.2	
	Costa Rica 2.5		
	Venezuela 2.3		
	Surinam 2.2		
	Panama 2.2	Brazil 1.9	
	Colombia 2.0	Guyana 1.9	
	Trinidad and Tobago 1.9		
Low			
	Jamaica 1.7		
	Chile 1.7		
	Bahamas 1.5		
		Guadeloupe 1.3	
		Argentina 1.3	
	Martinique 1.2	Puerto Rico 1.1	
	Cuba 1.1	Uruguay 0.8	
		Barbados 0.7	

Note: The figures next to country names correspond to the natural growth rate, expressed as percentages. The countries included are those for which the United Nations prepares population estimates and projections, which are those with at least 200,000 inhabitants.
*Birthrate (per thousand)   high: 32–45; moderate: 24–32; low   10–24
†Mortality rate (per thousand)   high: 11–16; moderate: 7–11; low: 4–7

Source: Economic Commission for Latin America and the Caribbean, "Latin America and the Caribbean: Country Situation According to Stage of Demographic Transition, 1985–1990," *Population, Social Equity and Changing Production Patterns* (New York: United Nations, 1993). (LC/DEM/G.131/REV.1, Series E, No. 37), Santiago, Chile, 1993, diagram I.1, p. 17, United Nations Publications, Sales No. E.93.\, II, G.8.

TABLE 10–2

Relationships between Demographic Transition
and Modernization

Stage of Demographic Transition	Modernization Level in the 1960s and 1970s		
	Advanced	Partial and Accelerated	Incipient
Advanced			
	Argentina		
	Chile		
	Cuba		
	Uruguay		
Full Transition			
	Venezuela	Costa Rica	
		Panama	
		Brazil	
		Colombia	
		Dominican Republic	
		Ecuador	
		Mexico	
		Peru	
Moderate			
		Paraguay	El Salvador
			Guatemala
			Honduras
			Nicaragua
Incipient			
			Bolivia
			Haiti

Source: ECLAC, "Relationships between Demographic Transition and Modernization," *Population, Social Equity and Changing Production Patterns* (New York: United Nations, 1993). (LC/G.1758/Rev.1-P; LC/DEM/G.131/Rev.1, Series E, No. 37), Santiago, Chile, 1993, diagram I.2, p. 20. United Nations Publications, Sales No. E. 93. II. G.8.

rates have an impact on every economic, political, and social question in Mexico. Labor relations, public health, family, education, values, and the dynamics of political struggle must be understood in light of the powerful impact of these population dynamics.

Large regional differences characterize fertility, infant mortality, and use of family planning in Mexico. In part, these differences reflect variation in regional patterns of urbanization and industrial development. Mexico is a very heterogeneous country. Geography, social and economic divisions, and ethnic and cultural contrasts are extreme. In some zones, especially in rural and southern Mexico, Amerindian communities exist where regional languages prevail and few people speak Spanish. Some groups are of pure European descent, especially among the economic and political elite. *Mestizos,* people of mixed Amerindian and European ancestry, comprise the vast majority of Mexicans (see Chapter 6, "Race and Ethnic Relations"). In Mexico's poorest and most rural regions, poverty, high levels of inequality, and political marginality all contribute to the maintenance of traditional patterns of high fertility and mortality.

The impact of extreme inequality on Mexico's population becomes clearer when we examine such demographic issues as teenage pregnancy and family formation, extreme rural poverty, and the heavy flow of Mexican migrants north seeking work in border factories or the United States. These patterns produce profound changes within Mexico, as the ethnic Amerindian population grows much faster than other Mexican groups. During the 1980s, the average Mexican faced unemployment and lower real income as the price for government austerity policies (see Chapter 3, "The Mexican Economy"). This significant decline in the average Mexican's standard of living produced changes in population characteristics such as family formation, migration, birthrates, and employment.

Mexico has witnessed great changes in family structure and work patterns due to its failure to produce sufficient new jobs for the young people entering the labor markets. A much higher proportion of women have entered the wage labor force. As the economy produced too few new jobs, more and more workers were driven into low-wage manual employment. Thus, we have seen an increased social and economic polarization in Mexico as employers take advantage of the vast supply of workers. In response, Mexican workers by the millions have sought economic opportunity and relief from poverty by migrating to the United States. In the following sections of this chapter, we will examine Mexico's demographic profile and consider a number of the social, economic, and political consequences.

CITIES

As recently as 1980, Mexico had only seven cities with more than 500,000 residents. By 2000, over 25 cities will reach this size, and the national capital, Mexico City, is already the largest metropolitan area in the world at well above 20 million. Large regional cities—for example, Guadalajara in the west and Monterrey in the east—provide services and products for local consumption and serve as transportation and communication hubs. Other urban areas have developed around Mexico's tourist economy. Thus, Acapulco, once a lazy Pacific retreat, serves millions of tourists each year, and other now substantial cities—for example, Cancun, Cozumel, Puerto Vallarta, and Ixtapa—have become well known to North Americans seeking relief from frigid winter weather. These tourist centers typically have an enclave for foreign tourists attached to a "real city" where Mexicans live. For example, Ixtapa is paired with Zihuatanejo in just such a relationship.

Perhaps most impressive, if one turns attention from the enormous concentration of Mexico City itself, border industrialization has produced extremely fast urban growth from Tijuana to Juarez. Tijuana's deep integration with Southern California's economy attracted migrants, and its 1990 population swelled to approximately 1.5 million. In the late 1980s, the countryside east of Tijuana was empty fields. By 1997, 250,000 Mexicans lived there in a town called El Florido.

More than 70 percent of all Latin Americans live in cities. The social and environmental problems associated with rapid and extreme urbanization—for example, sanitation, transportation, and air pollution problems—seem to be magnified in Mexico City (see Chapter 11, "Social Problems and Social Movements"). Unplanned and uncontrolled growth produced an urban sprawl filling up a 6,300-foot-high valley framed by mountains and built on dry lake beds. The air in Mexico City becomes almost unbreathable when frequent thermal inversions trap air in the valley. The ultimate cause of Mexico City's problems, however, rests with uncontrolled high levels of population growth.

In Mexico's government-controlled economy, from World War II until the 1980s economic crisis, for millions of Mexicans the chance to escape poverty had two roads. One led north across the border. The other led to Mexico City. Latin American economies driven by import substitution industrialization (ISI) often produced such economic and population concentration in national capitals. These cities become virtually unmanageable as public officials with few resources are overwhelmed by the sheer numbers of people. As Mexico City's population doubled each decade after World War II, the urban infrastructure failed to expand. Migrants were drawn there because 45 percent of all Mexican industry located in Mexico City by 1975 (Schteingart 1989). They created vast squatter settlements where high density and lack of legal claims to property produced widespread corruption and social conflicts. Instead of learning from experience, Mexico has continued to focus on economic growth, and this pattern of uncontrolled growth has been reproduced in its rapidly growing regional cities.

FERTILITY

Mexico's birthrate has powerfully influenced its population trends in recent decades. In the 1970s, the fertility rate began to decline, and this pattern has continued. Between 1973 and 1986, the **crude fertility rate** (total number of births for a year divided by the total population) declined from 6.3 to 3.8, an abrupt change after roughly 40 years of stable high rates that contributed to Mexico's rapid population growth (Palma and Echarri Cánovas 1992). For most age groups, these declines were higher in the 1970s and continued, but at a slower rate, in the 1980s. Older women, those over 35, reduced their childbearing more than younger women. Since this age group has lower fertility levels in general, however, the impact on overall fertility was small.

Mexico's teenage mothers exhibit many patterns identical to their counterparts in the United States. Complications during teen pregnancy and delivery are associated with relatively high rates of mortality, premature births, low birth weight, and congenital defects. A national survey of **fecundity** and health (Dirección General de Planificación Familiar [DGPF] 1988) concluded that 39.8 percent of all women over age 20 had their first birth when they were teenagers. Very young adolescent mothers are much more likely to be unmarried than Mexican mothers 20 years and older. Some 21.2 percent of births to mothers 15 years and younger occur prior to marriage, while only 7.5 percent of all mothers are unmarried.

As with other demographic processes in Mexico, there are great regional variations in fertility. In the northwestern and northeastern Mexican border states fecundity was lowest, ranging from 3.2 to 3.8 children per woman; in the southeast and west, fecundity was highest, ranging from 4.6 to 4.9 children per woman. This follows the worldwide pattern of lower fecundity where urbanism and industrial economic development are most advanced. The impact of formal schooling on birthrates in Mexico conforms to the general rule: more education, fewer children. Thus, we find that 1987 average lifetime births for women aged 45–49 was 7.88 for those without schooling, 6.70 for women who did not complete primary school, 4.65 for those with a primary school education, and 3.58 for women whose education was at the secondary level or higher.

MORTALITY

Since the beginning of this century, Mexico has experienced a continual decline in mortality rates interrupted only by the Mexican Revolution and by a period of political instability during the 1920s. As with other demographic trends, however, within Mexico we encounter striking contrasts between regions and socioeconomic groups. The **crude mortality rate** (the total number of deaths in a year divided by the population) stood at 33 per 1,000 population in 1900, 22.0 in 1944, 15.1 in 1954, 10.4 in 1964, 8.6 in 1974, and 6 per 1,000 population by the mid-1980s (Centro de Estudios Económicos y Demográficos 1981). In common with similar rapid declines in developing countries elsewhere, Mexico benefited greatly from advances in medicine and public health policies first developed in the United States and Europe. Especially important have been the methods for cheaply producing insecticides and antibiotics, as well as the availability of improved sanitation, fresh water, and food storage. Declines in mortality also have been influenced strongly by economic development after the 1930s and the emergence of an activist government that enacted many reform projects.

Mexican life expectancy greatly increased during this century. In 1930, life expectancy at birth was 36.9 years. This increased to 49.6 years in 1950, 62.0 in 1970, and 66.4 in 1987 (Jiménez 1992, p. 86). Gains in life expectancy were especially strong during the 1940–60 decades and have continued at a declining rate since then. This pattern is similar to that of other Latin American countries. Rapid gains in life expectancy can be expected when governments implement social programs targeting basic needs such as potable water supplies, sanitation, and access to basic medical services.

Infant Mortality

The greatest gains in life expectancy reflect substantial declines in **infant mortality**. In recent decades, international agencies have targeted infant mortality as a key modernization indicator. This has motivated governments in **peripheral nations** of the world system to implement policies to decrease infant mortality. Mexico is no exception, and we see that Mexico's infant mortality rates have declined even faster than mortality for the general population. In this century, Mexico's rate of infant mortality has declined from 288.6 per thousand population to 124.5 in 1940, 73.8 in 1960, and 56.8 in 1980. By the end of the 1980s, it was about 46 per thousand (Alba 1978; SSA 1988). Despite this rapid decline, Mexico's infant mortality rate today remains much higher than prevailing rates in developed core nations of the world system and even some Central American countries. Japan and Canada, for example, had infant mortality rates below 15 per thousand in 1975 and today they have mortality rates well below 8 per thousand. The United States infant mortality rate stood at 8.9 in 1990–92, a reduction from 12.0 in 1980–82 (National Center for Health Statistics 1994). Costa Rica, with a national health care system established in the 1950s, was able to reduce infant mortality to below 20 per thousand in 1980.

Causes of Mortality

Roughly half of infant deaths in Mexico are caused by infectious diseases, parasites, diarrhea, enteritis, influenza, and pneumonia. (Jiménez Ornelas 1992, p. 88). All these factors reflect the poor nutrition, lack of sanitation, and low levels of education that define life for much of Mexico's population, especially in rural areas and urban zones of poverty. In developed countries where lower mortality rates prevail, cardiovascular diseases and cancer are the principal causes of death because these are associated with death among the elderly. In Mexico and much of Latin America, we see a much stronger role played by contagious diseases and respiratory illnesses associated with poverty and lack of access to basic medical services. This role, however, has been declining since 1960, reflecting an improved standard of living for Mexicans.

Regions and Social Groups

We lack good **public health** data for Mexico. Thus, it is difficult to analyze and compare mortality causes for distinct social groups and regions. We do have national data for political subdivisions, and some surveys have included socioeconomic status of respondents when examining health. Paralleling the United States, we see the development of an increasing gap between female and male life expectancy. In 1900, U.S. women lived approximately 4 percent longer than males; however, in the census of 1990, this gap approached

10 percent. In Mexico, the mean life expectancy gap between men and women grew from two years in 1940 to 4.12 in 1970, 6.18 in 1980, and remained high at 6.12 years in 1987. This is mainly explained by increases in male deaths for ages 15–44, where in 1980 three males died for every two female deaths. This difference grew rapidly during the debt crisis years of the 1980s, when real wages were rapidly declining in Mexico. By 1987, for the 15–44 age cohorts, 203 males died for every 100 females. The difference was mostly attributable to high male death rates resulting from violence, accidents, suicides, and homicides (Jiménez Ornelas 1992, p. 90).

Mexico has substantial regional variations in mortality rates, too. Baja California, the state with the lowest mortality rate, has a 40 percent lower total mortality rate and a 50 percent lower infant mortality rate than Oaxaca, the state with the highest mortality rate. Thus, the life expectancy in Oaxaca is only 49.3 years, roughly equal to that in the United States in 1900, but in Baja California it is 68.6. Within the state of Oaxaca itself, the story is more complicated and reveals the extraordinary differences in material conditions and access to government services in Mexico. In the central valley near the city of Oaxaca, the state's capital, infant mortality was about 84 per 1,000 births in 1970. However, in Sierra Norte, the rate climbed to 249 deaths for every 1,000 births. In other words, nearly 25 percent of all children in Sierra Norte died before their first birthday, a rate 300 percent higher than that of children near the capital of the same state (Jiménez Ornelas 1992).

Social group affiliation and economic status also define extreme differences in Mexican mortality rates at all ages. For the Mexican middle class and wealthy, only one infant dies for every three deaths to children of rural and urban working-class families (Minujin, Vera, Jiménez, and Ruiz 1984). In comparative studies, researchers have found that differences between groups are also influenced by **demographic variables,** not just socioeconomic differences. Higher infant mortality rates among working-class groups were thus linked also to the age of the mother, the spacing between births, and the age of the mother when her first child was born. Social factors explaining differences in mortality rates were education of the mother and access to medical services (Jiménez, Vera, and Ruiz 1986).

MIGRATION

Since the 1940s, Mexican economic development and government programs have focused on urban areas. This produced a tremendous pressure for migration from rural to urban areas within Mexico as people searched for employment and the superior health care, education, social security, and higher standard of living of the cities. For this population of new urban residents, mortality rates were much lower than for comparable rural populations. Birthrates, however, remained high. As a result, by the 1970s, Mexico was becoming a proportionally younger population and mortality rates continued to drop, reflecting not only improving physical and social conditions but this change in the age pyramid.

Urbanward migration is one response to Latin American economic development policies such as import substitution industrialization (ISI) that focused economic opportunity in cities. At the same time, rural development patterns were undermining economic security for agrarian workers. Agribusiness expanded, and land ownership became more concentrated. Government policies for prices and taxes transferred wealth to urban areas. Mass-produced consumer products undermined local and regional producers. Rapid population growth placed additional pressure on rural labor markets. The result has been a massive increase in rural-to-urban migration. In this context, migration must be seen as a rational cost–benefit response by households seeking to meet economic needs, improve their life circumstances, and exploit economic opportunities (Grindle 1988, p. 28).

Economic opportunity, especially jobs, and the availability of services have been identified as the major reasons for migration to the United States. Mexican migration to the United States expresses family survival strategies that lead households and individuals to take advantage of their skills and available opportunities in different economic locations, even if that means migration across national borders (Massey, Alarcón, Durand, and González 1987).

Although economic calculations are significant, this does not mean that the poorest families or the most impoverished regions produce the highest migration rates. Migrants move where they can calculate costs and risks and seek to maximize gains. Knowledge of the city and social contacts who can offer support are important components of this calculus. As a result, migrants are more likely to come from backgrounds where they have resources to support their migration costs and knowledge about the conditions they will face. The poorest and most isolated regions and families do not fit this profile. When compared with nonmigrants from their communities, migrants tend to have more education and better job skills, and be younger and unmarried. They also tend to follow the path of earlier migrants from their village and region. Thus, in urban zones, whether in Mexico or the United States, we tend to find microcommunities of migrants whose social relationships began where they started. These networks facilitate not only migration but the flow of resources between rural origins and urban destinations.

However, Latin American migration differs from that elsewhere in the world system in one important respect: gender. The largest Latin American countries have migration streams dominated by women (United Nations 1993, Table 7). Mexico shares this gender bias with Brazil, Argentina, Colombia, and Venezuela. A gender-based labor market in rural areas restricts women's opportunities even as the market for products produced in households declines. This is a push factor. Economic opportunities, pull factors, draw women to urban areas where they work in factories, the service sector, and as maids in private homes.

Mexican migration to the United States, in particular undocumented labor migration, has become one of the most politically volatile and socially contentious aspects of relations between the two nations. The long history of Mexican migration, legal and illegal, to the United States confirms the economic and social integration of the two countries. Deeply established family and social ties facilitate the flow of labor from Mexico where unemployment, underemployment, and low real wages magnify the pull of salary differentials.

Current cross-border migration patterns build on a long history of legal migration that took place under treaties between the two nations. Drawn by employment and higher wages, from 1910 to 1930 as many as 800,000 Mexicans may have moved to the United States, but most of these returned during the Depression years of the 1930s. During World War II, U.S. labor shortages led to a treaty, the 1942 Bracero Program, that allowed Mexicans to work for limited periods. The Bracero Program continued until 1964 and created a deeply entrenched cross-border culture, economic habits of working in the United States, and knowledge about U.S. society that facilitated and encouraged Mexicans to continue seeking work in the United States even after the program ended.

Two pull factors influence migration northward. First, the difference in wage rates creates a powerful magnet drawing Mexico's impoverished and underemployed. Second, border industrialization, stimulated by the North American Free Trade Agreement and earlier treaties that encouraged *maquiladoras* (see Chapter 3, "The Mexican Economy") gives workers hope for jobs. Most Mexican migrants to the border originate in a few poor

states: Jalisco, Durango, Guanajuato, Michoacan, Sinaloa, and Zacatecas each contributes migrants well in excess of their proportion of Mexico's overall population. These poor rural states have
lagged in urbanization, industrialization, and the benefits of government expenditures. This strong migration has contributed to
roughly half of the population growth along the border (Ham-
Chande and Weeks 1992, p. 19).

Martin (1996) concludes that roughly 10 percent of Mexican
workers earn most of their income in the United States. Over the
past decade, some 3 million Mexicans migrated across the northern border, equal to 20 percent of Mexico's net population growth
(Martin 1996, p. 145). Structural changes in the Mexican economy,
causing workers to leave rural agricultural employment and
drawing millions north to border factories, interact with highly integrated institutions that facilitate migration across the border.
Simply put, Mexicans migrate to the United States in search of
work. Long-standing cross-border migration patterns have created
a network of family and community ties that also motivate migration. In short, Mexicans now also migrate to reunite families.

Mexico's highly concentrated income distribution and the
enormous difference in absolute wages also contribute to migration
pressures. While Mexican migrants receive media attention and are
the object of negative political rhetoric, little attention is paid to the
hundreds of thousands of U.S. citizens who migrate to Mexico in
search of lower living costs. Mexico itself draws unskilled workers
from Central America. Mexican government complaints about the
treatment of Mexican migrants are not complemented by similar
concerns for the treatment of Central American workers in Mexico.

POPULATION PLANNING IN MEXICO

Latin American population policy reached a watershed at the 1974
San José, Costa Rica, United Nations Regional meeting. This first-
ever Latin American focus on population was followed by several
more during the 1980s and a series of meetings in the 1990s. Latin
American governments adopted the World Population Plan of Action recognizing population policy as a central component of economic and social development plans. While many of the fundamental goals for population policy outlined at these regional
conferences have not been met, Mexico has one of the most successful and well-established administrative structures and coherent, well-defined programs to reduce rates of population growth.

Mexico's 1973 general law on population established the National Population Council (CONAPO), and since 1976 national family planning programs have been implemented. This contrasts with Brazil's and Colombia's experiences, where private and commercial family planning have led to dramatic reductions in fertility, especially among the poor. Sterilization and birth control pills are the most common means of birth control available in Mexico through the national health care system. Today, over 50 percent of married women in Mexico use some form of birth control. Condom usage in Mexico has increased due to government-based public information campaigns explaining the role of condoms in both AIDS prevention and family planning (see Chapter 11, "Social Problems and Social Movements," for a fuller discussion of population planning limitations).

In Mexico, however, as in many developing countries, social and population policies have been subordinated to development and economic policies. This neglect strongly influenced Mexico's health care sector and its approach to family planning. Political leaders were concerned with population distribution, especially important when one looks at Mexico's rapidly growing cities and population flows to the border region and the composition of marginal populations. In the 1980s, Mexico's government cut public health budgets from 2.6 percent of the gross domestic product (GDP) in 1982 to 1.7 percent in 1986. As a result, we see dramatic contrasts in mortality rates between classes and regions. Birth control usage is higher in urban areas and among the middle class, in part because government policies provide greater access.

CONAPO's policies target population growth and migration that threaten to overwhelm government's capacity to cope. Mexico's population policy has targeted the two issues of growth and migration. Mexico has sought to reduce regional fertility rate differences by coordinating federal, state, and city programs. It has recognized that internal migration patterns are concentrating population in a few large cities because of extreme inequality between regions. To influence migration, for example, the Mexican government has sought to decentralize federal government workers, previously concentrated in Mexico City. Training programs have aimed to increase marketable skills in poor regions and attract investment and thus retain population in the areas that have been producing high outmigration.

In the 1980s, each state created a population council. During the 1990s, these councils have coordinated population programs to ensure that local information and programs are consistent with national guidelines. Responding to these programs, we have begun to see changes in both fertility behavior and migration patterns. Most important, rural–urban migration is now less important than migration between cities, and migration from Mexico City to other urban zones has been on the rise.

Sex education in Mexico has a long history of rhetorical government support. The modern period of Mexican sex education dates to the 1960s when formal national sex education information campaigns began to target women's knowledge of their own biology and control of reproduction. School systems incorporated textbooks that dealt with puberty, human reproduction, contraceptives, and sexually transmitted diseases. Thus, educational programs have been an important part of the National Population Program and have been implemented throughout Mexico under federal government initiatives. Poor Mexicans, however, given low school participation rates, may not benefit from these programs.

CONCLUSION

Mexico's demographic profile is much younger than we find in the United States and other developed countries. This young population exerts tremendous pressure on the economy as it ages and enters the labor force. Mexico's government pursues policies that seek to maximize job growth, often at the expense of wages and environmental security. Moreover, Mexico has little incentive to inhibit migration, whether legal or illegal, to the United States. On the one hand, migration acts as a relief valve for population pressures; on the other hand, it brings new resources to the economy in the form of wages sent home to families dependent on wage earners in the United States.

Migration to the United States has a complicated relationship with Mexico's politics. Legal and illegal opposition to the PRI may "exit" instead of voicing protest to political repression, corruption, and corporatism. Migration thus also serves as a relief valve for political pressures. More recently, however, Mexicans living in the United States have become an important political pressure group demanding reform and supporting opposition political parties (see Chapter 2, "Politics and Political Institutions").

Mexico's rapidly growing population partly reflects historically rapid declines in mortality. At the heart of these declines are public health measures that reduced infant mortality. Nevertheless,

Mexicans continue to experience much higher infant mortality rates than are encountered in Europe, Japan, or the United States. Mortality rates, however, vary between social groups. Poor rural peasants and urban working-class families have much less access to Mexico's health care system, have poor nutrition, and are more likely to be exposed to industrial and environmental pollution. Thus, they experience much higher mortality rates than better educated and more affluent Mexicans.

In response to these demographic pressures, Mexicans engage in a variety of individual and collective family survival strategies. Migration to urban economic zones or to the United States reflects Mexicans' efforts to cope with population pressures on labor markets and low wages. Migration to the United States is often illegal, but it reflects a long-term and very intense integration of the two nations' economies. Often in the past Mexico and the United States have signed treaties to encourage and control Mexican migration to the United States. Problems emerge when the United States and Mexico try to shut down such migration after economic, social, and cultural networks have become well established.

Finally, Mexico has implemented a broad range of population planning and public health policies aimed at reducing the birthrate and decreasing mortality. In a predominantly Roman Catholic country, birth control policies and sex education in schools confront possible opposition. Most Mexicans, however, both want and demand access to this information and other resources that will allow them to control reproductive behavior. Recent cutbacks in government budgets associated with the promotion of economic development through expanded trade have begun to negatively affect many Mexicans' health, and we see declines in the health levels for those social groups that are most vulnerable—women, children, and the poor.

Social Problems and Social Movements

The conditions defined as social problems vary between societies and over time as values change. Social problems in one society (e.g., spousal abuse, immigration, infant mortality) may be considered normal and unproblematic elsewhere. Mexicans confront a number of long-term and emergent social problems. The severe depth of **poverty,** however, outweighs any other social problem. Poverty defines the risk of violent crime, domestic violence, pollution-related illness, malnutrition, AIDS infection, and access to health care and adequate housing (see Chapter 4, "Mexican Stratification and Mobility").

More than other Latin American nations, Mexico has directly addressed its chronic poverty problem. The ideas of social justice, demanded in Revolutionary rhetoric, are written into the Mexican Constitution. Almost every presidential administration has criticized the excessive concentration of wealth in the hands of a few and the economic impoverishment of many. Social programs were created in response to this problem, including a mass educational system, a government-run program to supply subsidized food to the poor (CONASUP), and most recently, **PROSONAL,** created by the Salinas administration to improve the living conditions of the poor.

These social programs, however, produced meager results. Over two-thirds of the population lack adequate housing; the majority of the population suffers from varying degrees of malnutrition; educational achievement past primary school is limited to the middle and upper classes. Programs fail for a number of reasons. First, heavy government bureaucratization impedes practical solutions. Second, programs are frequently created and/or used by politicians for political gain rather than social progress. Finally, government social programs, like other areas of the government, are fraught with corruption. Government employees often use their position for private gain—for example, requiring a bribe before placing an individual's name on lists for government services (Riding 1984).

Selby (1990) calls Mexico a "rich land with a poor people." Poverty, social inequality, and government corruption instigate urban and rural social movements. Some of the most powerful social movements in the world have emerged in Mexico, particularly in rural areas. Today, hundreds of thousands of Mexicans participate in different **rural** and **urban popular movements.** Rural Mexico's Amerindian (indigenous) groups have mobilized to protest their historical and continuing marginalization from the Mexican social structure (Nash 1995a; b). Urban Mexicans have responded to inequality, poor living conditions, and inadequate housing by organizing numerous democratic social movements (Angotti 1995; Bennett 1992).

SOCIAL PROBLEMS

Crime, Violence, and Corruption

Profound economic inequality and the long-standing tradition of minority elite rule over an impoverished majority aggravate the incidence of human rights abuses in Mexico. Nations with high rates of economic inequality typically have higher rates of crime and human rights violations (Pinheiro 1996). NAFTA supporters argue that human rights abuses will decline with economic modernization. To the contrary, foreign investment makes Mexico's government more anxious about political stability. Human rights abuses during Salinas's administration (1988–94) increased with the harassment, kidnapping, torture, disappearance, and murder of hundreds of Mexicans.

Latin America's poorest populations suffer most from human rights abuses. In cities, violent death rates are higher in poor neighborhoods where people face desperate living conditions. According to Amnesty International, Mexican human rights abuses, including death, disappearance, arbitrary arrest, and torture, are reported most frequently in southern states where poverty (and the Amerindian population) is concentrated. The middle and upper classes, however, view crime as "their" problem. They see crime as a lower-class threat—thus justifying official police and paramilitary violence against the rural and urban poor (Pinheiro 1996).

Police brutality and corruption are widespread. Latin American and Mexican police routinely torture suspects and force confessions ("Mexico under Fire for Human Rights Abuses" 1995). In rural areas, a type of vigilante justice often prevails, with local police and/or private armies of wealthy landowners arresting alleged criminals, then acting as judge and jury. The police bypass the formal judicial system, sometimes choosing to hang suspects in the public square before they are legally proven guilty. The poor typically view police and military as oppressive forces for use by the elite. The ever-present corruption in the political and judicial systems intensifies this attitude (Pinheiro 1996).

Corruption in Mexico is not limited to the political system and ballot stuffing or other electoral fraud. Corruption is present throughout Mexican society—by police, unions, border guards, the military, and so on (Hellman 1994). An entire **informal economy** is built upon an elaborate system of bribes or *la mordida* (the bite). Government officials and police regularly supplement their often low salaries with bribe payments. For example, motorists stopped for traffic violations routinely pay the officer *la mordida*, a duty, rather than paying the official fine, which is usually much higher (Dubois 1993).

The Drug Trade

Drug production, trafficking, and/or money-laundering activities are found in almost all Latin American nations. Mexico's drug economy centers around the production and exportation of drugs. In contrast, the U.S. drug economy centers around consumption, retailing, and importation of drugs. The drug connection between Mexico and the United States dates to the 1800s, when marijuana was legally imported to the United States for use in experimental medicines (Barry, Browne, and Sims 1994). Exporting marijuana was legal until 1927.

Illegal trafficking to the United States appeared minimal until the 1960s. Drug production and trafficking dropped from the late 1960s to the 1980s due to joint efforts between the U.S. and Mexican governments. The drug trade in Mexico, however, saw a resurgence during the 1980s. Drug abuse and trafficking (*traficante*) have become national security issues in recent years. Mexico, as both a producer and transshipment point for drugs produced in other countries, has been a target of U.S. international drug policy since the late 1960s (Craig 1989).

Seven Latin American and Caribbean countries produce the majority of illegal marijuana, cocaine, and heroin smuggled into the United States. Approximately 90 percent of all the marijuana smuggled into the United States comes from Latin America and the Caribbean. Mexico supplies 35 to 40 percent (Bagley 1989, p. 44). Cocaine is mainly produced in South America, but approximately 40 percent is shipped through Mexico (Craig 1989, p. 28). In addition, Mexico is the most significant opium-poppy producer in the Western Hemisphere. Opium-poppy is produced into black tar heroin (Del Villar 1989).

The drug trade (*la droga*) feeds an apparently insatiable demand for drugs by United States consumers. The U.S. State Department reported in 1989 that the United States consumes 60 percent of the world's illegal drug supply (Barry, Browne, and Sims 1994). U.S. antidrug policy, however, primarily concentrates on the foreign sources of drug production and transport. More than 40 U.S. Drug Enforcement Agents (DEA) are assigned to Mexico, which makes it the largest foreign DEA operation. Mexican citizens often express resentment over the level of authority Mexico grants U.S. drug agents when searching for *narcotraficantes* (drug traffickers). Imagine if the United States offered Mexican drug agents similar freedom to search for U.S. drug consumers (Reyna 1989).

Mexico has closely cooperated with the U.S. government in the fight against drug production and export (Del Villar 1989). Since 1993, Mexico has financed its own *compaña antidroga* (antidrug campaign). Mexico's antidrug federal budget often exceeds the proportion spent by the U.S. government (Reyna 1989). Mexico has drained scarce resources from other programs to fund antidrug efforts. For these reasons, Mexico resents U.S. criticism and controversy each year during the "certification" process. The U.S. initiated a certification process in the early 1980s as part of President Reagan's "war on drugs." This process requires the president to decide each year whether to certify particular countries (those identified as major trafficking routes) as cooperating with the United States in the fight against illegal drug trafficking. Nations that are not certified face the possibility of international economic sanction. Anti-U.S. sentiment in Mexico is highest during the certification process. Each year, the process triggers the United States to press for greater results from Mexico in the war on drugs. In 1997, for example, the United States pressed Mexico to extradite Mexican citizens charged with drug trafficking and to allow DEA agents to carry weapons (currently, they are only information-gathering forces) (Dillon 1997). Mexicans view these and many other U.S. demands as a threat to their nation's sovereignty.

In addition to its relationship with the United States, Mexico has other reasons to curb *narcotráfico*. Craig (1989) argues that drug trafficking and production destabilize Latin American nations. Mexican judges, police, governors, and other state personnel have been linked directly and indirectly to the drug trade. Government officials are bribed or placed directly on the payroll of the *narcomafia*. They ignore shipments of cocaine and heroin; they avoid the marijuana farms and processing centers in rural areas; they help free or do not convict known drug traffickers. Three of Mexico's national drug coordinators (the highest level government position in the antidrug effort and a position similar to the U.S. drug czar) were discovered to be collaborating with drug traffickers. Drug-related corruption and violence damage Mexico's relationship with the United States and in Mexico produce greater cynicism toward politicians, bureaucrats, police, and judges. In addition, the drug trade in Mexico worsens domestic drug abuse.

Despite a lack of official statistics, Mexican government spokespeople estimate that there are between 10,000 and 100,000 *drogadictos* in Mexico. The most significant drug problem in Mexico is glue and solvents, however, not marijuana or heroin. In fact, Mexico is the only major source country of a drug (heroin) that lacks a serious addiction problem with that drug. Glues and solvents are chosen because they are cheap and even the poorest addict can afford them. The addiction to glues and solvents is fierce and rehabilitation rates are extremely poor (Craig 1989). Alcohol abuse is also extremely problematic, particularly for Mexican men. Illnesses related to alcoholism proliferate in Mexico, including cirrhosis of the liver and indirect health risks such as violence and homicide (Gutmann 1996).

Narcoterror

Drug-related violence, *narcoterror*, reached record levels in the 1980s. Well-armed gangs of *traficantes* controlled many rural areas. The death toll for both antidrug forces and *traficantes* is high. State and federal police, soldiers, priests, journalists, and a U.S. DEA agent have died at the hands of Mexico's *narcomafia*. Drug-related murders often involve torture, mutilation, and execution-style killing. Kidnappings, a common crime in Mexico, are frequently connected to the drug trade. In the last three years, at least 51 Mexicans have disappeared in suspected kidnappings (Preston 1997).

The Mexican army is charged with the responsibility of combating drug production and trafficking, *compaña antidroga*. Mexico's army, however, is not trained for national defense. It is a domestic "pacification" force used predominately to maintain government control in rural areas. The weapons used by drug *traficantes* are often more sophisticated than those of the army (Craig 1989). Further, military officials are frequently charged with taking bribes from *traficantes* and are sometimes linked to drug-related murders and kidnappings.

Domestic Violence

Violence against women, including both domestic violence and rape, pervades Latin America. One-fifth of Latin American women interviewed by the World Bank in 1993 reported abuse by their partners (Inter-American Development Bank [IDB] 1995, p. 28). One nongovernmental organization (NGO) in Mexico estimates that domestic violence occurs in at least 70 percent of Mexican families (Economic Commission for Latin America and the Caribbean [ECLAC] 1995, p. 43). Poor women are most likely to live in a violent home.

Most domestic violence in Mexico, as in the United States, goes unreported. Public attitudes contribute to underreporting. Violence against women, particularly wives, is not considered a crime by many Mexicans. Most Latin American countries lack laws dealing with sexual violence, and many lack laws that deal with family violence (IDB 1995). Mexican women have equal protection under the law, but their legal status is often ignored. There is no specific penal code for domestic violence. Judicial decisions reflect public attitudes, which regard domestic violence as a private matter. Further, women must maneuver an extremely complicated legal process when placing a domestic violence charge. Current Mexican law requires that the woman show motive for the abuse even when physical evidence is obvious. Any woman filing a complaint must be accompanied by a witness who must testify that the physical evidence actually resulted from abuse by the woman's husband or partner (Olavarrieta and Sotelo 1996).

Most of the world ignored domestic violence until recent years. In many nations, a husband's abuse of his wife was not a crime but instead was considered his right—as "his" woman was "his" property. Mexico's patriarchal culture influences family relations by granting men the right to control their wives' behavior.

Cultures that legitimate male control over women typically define a certain level of abuse as normal. The *cult of machismo* in Mexican society encourages violent male behavior. The violent actions of husbands toward their wives often receive unwritten cultural acceptance. Mexican men sometimes boast of violent acts against their unruly wives or partners. Violence publicly confirms a man's status. Thus, men often beat their partners in front of family, friends, and neighbors (Olavarrieta and Sotelo 1996; LeVine and Correa 1993). LeVine and Correa (1993), for example, observed a man repeatedly punching a woman in the face on a busy street in Cuernavaca. The incident was ignored by passersby, and the woman did not attempt to protect herself. "When the man turned and walked away, the woman wiped her bruised and bleeding face with her apron, took a deep breath, and followed him" (pp. 86–87).

Latin American activists are dedicated to changing public and judicial attitudes toward domestic violence. Grassroots feminist organizations began to open shelters for battered women in the 1980s. Shelters and other services, however, are concentrated in state capitals, particularly Mexico City. Mexico's Congress also has responded to the problem with new consideration of domestic violence and associated penalties. In early 1995, Mexico signed the Interamerican Convention to Prevent, Sanction, and Eradicate Violence against Women. Mexican women less often accept violence in the home today. They receive an increasing amount of information through television and human rights agencies. In addition, as women work outside the home in greater numbers, they are more financially independent and thus have a better chance of leaving a violent situation (Olavarrieta and Sotelo 1996).

Health and Health Care

Public health levels depend on living conditions and access to quality health care and health care professionals. Living conditions vary throughout Mexico, but the majority of Mexicans live in poverty, many without adequate access to health services. Economic class and locale (rural or urban) determine the risk of illness. Thus, health care is a social problem in Mexico because of the unequal distribution of quality health care services.

Article four of the Mexican Constitution guarantees every citizen the right to health care. Private and public health care institutions function independently to meet health care needs. Private sector health care services include physicians working alone and/or in hospitals. Public sector health service organizations include the Ministry of Health, Integral Family Development institutions (DIF), and Social Security Health Insurance. Both the DIF and Social Security Health Insurance have separate services for private employees and government employees. Services provided by the Ministry of Health and DIF are free or discounted and available to anyone, but they primarily serve the uninsured (Guendelman and Jasis 1990).

In theory, Mexico has a national health care system, but in reality large gaps exist. Fifteen million Mexicans live in areas completely lacking public or private medical services (Allensworth and De Wit Greene 1990, p. 337). Health care services are distributed unequally between the wealthy and poor. Urban and rural areas enjoy vastly different health care access. Upper-class individuals use a private system. Many pay for services elsewhere (e.g., in the United States) when they feel Mexican services are deficient. The middle class generally has access to Social Security insurance or government employee clinics and hospitals.

The majority of Mexicans, the poor, receive care from Ministry of Health services. In urban areas, Ministry of Health clinics and hospitals are well staffed with recent medical school graduates. The clinics, however, are concentrated in city centers far from economically depressed *barrios.* A nurse services most rural areas (Warner 1991). Government expenditures for health care services were cut after the economic crisis, placing many services out of the general public's reach. Financial cuts particularly affected the Ministry of Heath and DIF, which provide health care to those most in need (Guendelman and Jasis 1990).

In recent years, significant improvements have occurred in both **life expectancy** at birth and **infant mortality rates,** both indicators of national health and wellness. By 1990, life expectancy at birth rose from the low 40s to 66 for men and 73 for women (LeVine and Correa 1993, p. 178). Infant mortality rates in Mexico improved from 84.7 deaths for 1,000 live births in the period between 1967 to 1971 to 47 deaths for 1,000 live births in the period between 1982 and 1987 (Warner 1991, p. 246). Life expectancy and infant mortality rates vary by locale and by parental income. Those in rural areas or with lower incomes have lower life expectancy and higher infant mortality rates (Reynolds 1996). The highest death rates are found in the largely Amerindian states of Guerrero, Oaxaca, Chiapas, and Puebla.

Despite measured public health improvements, Mexico continues to have serious health problems. The illnesses with the highest death rates are curable and treatable diseases such as pneumonia, influenza, bronchitis, tuberculosis, and gastrointestinal infections such as salmonella or diarrheal diseases including typhoid and cholera. In addition, 40 million people are undernourished. Many Mexicans consume little or no meat, eggs, or milk, particularly in rural areas. Malnutrition often leads to greater health problems, particularly for child-bearing women. On average, one-third of pregnant women in Latin America suffer from **anemia** (IDB 1995, p. 27).

Sexuality and Health

Recent changes in sexual norms, most evident in Europe and the United States, also have occurred in Mexico. Teens are becoming sexually active at earlier ages. Marital infidelity, always common for Mexican men, has become more common for Mexican women as well. Thus, the risk of teen pregnancy and sexually transmitted disease (STD) infection, including the AIDS virus, is considerable in the region (ECLAC 1995).

AIDS/HIV

The AIDS epidemic is a serious Latin American public health problem. Millions of people are infected with HIV. At this date, no cure or vaccine exists. The Latin American region has an estimated 1.7 million infected individuals (Bongaarts 1996, p. 23). Mexico, along with Brazil and Haiti, has one of the highest infection rates of the Latin American countries (Oxford Analytica 1991). Africa and Asia have the first and second highest infection rates in the world. In North America and Europe, the number infected is estimated at less than 1 million for each region (Bongaarts 1996, p. 23).

When the AIDS virus was first discovered in the early 1980s, it was thought to be a disease that predominately affected homosexuals and injection drug users. Today, however, a majority of AIDS infections across the world are known to be the result of heterosexual transmission (Bongaarts 1996). In Mexico, approximately 22 percent of reported AIDS cases are female, while 35 percent are homosexual males. AIDS has become the sixth leading killer of Mexican men between 20 and 44 ("The Face of AIDS in Latin America" 1996, p. 4).

The AIDS epidemic received little attention from the Mexican government until very recently. Most Latin American governments have considered **taboo** the discussion of AIDS. Initially in Latin America, as in the United States, the disease was predominantly found in homosexuals, prostitutes, drug abusers, and those receiving blood transfusions. Initially those infected had an above-average education and income. In recent years, however, the disease has become "pauperized," with an increasing number of poor, married women infected each year. Nevertheless, the Latin American governments and the public continue to attribute the virus to homosexual behavior, drug abuse, and prostitution ("The Face of AIDS in Latin America" 1996).

The behavioral norms that accompany *machismo* contribute to the spread of AIDS in Latin America. The popular *macho* image reinforces men's illicit sexual behavior and encourages sexual relations with many women. At the same time, these notions make it difficult for women to purchase condoms or to ask their partners to use condoms. Women are often called dirty or considered to be prostituting or cheating on their partners when they request condom use (see Chapter 7, "The Mexican Family").

Discrimination and ignorance compound the spread of AIDS. In Mexico, those with AIDS are often rejected by their community and face abuse. AIDS patients are often refused health care or receive negligent care. Workers known to be infected with HIV are frequently discharged from their job and evicted from their homes by landlords ("The Face of AIDS in Latin America" 1996). Because of this discrimination, underreporting of the disease is common. Death certificates frequently list tuberculosis or pneumonia as the cause of death rather than AIDS.

AIDS patients in Mexico are better off than in other Latin American nations, particularly Ecuador and Peru, where homosexuality is illegal. In 1988, the Mexican government founded the National AIDS Prevention and Control Council (CONSIDA). The Health Minister organized the council to generate greater understanding of the disease, promote more humane treatment of victims, and counter the further spread of the disease through educational programs. The cost of government negligence and public ignorance is high. CONSIDA asserts that the 23,000 reported AIDS cases in Mexico have already cost the nation close to US $700 million ("The Face of AIDS in Latin America" 1996).

Abortion

Abortion is illegal in Mexico (except to save a mother's life and in cases of rape), as it is in every other Latin American nation except for Cuba. The Catholic church and the religious right have impeded attempts to legalize abortion. Abortion, however, is still routinely practiced. A number of illegal abortion clinics operate in Mexican cities. Although few doctors or women have been jailed for performing or having abortions, doctors fear the damage to their medical reputation that often comes with being labeled an abortionist. Women fear being ostracized by family, friends, and the church. Mexican women who have illegal abortions risk their health, excommunication, and isolation from their communities (Honey 1994).

Wealthy and middle-class women can undergo abortion procedures at clandestine clinics in Mexican cities or they can go abroad to the United States. Poor women, who cannot afford either option, often attempt the procedure themselves. Unsafe or self-performed abortions are considered by some Mexican physicians and organizations as one of Mexico's principal health problems (Honey 1994). Complications from illegal abortions contribute to roughly half the deaths of pregnant women in Latin America (IDB 1995 p. 26). In Mexico, the law now requires government hospitals and clinics to aid women with abortions in progress or abortion complications. This law has saved the lives of many women.

Environmental Pollution and Health

Urban environmental pollution is rampant throughout Latin America. A perpetual brown haze lingers above Mexico City. By the late 1980s, Mexico City claimed title to the foulest urban air in the world. Carbon monoxide levels are dangerously high—much higher than in Los Angeles or New York. According to the World Health Organization, Mexico City has unacceptable levels of ozone 320 days of the year (Hamill 1993). Residents of Mexico City routinely wear surgical masks over their faces when walking or working outside. They often restrict the amount of time they spend outside.

Mexico City's geographic location intensifies the pollution problem. The city rests in a 7,800-foot-high valley surrounded by mountains. The wind blows into Mexico City from the north and northeast across concentrations of roads, railroads, and industry and a number of squatter settlements. Winds carry to the city industrial smoke and particulates from more than 30,000 factories, dry human waste from settlements without sewage systems, and salt sediment from dry lake beds (Collins and Scott 1993). Mountain ranges trap this filth-laden air.

Public discussion of Mexico City's pollution problem has focused on automobile exhaust from cars, trucks, and buses (Collins and Scott 1993; Hamill 1993). Cars in Mexico tend to be older than those in the United States and most of Europe, generally more than 10 years old, and thus have inadequate emission systems and burn cruder fuel. The government has consciously kept gas prices low in order to maintain the national oil industry **(PEMEX)** and to gain popular support (see Chapter 3, "The Mexican Economy"). This allows more of the population to afford to drive cars. PEMEX first produced lead-free fuel in 1986. Prior to this change, PEMEX's gasoline was the most highly leaded in the world. Buses provide Mexicans with their main public transportation source. Mexico City's subway system is limited and overcrowded. In addition, most freight moves through the nation by truck, not rail.

Recent studies have linked the ozone problem in Mexico City to urban households (particularly squatter settlements) heating and cooking with liquefied petroleum gas. Some researchers attribute pollution to the slow but massive leakage of unburned liquefied petroleum gas into the atmosphere from heating and cooking sources in and around Mexico City (Blake and Rowland 1995). Overpopulation and poor urban planning also contribute to pollution.

The brown haze that covers most of Mexico City is credited to **suspended particulates.** Such particles are smaller than 50 microns in diameter (small enough to be inhaled or swallowed). Recent research links the inhalation of particulates to a range of illnesses, particularly respiratory problems such as bronchitis, emphysema, and lung cancer. Infections of the eyes, ears, nose, and throat are common for residents of Mexico City. A constant cough and nausea, the price of urban life, are attributed to high ground-level ozone (Collins and Scott 1993). Pollution is not limited to Mexico City. Almost every Mexican city has open-air landfills and polluted bodies of water (Barkin 1993). The border cities that house over 1,000 *maquiladora* plants suffer from severe air and water pollution as well as high rates of communicable disease. Unregulated growth of the border industries creates an environmental mess. According to the Council on Scientific Affairs (1990), the border area is "a virtual cesspool and breeding ground for infectious disease" (p. 3320). Forty-six million liters of raw sewage flow daily into the Tijuana River, 76 million liters are dumped into the New River, and 84 million liters are dumped into the Rio Grande. The Nogales Wash is so polluted with toxic chemicals like mercury, nitrates, and cyanide that it exploded and caught fire in 1991 (Barry, Browne, and Sims 1994). Many Mexican border cities and towns actually draw their public drinking water from these rivers.

These conditions compel U.S. policymakers to consider the need to monitor Mexican environmental pollution. Many border industries are owned and operated by U.S. corporations. Further, pollution along the border is difficult for the United States to ignore, especially for states such as Texas, New Mexico, and California. Communities on the U.S. side of the *maquila*-lined border have witnessed an increase in health problems, including birth defects and cancer (Barkin 1993). From 1988 to 1992 in Brownsville, Texas, 25 children were born with spina bifida; over 30 more were born with almost no brain at all (anencephaly). Though the cause of this "epidemic" of birth defects was never definitively determined, a lawsuit by the parents of the children blamed pollution from dozens of U.S.-owned *maquila* companies on the Mexican side of the border. The companies denied causing the epidemic, but the case was settled out of court (Feldstein and Singer 1997).

Although pollution seriously affects the health and future economic vitality of Mexico's border region, daily survival simply outweighs long-term environmental concerns. The first environmental laws were passed in 1971, but these laws have been weakly enforced. In the 1980s, the government began introducing measures to cut pollution. Lead-free gas was introduced by PEMEX in 1986, but for unknown reasons ozone levels actually increased after lead levels were reduced (Collins and Scott 1993).

The 1990s brought strict environmental legislation. Auto emission testing is mandatory. Catalytic converters (antipollution devices) are required in automobiles manufactured after 1993. All vehicles were to convert to clean-burning fuels by 1996. The mass transit system has improved somewhat with expansions to the Mexico City subway system. New buses burn cleaner fuel. Nevertheless, few professionals are employed to police these measures or gauge their effectiveness. Furthermore, industry is rarely a target for environmental criticism. Most factories lack emission controls. The costs of fines for noncompliance are lower than those for installation of antipollution equipment. Only nine inspectors monitor 30,000-plus factories in Mexico City (Collins and Scott 1993). The government still grants higher priority to job growth and unemployment than it does to air quality. Concern over environmental pollution ranks behind Mexico's struggle with poverty.

The Housing Crisis

Mexico lacks adequate and affordable housing, as do most developing nations. The Mexican Constitution entitles all Mexicans to a "dignified home," but the government does little to ensure it (Riding 1984). Social programs to improve the urban housing situation exist, including the National Housing Institute (INFONAVIT), which funds the construction of low-income housing. The rent payments on low-income housing, however, are often still too high for poor and working-class families. Further, in the 1980s, INFONAVIT increasingly allocated its housing efforts to working-class public sector employees and middle-income families connected to the PRI (González 1994).

The middle class takes advantage of subsidized low-income housing because they cannot afford the down payment or interest rates on a new home. Mortgages in Mexico cover only 50 percent of the house price and interest payments are notoriously high (Riding 1984). Banks sometimes charge annual interest rates of 80 percent on mortgages (DePalma 1995). Thus, the middle class consumes housing targeted for the lower classes rather than constructing more expensive homes. In addition to high rents, population booms, the 1985 earthquake, and the 1994 peso crisis worsened the already-existing housing crisis.

The housing crisis forces urban migrants and slum dwellers to adopt informal strategies to find a home. They invade private or government-owned land and create "squatter" settlements (shanty-

Squatters use scavenged materials to quickly section off land and build on abandoned sites. These community members are building a kindergarten so they can petition authorities to assign teachers to their community. (Courtesy of the Inter-American Foundation; photographer, David Melody)

CHAPTER 11

towns) or *colonias perdidas*. Each family constructs a small dwelling with whatever resources it possesses (cardboard, packing crates, salvaged tin, worn tires, etc.) on an "invaded" plot of land. Eventually, the temporary structure is made permanent with brick or stone (see Chapter 7, "The Mexican Family"). Once a squatter settlement is established, residents collectively petition authorities for legal title of the land and for the extension of public services (i.e., electricity, sewage, etc.) to the settlements. This process is usually lengthy. Thus, squatters frequently steal electricity by tapping into the electric wires of neighboring communities—often overloading electrical circuits and causing massive blackouts. A number of large Mexican cities began as squatter settlements. For example, Netzahualcóyotl on the outskirts of Mexico City was "invaded" by squatters in the 1960s and today is home to over 2 million people.

La Frontera (The Border)

The U.S.–Mexico border is the only place in the world where the First World "meets face to face" with the Third World (Langewiesche 1993). The border is 2,000 miles long, but the population is concentrated in 28 "twin cities." The border separates them, one in Mexico, the other in the United States. *Maquiladora* factories concentrate on the Mexican side in the twin cities. The heavily industrialized sections of the border may allow easy economic trade, but human migration is more difficult. The border in urban areas is well-protected with visible barriers and hundreds of border police. The rest of the border, however, remains almost deserted, with little more than a barbed wire fence as a marker (Barry, Brown, and Sims 1994; Langewiesche 1993).

The border is included in the social problems section for a couple of reasons. First, the social problems discussed in this chapter are magnified in border cities. Second, U.S. citizens increasingly view the border and the thousands of Mexicans that attempt to illegally cross it everyday a pressing social problem. Most Mexicans who cross the border do so in search of higher wages. Some Mexicans cross each day to work in higher-paying U.S. jobs and return to their homes on the Mexican side each evening. There is a growing U.S. concern that Mexican immigrants are "invading" the United States, accepting jobs and social services that belong to U.S. citizens.

The Mexican–U.S. migration pattern that began during World War II with the Bracero Program continues today. The Bracero Program was established to recruit Mexican laborers to temporarily fill U.S. agricultural jobs during the war. Mexican workers were swiftly deported in 1954, however, after U.S. workers and unions expressed concern with the continuous importation of cheap labor. Today Mexicans, particularly skilled laborers, are again encouraged to migrate to areas with labor shortages. This trend worries many in the United States who believe that U.S. citizens should be trained and recruited to fill available jobs. The economic contributions of Mexican immigrants (legal and illegal) to the United States are often ignored. It is obvious, however, that the United States cannot tolerate an open border that would allow mass northward immigration (Langewiesche 1993).

The border is often a violent place, especially for those seeking to cross illegally into the United States. Border guards (*la migra*) and local police on both sides are frequently described as "brutal." Between 1989 and 1992, 11 illegals died and 10 were permanently disabled in the San Diego area alone after being shot by border patrols. The Binational Center for Human Rights claims that they have 109 documented cases of child torture by Tijuanan police, 826 disappearances of Mexican people, and 1,500 dead along the California–Mexico border from 1984 to 1989 ("Rescuing the Tunnel Rat: The Mexican Border" 1997, p. 78).

Before making it to the border, prospective illegals encounter a path of brutality. The popular routes through Mexico are littered with thieves and *bandidos* who rape, rob, and murder their victims. The strong may choose the desert and mountain routes where *bandidos* and border patrol are scarce. But they risk dehydration, sunstroke, and death. Most travel and cross the more popular routes. Crossing the border by waterway such as the Rio Grande is popular, as is crossing the North–South freeways in San Diego County. Both of these routes are dangerous. In 1989, 117 drownings occurred in the Rio Grande. Between 1987 and 1991, 127 deaths occurred on San Diego freeways (Barry, Browne, and Sims 1994, p. 38).

Mexicans accept the risks involved with crossing the border because they seek better wages and a better life. Although wages are higher in the United States, illegals face a higher cost of living and often live in conditions not unlike those on the Mexican side. Shantytowns (*colonias perdidas*) are common to both sides of the border. *Colonias perdidas* rarely have electricity, running water, plumbing, or adequate sewage facilities. Other than San Diego, the U.S. border cities are among the poorest cities in the United States. One-quarter of the families in these cities have incomes below the poverty line. El Paso is home to approximately 5,000 homeless, and an estimated 50,000 live in shantytowns (Barry, Browne, and Sims 1994; Langewiesche 1993).

Pollution, as described above (in the section "Environmental Pollution and Health"), is rampant along the border. Anyone who visits the area is immediately aware that the border does not prevent the passage of pollution. According to Mary Kelly, director of the Texas Center for Policy Studies (quoted in Barry, Browne, and Sims 1994): "In the rush to sign a free trade agreement, both the U.S. and Mexican government are on the verge of relegating the border environmental issues to a high-profile sideshow, long on promises, but very short on meaningful changes and enforceable commitments to action" (p. 173). Mexican border communities simply do not have the funds to enforce environmental laws or to make the infrastructural improvements necessary to protect the environment. Numerous health problems (on both sides) stem from the environmental pollution in the area. People on both sides of the border suffer from gastrointestinal problems related to contaminated drinking water. In Nogales, Arizona, the hepatitis rate is almost 20 times the U.S. average. In San Elizario, near El Paso, 90 percent of adults will contract hepatitis before age 35 (Barry, Browne, and Sims 1994, p. 185).

SOCIAL MOVEMENTS

Rural Popular Movements

After centuries of degradation and oppression, Mexico's rural peasants have organized to demand access to land and protest gross inequities and corruption in politics. Beginning in the 1970s, people from distinct Amerindian cultures, including Tzeltales, Tzotzl, Choles, Tojolabales, Zoques, and Mayas, united to form rebel armies. Eventually, they declared war on Mexico's economic and political elite. This plurality of Indian cultures enables indigenous rebel groups to mobilize more successfully for resources (Nash 1995a). The groups focus on political issues such as land, fair wages, control and defense of natural resources, and the right to self-determination (Tresierra 1994). Amerindian groups in Mexico oppose agricultural policies that favor large commercial agricultural interests over small family farmers. They are particularly concerned that NAFTA, which increased the number of U.S. food imports to Mexico, will hurt small farmers and create prosperity solely for the Mexican elite.

At the fore of these rural social movements is the *Ejército Zapitista Liberación Nacional* (EZLN). The EZLN was formed, according to one of its leaders, because Indians "have nothing, absolutely nothing. Not a decent roof, nor work, nor land, nor health care, nor education" (Nash 1995a, p. 7, quoting Subcommandante Marcos). The EZLN declared war on the PRI on New Year's Day 1994, then seized and held for a short period the municipal buildings in the towns of San Cristóbal, Altamirano, Las Margaritas, and Ocosingo, located in the southern state of Chiapas. The military fought unsuccessfully for 11 days to end this uprising. A ceasefire was eventually declared by President Salinas, but not before 145 people were killed. The rebels justify their revolt in both economic and cultural terms. Indigenous Mexicans are excluded from decision-making roles simply because of their ethnic status as Amerindians. They lack access to public institutions such as education, health care, and land. Exclusion has reinforced their weak social position (Nash 1995a). The EZLN released the Declaration of the Lacandon Jungle during their uprisings, which included 11 demands: work, land, shelter, bread, health, education, democracy, liberty, peace, independence, and justice (Melendez and Conteras 1997).

Rebel social movements concentrate in Mexico's southernmost states where indigenous groups are a majority and poverty is most intense. The most publicized rebel activity, including that by the EZLN, is concentrated in Chiapas, where conditions are particularly distressed. Although 55 to 60 percent of the electricity for all Mexico is produced at hydroelectric stations located in Chiapas, 35 percent of the residents in the state live without electricity (Floyd 1996, p. 142). The people living in Chiapas are overwhelmingly classified as poor, yet 21 percent of Mexico's oil and 47 percent of the natural gas are found in Chiapas. Other indigenous movements, similar to the EZLN, may be found in southern states such as Oaxaca and Guerrero, where living conditions are similar to those in Chiapas. Approximately 23 percent of Mexico's poor live in Guerrero, Oaxaca, and Chiapas (McKinley and Alarcón 1995, p. 1579).

The indigenous cultures in Guerrero organized a collective movement in 1985, nine years before the armed uprisings in Chiapas. While the core demand of the EZLN is land, the indigenous cultures in Guerrero concentrate on political autonomy. The efforts in Guerrero are organized by the Guerrero Council of 500 Years of Indigenous Resistance (CG500ARI), which includes four indigenous cultures, Nahua, Mixtec, Tlapaneco, and Amuzgo. The Nahua were the first to propose the establishment of an indigenous-based municipality. The proposed Nahua municipality would give the Nahua community (which includes 67 villages within several hundred square miles in Chilapa, Guerrero) greater independence. The state of Guerrero is currently under PRI control. The current municipal government rarely petitions the state for municipal resources to make improvements in indigenous communities. Thus, the Amerindian villages often lack paved roads, electricity, and sanitation facilities. The Nahua are not attempting to secede from the Mexican state but instead seek greater political participation. The Nahua municipality, if granted, could elect its own leaders and petition the state for funds available to municipalities, thus allowing the Nahuas to invest in development projects for their community. The indigenous movements in Guerrero are much less known than the EZLN but no less significant. Moreover, the groups have similar goals but different strategies. The CG500ARI is strictly a peaceful movement. Some argue that the Zapatistas have been more successful because they are armed (Payne 1996).

Others argue that the Zapatistas' strength lies in their political message and unique ability to disseminate it internationally. Though headquartered deep in the Lacandon Jungle, they have captured international attention in a completely modern way. The leaders of the EZLN have communicated their message to the international press and the world via the Internet, using e-mail and creating Web sites (see "Webliography") (Melendez and Conteras 1997). This strategy sets this democratic movement apart from other movements in Latin America. The Zapatistas, through their media efforts, caught the attention of socially conscious activists and radical celebrities in the United States and Europe. U.S. movie director Oliver Stone and Hispanic actor Edward James Olmos have both met with EZLN leader Subcommandante Marcos, as has French First Lady Danielle Mitterrand (Oppenheimer 1996).

National and international attention have forced the Mexican government to participate in negotiations with the rebels. Rebel groups have gained momentum, acquiring the support of both an increasing number of Mexican urban dwellers and some foreigners. International recognition of rebel activities and government repression damages Mexico's relationship with foreign investors. Thus, peace talks between the EZLN and government officials have taken place since the 1994 uprisings.

A peace accord was signed between the Mexican government and the Zapatista rebels in 1996, but it was incomplete. It did not include the principal demands of indigenous groups—land redistribution and the reinstatement of **Article 27,** which legally protected Amerindian communal lands (*ejidos*). It is also questionable whether the government will actually carry out the promises of the accord. Further, military repression and human rights abuses against Amerindians continue. Amnesty International and other human rights groups vehemently criticize the military repression that has occurred in response to rural uprisings. According to the United Nations, hundreds of deaths have occurred in Mexico's rural regions since the beginning of the indigenous insurgencies. Mexico's army has occupied the city of San Cristóbal in Chiapas since 1994. The EZLN is headquartered in this same city. Military and local police often act in collusion with *cafeteros* (coffee growers), *finqueros* (landowners), and *ganaderos* (cattlemen) to suppress militant indigenous groups. Indigenous leaders have been captured, imprisoned, and often killed by paramilitary groups or the private armies of landed elites. Tresierra (1994) notes that from 1982 to 1989, 870 assassinations were reported in Mexico. Eighty-one percent occurred in those Mexican states with the largest indigenous populations (Chiapas, Oaxaca, Puebla, Hidalgo, Veracruz, and Guerrero). Since the 1994 uprisings, foreigners have been encouraged to avoid these areas for reasons of personal safety.

Urban Popular Movements

In 1968, a series of large-scale student demonstrations erupted in Mexico City to demand free and mass education. As the protests expanded to include workers, peasants, and unions, ideas of democracy and redistribution of wealth were adopted (see Chapter 9, "Mexican Education"). The student movement was significant for several reasons. First, participation in the demonstrations included approximately 400,000 people. Not since the Revolution had so many people participated in a social protest. Second, the student march to Tlatelolco Plaza in Mexico City, October 2, 1968, ended violently, with Mexican police and army attacking the group: 325 protesters were killed and thousands were injured. The protest represented the bloodiest civil conflict since the Revolution (Levy 1980). Third, a number of the students involved in the 1968 student movement influenced or became leaders of urban popular movements in the early 1970s (Bennett 1992).

Through the 1970s and 1980s, urban popular movements (UPMs) evolved from small groups scattered across many states. They mobilized around diverse interests such as utility rates, land acquisition, housing shortages, unemployment, and government indifference. UPMs emerged during both poor and prosperous periods. Their growth was uninterrupted because they did not form in response to changing economic conditions but rather as a response to ongoing poverty. By the 1980s, regional and national coalitions of UPMs emerged, including the *Confederación Nacional del Movimiento Urbano Popular* (CONAMUP). CONAMUP is a national level organization that collects and disseminates information to UPMs across Mexico. It organizes yearly meetings and handles negotiations between the UPMs and the government (Bennett 1992).

One of the most significant UPMs is the *Asamblea de Barrios*, a movement dedicated to housing rights. The movement organized after a 1985 earthquake in Mexico City that magnified the existing housing crisis. Following the earthquake, the *Asamblea de Barrios* expanded and organized slum dwellers around demands for affordable housing, potable water, sewer lines, and electricity. Active members of the *Asamblea de Barrios* are placed on a list for improved housing (Hellman 1994).

An important and interesting figure in the struggle for housing rights is "Super-Barrio." Super-Barrio is an extremely effective political activist in a super-hero costume. In Superman fashion, he dresses in red tights, a gold cape, face mask, and shirt with the letters "SB" emblazoned on it. He first appeared after the Mexico City earthquake. Like the EZLN, Super-Barrio has captured the attention of both the Mexican government and the international press. Super-Barrio travels to popular assembly meetings and demonstrations in his "Barrio-mobile." He is so popular that the police refuse to arrest him for fear of public unrest, and the Mexican government has even allowed him to testify before government housing committees. He refuses to reveal his true identity because he fears focus would shift away from the collective identity of the housing rights movement ("The Poor Man's Superman" 1988).

Government responses to urban movements are diverse and variable. Initially, the government tolerated and even supported a few. If leaders failed to cooperate with government officials, however, violent repression followed. By the late 1970s, violent government repression became the norm. Participants in the UPMs were frequently imprisoned or even killed. New popular movements emerged, however, and strengthened after the economic crisis—forcing new government responses. In the late 1980s, social programs began to directly address the needs expressed by both urban and rural popular movements. Most notably, Salinas created *Programe Nacional de Solidaridad* (PROSONAL) to improve the living conditions of the poor (Bennett 1992). PROSONAL, however, currently allots only one-third of its resources to the direct alleviation of poverty (McKinley and Alarcón 1995).

El Barzón

El Barzón, a protest movement started in 1993, has evolved into one of Mexico's largest popular movements. This popular movement, in contrast to those previously discussed, is organized around the demands of the middle class. Middle-class farmers in the state of Jalisco began the movement to protest obscenely high interest rates. Other property and business owners, although too proud initially, eventually joined as they began to sink under heavy debt burdens. The group spans both rural and urban areas and unites farmers, small business operators, and other middle-class property owners across the nation.

The tactics of the Barzonistas are often radical. The group captured the attention of the Mexican media and government during numerous protest activities. They have "tarred and feathered" a bank repo man in northern Mexico, "seized" bank lobbies by flooding them with hundreds of people, and threatened prospective U.S. investors interested in repossessed Mexican real estate. The Barzonistas have carefully avoided radical or leftist rhetoric, however, focusing only on the issue of "economic mismanagement" rather than on demands for political or social structural change. Their primary demands are a moratorium on bank repossessions and a grace period for debtors (DePalma 1995; Solis 1995).

El Barzón represents a unique threat to the Mexican government. The members of this popular movement are traditionally pro-government. A middle-class movement of this magnitude combined with the hundreds of thousands of poor rural and urban protesters represents a serious threat to Mexico's social order. With this in mind, in late 1995 the government allocated $1 billion to a program designed to ease the burdens of high interest rates on middle-class debtors (Solis 1995).

CONCLUSION

Mexican society faces a number of pressing social problems, including crime, violence, human rights abuses, corruption, massive housing shortages, environmental pollution, malnutrition, and the elevated incidence of other treatable and curable diseases. The severe depth of poverty in Mexico, however, outweighs any other social problem.

Each presidential administration designs its own strategies to alleviate these social ills, but most continue unresolved. Realizing that government services and programs are inadequate, hundreds of thousands of Mexican people have joined collective movements. Rural and urban popular movements protest and seek solutions to the problems that plague their members. Rural popular movements, most notably the EZLN, fight for land redistribution, access to necessary public services, indigenous autonomy, and political representation. Urban popular movements struggle for adequate housing, improved access to education, and basic public services.

NAFTA supporters argue that human rights abuses will decline with economic modernization, but the most common government response to rural and urban unrest in Mexico has been police and military repression. This is partially because the economic relationship between the United States (and other foreign investors) and Mexico waivers during periods of political chaos. Foreign investment, so important to Mexico's modern economy, is threatened by political instability. Thus, political leaders in Mexico aggressively work to maintain social order—sometimes through negotiations with protesters, sometimes through social programs, sometimes through violent repression.

Webliography

The World Wide Web (WWW) is a dynamic and rapidly developing communications medium. The sites listed below are currently
available, but others surely will be functioning before this text is
published. We offer these sites as a starting point and recommend
that students explore more information bases using various search
engines. Many of the sites below have links to other databases that
will help students access current information about Mexico and
Latin America. Most have text available in English, but some, such
as daily newspapers from Mexico, have only Spanish text. Given
the volatile and rapidly changing characteristics of the World
Wide Web, readers should note some Web sites may cease operating or change addresses.

Arts and Humanities

Mexican art and culture
    http://www.udg.mx/cultfolk/mexico.html
    http://www.trace-sc.com/museums.htm
Museo de Arte Contemporaneo
    http://www.conet.com.mx/macg
Curare
    http://www.laneta.apc.org/curare/index.html
Dance, music, art and culture Web sites
    http://www.alegria.org/mxother.html
        Homepage with special focus on dance, but includes
        links to other culture-oriented sites

Demography

Instituto Nacional de Estadística Geográfia y Informática
(INEGI).   Statistical data on population, economic
indicators, communications and transportation
infrastructure, industry, geography, and a copy of the
National Development Plan, 1995–2000.
    http://ags.inegi.gob.mx
Health statistics
    gopher://gaia.info.usaid.gov:70/00/regional_country/
    lac/mexico/

National Center for Health Information and Documentation
http://cenids.ssa.gob.mx/

General population data
http://secac.ciesin.org/home-page/mexico.html
http://www.worldonline.nl/~america/mexico.html

Economy

Business, finance, and economy
http://www.trace-sc.com/trademon.htm

Basic socioeconomic data (Inter-American Development Bank)
http://iadb6000.iadb.org/~http/mexico/mebsed.html

Trade data (IADB)
http://iadb6000.org/~http/mexico/trade.html
http://lanic.utexas.edu/cswht/tradeindex.html

Economic indicators (Bank of Mexico)
http://www.quicklink.com/mexico/bm/agregad.htm

Statistical information (INEGI)
http://www.inegi.gob.mx.homepages/estadistica/
estadistica.html

Daily financial indicators
http://www.spin.com.mx.noticias.fina

Selected economic data (U.S. Agency for International Development—USAID)
http://lanic.utexas.edu.80/la/region/aid/aid94/
Country/MEXCAR.html

Trade data (USAID)
http://lanic.utexas.edu.80/la/region/aid/aid94/
Intraregional/MEX.html

Nafinsa Securities
http://www.quicklink.com/mexico/nafinsa.htm

Banco de Mexico
http://www.quicklink.com/bm/bm1.htm

North American Development Bank
http://www.quicklink.com/nadbank/ning1.htm

Mexican Investment Board
http://www.quicklink.com/mexico/mib/mib1.htm

Bancomext
http://www.quicklink.com/bancomext/banc1.htm

Mexican Stock Exchange (U.S.)
http://www.mexico/bmv/bmv1.htm

Environment

U.S.-Mexico Border XXI Program
http://www.epa.gov/region09/cross_pr/usmex/index.htm
Homepage of a binational interagency program with many links to other Mexico environment-oriented sites.

Mexican Daily Newspapers

The News (Eng)
http://www.novedades.com/the-news.htm

La Jornada
http://serpiente.dgsca.unam.mx/jornada/index.html

Excelsior
http://worldnews.nte/excelsior/excelsior.html

El Diario de Monterrey
http://pixel.com.mx/diariomty/index.html

El Economista
http://condor.dgsca.unam.mx:2500/notimex.html

News Summaries

The General Information category below includes access to numerous Web sites that include links to many Mexican news summaries and daily newspapers. A few important news sources, but not all, are listed in this section.

Mexico National
http://www.infosel.com.mx/newsfax/newsfaxe.html

North, South & Central America
http://www.spin.com.mx/noticias.html

Chiapas
http://lanic.utexas.edu:80/la/region/news/arc/amdh/1995/

BorderLines Interhemispheric Resource Center
http://lib.NMSU.edu/subject/bord/bordline/

News
http://www.internet.com.mx/medios/index.html

General Information on Mexico and Latin America

The following list of sites may be used to access links to numerous databases with information on the Latin American region and individual nation-states.

Information Mexico.   Links to Web sites covering such topics as business, travel, finance, news and analysis, trade, and tariffs.
http://www.mexicosi.com/

Iowa State University.   Categories of Web site links include an almanac of events, Web guide, rural Mexico, and frequently asked questions (FAQs).
http://www.public.iastate.edu/~rjsalvad/scmfaq/semfaq.html

Mexico Web Guide.   General categories of Web sites include art and culture, science and technology, computers and the Internet, education, companies, entertainment, events, government, news, personal pages, states, tourism, and health.
http://mexico.web.com.mx/

New Mexico State University.   Links to Web sites focusing on Mexican government and politics, culture and society, Tijuana, various states, some universities, and daily newspapers.
http://www.nmsu.edu/~bri/mexico.html

University of North Texas.   Links to Mexican Web sites on many topics, including politics, economics and tourism, regions, cities, culture, food, and universities.
http://www.hist.unt.edu/09w-la2.htm

Stanford University Mexico Web Page.   Links to Mexican Web sites focusing on Mexican history and origins, culture, general facts, food, and other topics.
http://www-leland.stanford.edu/~flyhigh/mexico/mexico.html

University of Birmingham Mexican Society Home Page.   Links to Mexican Web sites with maps, subway system, newsgroups, tourist information, government, and economy.
http://sun1.bham.ac.uk/glp510/mexico.htm

Mexico's Index.   A searchable index with Web sites listed by organization type, including colleges, universities, and technical schools; research centers; and official institutions.
http://www.trace-sc.com/lista.htm

Organization of American States
http:/www/oas.org/

Latinworld
http://www.latinworld.com

University of New Mexico
http://lib.nmsu.edu/subject/bord/laguia/lag1.html

University of Texas
http://lanic.utexas.edu/ilas/mexcenter/mexicenter.html

North American Congress on Latin America (NACLA)
http://www.igc.apc.org/nacla/ladb/ladb.html

Congreso Nacional Indigena.   Information on Mexican
Indian groups from their official homepage in Mexico City.
http://www.laneta.apc.org/cni

Frequently asked questions (FAQs about Mexico)
http://www.public.iastate.edu/~rjsalvad/scmfaq/
faqindex.html

Mexican Government Websites

Federal Government.   Icon links to Web sites for most
federal government ministries and the office of the president.
http://www.quicklink.com/mexico/gobfedin.htm

President
http://www.quicklink.com/mexico/presidency.htm
http://www.dash.com/netro/int/mx/mexico.htm

Foreign affairs
http://www.com/mexico/secretin.htm

Mexican Consulate, New York
http://www.quicklink.com/mexico/

Cabinet of the President
http://www.udg.mx/Gabinete/Info/gabinete.htm

National Institute of Statistical and Geographical Information
http://ags.inegi.gob.mx/

Federal and state constitutions
http://info.juridicas.unam.mx/cnsinfo/indice.htm

Travel and Tourism

Cancun
http://www.cancun.com/

Mexicana Airlines
http://www.catalog.com/cgibin/var/mx/index.html

Mexico City subways
http://metro.jussieu.fr:10001/bin/select/english/
mexico/mexico

Mexico Tourism Web
http://ss20.mty.itesm.mx/turweb/

Mexican Tourist Information
http://www.reidgroup.com/~dmg/mexico/

Social Movements

EZLN
http://www.ezln.org/
http://www.peak.org/~joshua/fzln

Universities
http://acm.org/~ops/w3vlmex/universities.html

Mexico's Index.   Extensive links to Mexican colleges,
universities, technical schools, research centers, and official
institutions.
http://www.trace-sc.com/lista.htm

GLOSSARY

abnegada   Self denial.

age cohorts   Persons born within a specific period of time, usually one year.

aguantadora   Capable of almost infinite emotional and physical tolerance.

ahijado   A godchild.

ahorradora   Frugal.

amalgamation (demographic)   The blending of many different racial groups to form one dominant race.

Amerindian (indigenous)   A term referring to the population living in the Americas when Spanish *conquistadores* first arrived in the 15th and 16th centuries. This term also is used to describe the descendants of that population.

anemia   A deficiency in the number of red blood cells that carry oxygen; generally attributed to malnutrition and one cause of physical weakness.

anticlerical   Opposed to church or clergy influence in political or state affairs.

Article 27   A constitutional provision that governed agrarian reform and protected Amerindian communal lands known as *ejidos*. Article 27 was altered to allow the sale of communal properties to international agribusiness and other buyers during the Salinas administration (1988–1994).

assimilation (acculturation)   Process through which a subordinate group becomes integrated into the dominant group and society.

authoritarian   A political system with a small, very powerful leadership group exercising power and excluding most of the population from significant means to influence policy.

automático pase   Automatic admittance to a particular university; sometimes awarded to students who attend the *prepa* linked to the university.

autonomous university   A university that makes independent administrative decisions free of the government, including selection of its president and board of directors.

ayuntamiento   City council.

barrio   Neighborhood.

basic needs programs   Government and nongovernment organization (NGO) activities aimed at improving nutrition, housing, education, security, and other defined subsistence requirements.

binational labor markets   A stable process linking job opportunities and workers seeking work that extends across two nations.

cacique   A chief or political boss.

cafeteros Coffee growers.

camarilla A group with common political interests where members share loyalty and resources to improve their prospects for economic gain, political power, and upward social mobility.

campesinas (See **peasants.**) A female peasant farmer.

campesinos (See **peasants.**) A male peasant farmer.

cannonization To officially designate an individual as a saint.

carrera Career.

casa chica A woman who establishes a second household with a married man.

central business district (CBD) Urban zone with the principal concentration of office buildings and retail trade.

church A large, bureaucratic, and hierarchical religious organization with a trained ministry and/or priesthood and a formal and ritualistic liturgy. Churches tend to recruit from the middle and upper classes through socialization rather than conversion; typically act in accommodation with the state, and are conservative in belief and social standing.

civil servants Public employees whose jobs are formally defined as apolitical administrative functions.

class-based stratification Systematic inequality between groups of different socioeconomic backgrounds.

class consciousness Awareness of one's individual economic interests and how they relate to a group that shares those interests.

clientalism The distribution of resources, such as jobs, political power, social prestige, and the determination of political decisions, in return for support. A system of patronage and loyalty that is linked to *camarillas.*

colonia A city district.

communidades eclisial de base (**CEBs—Ecclesial Base Communities**) Small grassroots religious communities that meet to read and discuss the Bible and church doctrine and to discuss other political, social, and economic issues.

compadres Name used to express kinship between parents and godparents.

compaña antidroga Antidrug policies by government.

compadrazgo Relations between the godparents and natural parents of a child; also used to describe cliques or groups of friends.

Confederación Nacional Campesina (**CNC**) National Peasants Confederation, the peasant organization supporting the National Revolutionary Party, later the *Partido Revolucionario Institucional* (PRI).

Confederación Nacional del Movimiento Urbano Popular (**CONAMUP**) A national level organization that collects and disseminates information to UPMs across Mexico.

Confederation of Mexican Workers (CTM) Established during the 1930s, this is the largest formal organization of unionized employees in Mexico and became one of the three important groups supporting the National Revolutionary Party, later the *Partido Revolutionario Institucional* (PRI).

conflict theory General social theory that focuses on antagonism between groups as the principal factor defining social structure and social change.

conjugal nuclear family A family unit that consists of a married couple and their dependent children, with family emphasis placed on the marital relationship rather than the wider kinship network.

conquistadores Spanish military expeditions sent by the monarch to subjugate indigenous Amerindian populations. The majority of these men sought wealth and upward social mobility unavailable to them in Spain.

consanguine kin Relationships based on common ancestral descent.

consensual union Couples who live together and sometimes have children but do not legally marry.

COPARMEX Employers Confederation of the Mexican Republic, a business employers organization that led 1990s' demands for increased protection for civil liberties (from the state), implementation of political reforms, reduced government, and reduced corruption by public officials.

core Those states in a world economy that dominate the world division of labor and appropriate most wealth.

corporatism Related to Mexican authoritarianism and common to many Latin American cultures; refers to the complex of officially recognized organizations that convey demands or petitions to political authorities and which, in turn, become umbrella organizations through which many social and economic policies are implemented.

cost of living The price in U.S. dollars of a typical household basket of consumption, including housing, food, transportation, and clothing.

criollo An individual of pure Spanish (white) descent, born in Mexico.

crude fertility rates The total number of births in a given year divided by the total population.

crude mortality rates The total number of deaths in a given year divided by the total population.

debt peonage A relationship between rural landowners and farmers who rent or sharecrop. Landowners extend credit to farmers to rent land and buy seed, tools, and other farming necessities. At harvest, landowners determine the value of crops and deduct what is owed. When the value of harvests is insufficient to pay the debt, farmers must continue to work the land in order to pay the debt and may not leave. This often becomes a lifelong debt, and obligations to pay may be enforced against a debtor's children who inherit the debt.

dedazo The process by which a Mexican president personally selects a successor, who then becomes the party candidate in the next election. Very little is known about this decision-making process, but it is clear that *camarilla* groups' power and interests are involved in the succession of presidential candidates.

demographic transition An evaluation of historical changes in population fertility and mortality rates associated with industrialization, urbanization, and rising literacy. This position contends that agrarian and nonurbanized societies with limited market relations strike a rough balance between fertility and mortality rates due to disease, famine, and war. As societies urbanize, develop extensive market relations, and improve literacy rates, population stability occurs at low levels of mortality and fertility. This occurs because children in traditional society are an economic asset, while in modern society they are an economic cost. Thus, families, as rational economic actors, have fewer children.

demographic variables   Quantitative measures of fertility, mortality, and migration (population structure), but also including quantitative measures of gender, location, education, and other factors (population composition).

denomination   Religious organization with voluntary association and loose individual commitment but with a formal bureaucracy and trained ministry.

dependency support ratios   The ratio of population less than 15 years of age and older than 65 to the population between 15 and 65. The latter is generally referred to as the economically active population (EAP) and is presumed to be available for work.

division of labor   Specialization of economic activity. This concept may be used to refer to specialization between nations, social categories (race and gender, for example), or social groups.

doble jornada   Double work day (two jobs).

dócil   Docile.

drogadicto   Drug addict.

dual economy   Describes economic activity in terms of a core of large, bureaucratic organizations where competitive markets are limited by the dominance of a few firms with national and international scope and a periphery of small, nonbureaucratic competitive organizations with local markets and low levels of capitalization.

egresados   Name for individuals who complete the coursework for the *licenciado* degree but do not finish the thesis or project required to graduate.

Ejército Zapatista Liberación Nacional **(EZLN—Zapatistas)**   A rural-based rebel movement dedicated to indigenous and political causes such as land rights, fair voting practices, fair wages, control of natural resources, and the right to self-determination.

ejidos (ejidatarios)   Originally an Indian concept of "common lands" owned by a village, the term was adopted by the Mexican government as part of a land redistribution policy that gave thousands of rural villages the right to use lands but not legal title or rights to sell the land. *Ejidatarios* are the rural villagers who work *ejido* lands.

encomienda   Spanish colonial policy granted individual *conquistadores* the right to demand tribute and free labor from Amerindians who were entrusted to their supervision. In return, the *conquistadores* were to maintain social order and supervise the conversion of the Amerindians to Christianity. It served to legitimate widespread economic, social, and physical abuse by Spaniards and was one factor leading to a steep decline in the Indian population during the first century of Spanish rule.

endogamous marriage   Marriage within a defined kinship group such as consanguine kin, the extended family network, social class, or ethnic group.

escuelas normal   Primary school.

estancias   A large farm or cattle ranch.

estrategies de sobrevivir   Survival strategies, usually of extended families, as they rationally allocate labor and other resources aimed at maintaining the family unit in a complex and volatile economic and political environment.

ethnicity   A distinction based on specific characteristics (cultural, religious, racial, national) that are shared by a group of people and that separate them from others in a society.

exogamous marriage   Marriage outside of a defined kinship group.

export production zone (EPZ)   An area wherein manufacturing facilities may import and export products without being subject to normal taxes and regulations that apply elsewhere in the national economy.

export sector agribusiness   Corporations that grow commercial crops for foreign export. In Mexico, this refers to northern Mexican fruit, vegetable, and cotton crops, for example, that are exported to the United States, and in southern Mexico to fruits, coffee, sugar, and other tropical crops exported to foreign markets.

extended family   A family unit that consists of more than one generation living together in a single household.

extended family network   Several nuclear family units that maintain separate households but live in close proximity and engage in reciprocal sharing of resources; these networks include both consanguine and fictive kin.

family economy   The collaboration of all members of a family, including husband, wife, children, and sometimes fictive kin, to the economic well-being of the family unit.

family survival strategies   An interpretation of economic behavior that uses the extended family network as a unit of analysis. Acting as an organization, the family allocates resources, including food, land, and labor, to various activities distributed across different economic sectors in order to maximize survival chances for all family members (see *estrategias de supervivencia*).

fecundity   The potential total births for a population. Fecundity is determined by the proportion of women of childbearing age.

feminism/feminist   A social movement that seeks to achieve equality between the sexes/one who advocates or demands the same rights for women as those granted to men.

fertility rates   The average number of children born to women of childbearing age or for women at specific age cohorts.

fictive kin   Nonkin members of extended family networks.

finqueros   Owners of farms, usually small farms, but also may refer to owners of larger rural land holdings when used as a euphemism.

folk Catholicism   The blending of pre-Hispanic (indigenous) beliefs with traditional Roman Catholicism.

formal sector   (See **informal sector**.) Economic activities regulated by the state.

functionalist sociology   Sociological theory and empirical research that view society as a system that tends toward equilibrium. Social institutions are parts of this system, and each exists to perform some adaptive purpose (function) when the society is challenged by external forces.

ganaderos   Cattlemen or ranchers.

gender   The socially constructed division into masculine and feminine (as compared to *sex*, which is the biological division into male and female).

gender division of labor   The division of tasks (social, religious, political, economic) into masculine tasks and feminine tasks such as male breadwinner and female homemaker.

global restructuring   Refers to recent changes in the structure of international political and economic relations, including the development of integrated financial markets, widespread migration across borders, and expansion of factory production to Third World nation-states. This general term may also be used to refer to such sweeping changes as the collapse of old colonial empires, the fall of the Soviet Union, the emergence of multinational corporations, and emergence of regional trading blocs such as the European Union, North American Free Trade Agreement, and others.

gross domestic product (GDP)   An economic term referring to the total value of economic goods and services produced within a nation-state.

guelaguetza   Nonmonetary exchange of goods and/or services.

hacendados   A Spanish word referring to owners of large ranches or estates. Generally, it implies that these individuals and families are part of the economic, social, and political elite.

haciendas   Large ranches or estates.

hectares   A metric system measure of land area equivalent to 2.7 acres.

horizontal kinship networks   Mutual assistance kinship networks comprised of both real and fictive kin.

IFE (Federal Electoral Institute)   A Mexican election "watchdog" group, formally part of the government but now independent.

import substitution industrialization (ISI)   A term referring to policies implemented by many Latin American governments during the 20th century. The goal was to reduce vulnerability to wild economic fluctuations—booms and busts—associated with a model of economic development based on exports of agriculture and minerals but without complementary development of industry. By using government subsidies to help investors and high tariff barriers (taxes on imports) to protect manufacturers from competition, Latin American governments hoped to keep more of their earnings from exports and thus increase their rate of economic development.

indigenismo   The policy of assimilating Amerindians into the dominant *mestizo* culture while maintaining certain traditional Amerindian practices.

indigenistas   Individuals supporting a policy of *indigenismo*.

indigenous Amerindian   A term that refers to peoples who were living in the Americas when Spanish and other European invaders and settlers arrived. Sometimes called Indians or Native Americans, we have used the terms *Amerindian* and *indigenous* or *indigenous Amerindian* in this text to express respect for and recognition of these distinct original inhabitants of Mexico and the Americas.

individual mobility   Change in social and/or economic status for a single person. This may refer to changes from the original status of one's birth family, but it may also refer to changes during the course of one's adult life.

industry groups   Sets of companies, often owned within an extended family, that operate by coordinating their economic, social, and political activities to maximize benefits to the group as a whole.

infant mortality rates   The proportion of infants who die before their first birthday. Typically high in traditional agrarian societies. The availability of public health measures such as clean water and sewers, as well as widespread availability of antibiotics and vaccinations, can rapidly reduce infant mortality rates.

informal economy   See **informal sector.**

informal polygamous arrangements   An arrangement in which one man maintains two households (typically one legal marriage and one consensual union).

informal sector   (See **formal sector.**) An economic term referring to economic production, distribution, and consumption activities that are unregulated by the government.

International Monetary Fund (IMF)   An international regulatory agency founded at the 1944 Breton Woods conference. Originally intended to serve as a "credit union" for governments, granting short-term loans to help them deal with fluctuations in revenues due to unstable trade, the IMF was based on an international agreement to set "fixed exchange rates" between national currencies. When President Richard Nixon twice unilaterally devalued U.S. currency in the early 1970s, international currency markets began to set exchange rates. Since that time, the IMF has taken on new functions, especially acting as a credit-rating agency and advisor, recommending reform policies to countries whose governments have high debts and face aggressive creditors (private banks, the IMF itself, the World Bank, and other governments).

jefe de familia   Male head of household.

labor segmentation   Division of job groups or markets according to some criterion such as gender, nationality, location, or race/ethnicity of potential job holders.

la droga   The drug trade.

land tenure   Land ownership pattern, including large and small holdings (*latifundia* and *minifundia*), renters and sharecroppers, *ejidos* (communal lands), and so on.

la raza   Literally "the race," used to refer to the unique *mestizo* (Hispanic) race that resulted from years of racial blending in Mexico.

latent function   A secondary social system consequence of a principal element of social structure. For example, the *ejido* system of communal landholding functions to allow peasant survival, but it has a latent function of legitimating the political power of the dominant political party.

liberalism   A political and economic policy position that asserts support for individual rights, private property, and limited government regulation of markets and social relations.

liberation theology   A Catholic theology that emerged following Vatican II and links church doctrine to the liberation of the oppressed.

libros de texto gratuitos   Free textbooks distributed by the Mexican government.

licenciado   Degree received after graduating from a Mexican university; roughly equivalent to an American bachelor of arts or sciences degree.

licenciatura   The license to practice a particular profession.

life expectancy   A quantitative aggregate measure of average life expected at birth for specific age cohorts or other social groups (gender, ethnicity, race, etc.).

machismo   A term representing the stereotypical behavioral norms associated with masculinity such as strength, virility, and aggressiveness.

macroeconomic policies   Broad government policies targeting interest rates, money supply, trade, and other factors that are not specific to individual markets, regions, or industries.

madre soltera   Unmarried mother.

malnutrition   Poor nutrition due to an insufficient or poorly balanced diet.

maquiladoras (maquilas)   Foreign-owned manufacturing plants along the U.S. Mexican border that are allowed to export products to the United States free of taxes and tariffs.

marianismo   A term representing the stereotypical behavioral norms associated with femininity such as patience, self-denial, sexual disinterest, and obedience.

materialist values   Emphasis on money and conspicuous consumption as indicators of success and well-being.

median age   For a given population, the age in years for which half the population is older and half the population younger.

mercantilism   A term referring to the policies of European states from the 15th to 18th centuries. Mercantilism viewed the world as a zero-sum game where nation-states compete and one nation's gain is another's loss. Policies focused on state intervention to gain wealth through acquisition of bullion. Increases in national production were viewed as more important than raising living standards and consumption.

mestizaje   Ethnic blending or the integration of cultures.

mestizo   Individual of mixed white/Amerindian descent.

modernization theory   General theory of national development that emphasizes the central role of entrepreneurs and values. Assumes that the development pattern and social, political, and economic institutions of Europe and the United States of America form a model that will be duplicated by later developing nation-states.

mortality rates   A quantitative measure of the total deaths in a social group divided by the population. Usually specified for a single year.

mulatto   Individual of mixed white/African descent.

municipio libre   A constitutionally defined local government entity, roughly the size of a county in the United States, which is governed by a council and president. While the constitution gives this political entity considerable local autonomy, in practice, PRI control of national politics, until the 1990s, limited the actual degree of freedom exercised by political officials at this local level.

NAFTA (North American Free Trade Agreement) A treaty between the United States of America, the United States of Mexico, and Canada to end all barriers to investment and trade in goods.

narcomafia Organized drug lords who control the production, transport and distribution of illegal narcotics.

narcoterror Violence associated with the illegal drug trade.

narcotraficantes Drug traffickers.

narcotráfico Drug trafficking.

national income Total national earnings from wages, capital gains, dividends, interest, rents, and royalties.

nationalism Belief in distinct interests and sense of identity linked to a nation-state and commitment to those interests against those of other nation-states.

neoliberal economic policies Government programs aimed at reducing restrictions on trade, reducing public ownership of industries (privatization), ending or minimizing social programs, and generally reducing the relative size of government in relationship to the private sector economy. In Latin America, these policies became an important and widespread feature of political reform in the 1980s and 1990s in response to pressure from international organizations such as the World Bank, the International Monetary Fund, and other creditors involved in global financial markets.

neoliberal reforms (See **neoliberal economic policies.**)

network A formal or informal linking of persons, organizations, or groups that share some interest and act to coordinate their activities and share resources for mutual gain.

nonautonomous university A university that makes administrative decisions in conjunction with the government.

norm A shared expectation of behavior.

nuclear family A family unit that consists of a married couple and their dependent children.

OPEC (Organization of Petroleum Exporting Countries) A cartel of national governments formed in the 1970s to control petroleum prices on world markets by restricting supply. Initially successful in producing significant short-term increases in prices during the 1970s, cheating by individual countries (producing more than their quota) and new oil reserve discoveries by private companies undermined the influence of the cartel during the late 1980s and 1990s.

padrino Patron or godfather.

PAN The National Action Party, the most important opposition party in Mexico. Founded in 1939, PAN's membership today represents conservative business leaders. PAN's electoral strength has never been great at the national level, but since 1988 it has gained strength in some states, even winning several governorships.

patria potestad   The legal authority of men over women and children during the colonial period.

patriarchy   Male domination.

patrilineal extended family   A family unit that consists of more than one generation living together in a single household with property passed from father to son (usually the firstborn).

patrineolocal residence   A married couple residing with the husband's family.

patron   Leader of small social group within a major institution—economic, social, or political—who demands loyalty in return for resources.

patron-client relations   (See **clientalism.**)   Institutional pattern of exchange between leaders and their supporters as loyalty and resources (jobs, money, access) form a bond. At the level of social structure patron-client relations form a social pyramid as leaders (patrons) become clients for leaders who operate at a higher level of power and prestige in major institutions of business, labor, and government.

peasants   (See *campesinos, campesinas.*)   Poor rural farmers who may own land, may be landless workers on property owned by others, or, in Mexico, may work on communal *ejido* lands.

PEMEX   Mexico's government-owned petroleum company, which has a monopoly on the production, refining, and sale of petroleum. In Mexico, as in most of Latin America, the Constitution defines all minerals as a public resource and prohibits private ownership, although concessions may be granted for private investors.

peninsulares   Individuals of Spanish (white) descent living in Mexico, born in Spain.

peripheral   A general concept referring to countries, economic sectors, and individuals not part of the core dominant nation-states, capital intensive sectors, or powerful institutions.

petit bourgeois   A concept referring to an economic class of independent small business owners.

PNR   National Revolutionary Party, the antecedent of Mexico's dominant political party, the PRI (Institutional Revolutionary Party).

polytheistic religion   A formal religion that recognizes the existence of and reveres multiple gods.

Porfiriato   A term referring to the years 1876–1910 when the dictator Porfirio Díaz ruled Mexico.

poverty   The inability to obtain a socially recognized minimal standard of living. The official poverty level serves as a measure identifying what proportion of the total population experiences incomes so low that they cannot purchase basic needs in the marketplace.

PRD   Mexico's second major opposition party. Drawing from parts of the Mexican Communist Party (PCM) and Mexican Socialist Party (PMS), it was founded in 1988 by PRI dissidents. In contrast to the PAN, PRD has backed economic policies less favorable to private business and has supported extensive state involvement in the economy.

prepa   Preparatory school whose graduates typically attend a university.

preparatoria   Preparatory (for the university) school.

presidente municipal   Local political leader of a constitutionally defined administrative district, roughly equivalent to a county.

PRI   Unique to Mexico, the party was created by Mexico's political leaders as a means to protect and ensure their power. The PRI was created and later controlled by Mexico's government bureaucrats. The PRI cannot be compared with political parties elsewhere because it does not produce political leaders who originate in the party or other organized interest groups. Rather, the party is a vehicle funded by the government, and policymaking and power are relatively independent of the party. Highly successful in its role, the PRI dominated virtually all political offices at national, state, and local levels from 1929 until 1988 and continues to exercise political dominance despite a few challenges during the 1990s.

primaria   Primary (elementary) school.

privatization   The process of selling government-owned companies to private owners, often foreign corporations.

PRONOSAL   The National Solidarity Program, an experimental social program aimed at bringing funds to local community projects targeting infrastructure and services bypassing PRI organizations and the federal bureaucracy. Viewed as a neoliberal social program acceptable to business, PRONOSAL was the PRI's response to resistance within its own ranks and demands for reform from without.

public health   Measures of general population physical well-being, on the one hand, and aggregate measures of illness, on the other. Public health agencies and programs target infectious diseases, nutrition, and access to medical care.

race   A group distinguished by genetically transmitted physical characteristics such as skin color, facial characteristics, and hair texture.

racial stratification   Systematic inequality between groups of different races.

reciprocity network   A network of extended nuclear families that exchange goods and services such as child care, food, transportation, housing assistance, and job and political connections.

regionalism   Focus on variations in culture, economic structure, and political interests linked to geographic areas within a nation-state. Mexico is marked by strong regional contrasts in wealth, economic activity, geography, and climate.

repartimiento   A system of labor controls implemented by the Spanish monarchy during the 16th century to replace the *encomienda*. This system of forced labor required male Amerindians to work for Spaniards about 45 days per year. Workers were to be paid by landowners, but physical abuse and fraud were commonly employed by Spanish colonists.

reproductive/household work   Childbearing, childrearing, and other unpaid domestic tasks.

rural popular movements   Grassroots social movements emerging in rural areas that are primarily dedicated to indigenous causes (See *Ejército Zapitista Liberación Nacional*).

rural social structure   A general term referring to the dominant economic, political, and cultural institutions of agrarian society.

sect   Small, evangelical religious organization that recruits members by conversion and adopts a radical stance towards the state and society.

secundaria   Secondary school.

semiperipheral   In world system theory, a concept that identified nation-states that occupy an intermediate position in unequal exchange networks, exploited when they trade with core nation-states but exploitative themselves when trading with peripheral nation-states. Semiperipheral nations exhibit core characteristics (urbanization, manufacturing employment, institutional strength, and stability) and peripheral processes (exploitative labor relations, nondemocratic politics, etc.).

serial monogamy   Where partners who once lived together in a monogamous relationship separate from one another and establish subsequent monogamous relationships with other individuals.

sex discrimination   Unfair discrimination on the basis of one's sex, specifically related to one's employment.

sexually transmitted diseases (STDs)   Bacteriological and viral illness spread through direct sexual contact—for example, AIDS (auto immune deficiency syndrome), gonorrhea, syphilis, chlamydia, venereal warts.

Sindicato Nacional de Trabajadores de la Educación   Mexican teachers union.

sin verguenza   Without shame.

socialization   The process through which individuals learn to become members of a society.

social legislation   Government policies and programs aimed at meeting basic needs (food, housing, health), addressing human rights (access to education, security), and building community institutions.

social mobility   Change in social status for individuals or groups. Change may include upward or downward processes; it may refer to individuals or structural processes. Individual social mobility typically refers to change in social position with reference to one's family origins. Structural mobility refers to changes in the stratification system itself as these influence the distribution of individuals to positions. For example, rural-to-urban migration produces a population shift that redefines the opportunities available to individuals and thus creates social mobility.

social norms   A shared expectation of behavior that may be formal, as in laws, or informal. Norms are typically accompanied by sanctions that may be imposed on individuals who violate norms. These may range from formal penalties (prison time and fines) to a "stare" indicating disapproval.

social status   Any particular defined position in a stratification system for which there are social norms. Social status may be ascribed, depending on social definitions of who you are. Social status may be achieved, depending on social definitions of an individual's accomplishments as an economic, cultural, or political actor.

social stratification   A characterization of society in terms of unequal distributions of economic, cultural, and political identity of individuals and groups. This social structure may vary in the degree of openness to individual and group mobility (change in status).

social structure   Any characteristic of groups as opposed to individuals. Components of social structure range from sex ratios (ratios of males to females in a given population) to economic classes, political systems, languages, and religions.

soldadera Female revolutionary suffrage/suffragist—the right or privilege of voting/an advocate of women's right to vote.

structural adjustment policies (See **neoliberal policies**.) A set of government reforms aimed at increasing the unregulated and untaxed proportion of market-based economic activity. These policies usually included reducing public sector employment (as a proportion of the total), devaluation of currencies, reduced tariffs, cutbacks on social programs, and privatization of publicly owned industries.

structural dualism A concept that defines national economic structures in terms of primary sector (agriculture and mining) export dominance, with little rationale for increasing wages or promoting democracy, or manufacturing/service sector domestic dominance, with strong rationale for expanding consumer demand and democratic politics.

structure functionalist A sociological theory that evaluates social institutions in terms of their contribution to group, community, or societal adaptation, thus allowing them to survive in a given environment.

structural mobility Social mobility that results from changes in economic structure, which in turn revise the social status distribution available. The shift from a rural agricultural society to an urban industrial and service society thus creates new status positions while reducing others.

subsistence crops Agricultural production oriented to consumption by farmers themselves. Corn and beans are examples of typical Mexican subsistence crops.

subsistence farmers Agricultural producers whose primary orientation is toward producing crops they and their family will consume. Such farmers may sell a small portion of their crop, but commercial goals are secondary.

supply-side economics An economic policy position that stresses the importance of government policies that increase economic gain for property owners, especially the wealthy, as a means to general economic growth. The position assumes that wealthy individuals and families will invest their gains in new productive enterprises and thus produce more jobs, distributing the gains downward in the society.

suspended particulates Particles in the atmosphere smaller than 50 microns in diameter.

taboo The social prohibition assigned to certain things that deems them untouchable and/or unmentionable.

talleres familiares Family workshops.

tanda A revolving credit association or savings strategy.

technocrat A term identifying well-educated government workers who staff planning and program agencies. They are often viewed as a "new class" whose economic interests are tied to their positions as public employees, in contrast to classes whose interests are rooted in the private economy itself.

unemployment/underemployment A quantitative measure of economically active adults who are without regular wage labor jobs or whose employment is so poorly paid and irregular that it fails to produce a living wage.

union libre   A union between a man and a woman in which the couple agree to establish a household, but do not legally or religiously marry.

urban popular movements (UPMs)   Grassroots social movements emerging in urban areas that are dedicated to diverse urban and political issues, including education, land acquisition, housing shortages, unemployment, and government indifference.

uuletik   Mayan curer-diviner.

Vatican   The central governing body of the Roman Catholic Church.

Vatican II (the Second Vatican Council)   Council held from 1962 to 1965 during which Vatican authorities and Catholic scholars and clergy discussed new interpretations of Catholic traditions and instituted a number of significant structural changes.

verguenza   Shame.

vertical kinship networks   Kinship networks that link families of different socioeconomic status into patron–client relationships.

World Bank   An international organization supported by contributions from national governments, the World Bank was founded at the 1944 Bretton Woods conference, which also produced the International Monetary Fund. The World Bank's principal goal is to provide loans at market rates, but for projects that private investors and creditors avoid as too risky or not profitable. World Bank loans target projects that will build national economic infrastructures or increase human resources available for economic activity.

world system theory   A general theory of historical change in the capitalist global economy that describes the relationship between nation-states and regions in terms of trade relations. Three zones—the core, semiperiphery, and periphery—define a continuum from powerful exploitative to weak and exploited nation-states. The theory emphasizes the importance of systemic relations between these zones as determining the experience of a nation-state within a zone.

REFERENCES

Editor's Preface

Horowitz, Irving Louis. C. *Wright Mills: An American Utopian*. New York: Free Press, 1983.

Lipset, Seymour Martin. *American Exceptionalism: A Double-Edged Sword*. New York: W.W. Norton, 1996.

Ragin, Charles; and David Zaret. "Theory and Method in Comparative Strategies." *Social Forces* 61 (1983), pp. 731–54.

Smelser, Neil J. *Comparative Methods in the Social Sciences*. Englewood Cliffs, NJ: Prentice Hall, 1976.

Chapter 1

Cockroft, James D. 1983. *Mexico: Class Formation, Capital Accumulation, and the State*. New York: Monthly Review Press.

Cornelius, Wayne A., and Ann L. Craig. 1991. *The Mexican Political System in Transition*. La Jolla, CA: Center for U.S.–Mexican Studies, University of California, San Diego.

INEGI. 1990. Instituto Nacional de Estadistica, Geografia e Informática. *XI Censo General de Población y Vivienda, resultados definitivos*.

Levy, Daniel, and Gabriel Szélkey. 1983. *Mexico: Paradoxes of Stability and Change*. Boulder, CO: Westview Press.

Lima-Dantas, Elizabeth de. 1985. "Historical Setting." In *Mexico: A Country Study*, ed. William Evans-Smith, pp. 1–80. Washington, D.C.: U.S. Government.

MacLachlan, Colin M., and William H. Beezley. 1994. *El Gran Pueblo: A History of Greater Mexico*. Englewood Cliffs, NJ: Prentice Hall.

Meyer, Michael C., and William L. Sherman. 1995. *The Course of Mexican History*. New York: Oxford University Press.

Miller, Robert Ryal. 1985. *Mexico: A History*. Norman, OK: University of Oklahoma Press.

Otero, Gerardo. 1996. *Neo-Liberalism Revisited: Economic Restructuring and Mexico's Political Future*. Boulder, CO: Westview Press.

Siembieda, William, and Ramon Rodríguez M. 1996. "One Country, Many Faces: The Regions of Mexico." In *Changing Structure of Mexico: Political, Social, and Economic Prospects*, ed. Laura Randall. Armonk, NY: M. E. Sharpe.

Skidmore, Thomas E., and Peter H. Smith. 1992. *Modern Latin America*. New York: Oxford University Press.

Stannard, David E. 1992. *American Holocaust: The Conquest of the New World*. New York: Oxford University Press.

Chapter 2

Bagley, Bruce M., and Sergio Aguayo Quezada, eds. 1995. *Mexico: In Search of Security*. New Brunswick, NJ: Transaction Publishers.

Blancarte, Roberto J. 1996. "The 1992 Reforms of Mexican Law on Religion: Prospects of Change in State-Church Relations." In *The Challenge of Institutional Reform in Mexico*, ed. Riordan Roett, pp. 95–113. Boulder, CO: Lynne Rienner Publishers.

Cornelius, Wayne. 1996. *Mexican Politics in Transition: The Breakdown of a One-Party Dominant Regime*. San Diego, CA: The Center for U.S.–Mexican Studies.

Domínguez, Jorge I., and James A. McCann. 1996. *Democratizing Mexico: Public Opinion and Electoral Choices*. Baltimore: The Johns Hopkins University Press.

Harvey, Neil, ed. 1993. *Mexico: Dilemmas of Transition*. London: The Institute of Latin American Studies and British Academic Press.

La Botz, Dan. 1995. *Democracy in Mexico: Peasant Rebellion and Political Reform*. Boston: South End Press.

"Latin American Arms: Toys for the Chicos?" 1996 (October 5). *The Economist*, p. 43.

"Mexicans Hand Major Electoral Defeats to Ruling Party." 1997 (July 7). *The Wall Street Journal*, p. A14.

"Mexico: Survey." 1987 (September 5). *The Economist* (special supplement).

———. 1993 (February 13). *The Economist* (special supplement).

———. 1995 (October 28). *The Economist* (special supplement).

Middlebrook, Kevin J. (ed.) 1995. *The Paradox of Revolution: Labor, The State, and Authoritarianism in Mexico*. Baltimore: The Johns Hopkins University Press.

Valdés Ugalde, Francisco. 1996. "The Private Sector and Political Regime Change in Mexico." In *Neo-Liberalism Revisited: Economic Restructuring and Mexico's Political Future*, ed. Gerardo Otero. Boulder, CO: Westview Press.

Chapter 3

Bronfenbrenner, Kate. 1997. "The Effects of Plant Closing or Threat of Plant Closing on the Right of Workers to Organize." A report submitted to the Labor Secretariat of the North American Commission for Labor Cooperation.

Canak, William. 1989. *Lost Promises: Debt, Austerity and Development in Latin America*. Boulder, CO: Westview Press.

Gates, Marilyn. 1996. "The Debt Crisis and Economic Restructuring: Prospects for Mexican Agriculture." In *Neo-Liberalism Revisited: Economic Restructuring and Mexico's Political Future*, ed. Gerardo Otero, pp. 43–62. Boulder, CO: Westview Press.

Gereffi, Gary. 1996. "Mexico's 'Old' and 'New' Maquiladora Industries: Contrasting Approaches to North American Integration," In *Neo-Liberalism Revisited*. *See* Gates 1996.

Hirschman, Albert O. 1970. *Exit, Voice, and Loyalty: Responses to Decline in Firms, Organizations and States*. Cambridge, MA: Harvard University Press.

Kopinak, Kathryn. 1996. *Desert Capitalism: Maquiladoras in North America's Western Industrial Corridor*. Tucson: University of Arizona Press.

"Mexico: Survey." 1987 (September 5). *The Economist* (special supplement).

———. 1993 (February 13). *The Economist* (special supplement).

———. 1995 (October 28). *The Economist* (special supplement).

Myhre, David. 1996. "Appropriate Agricultural Credit: A Missing Piece of Agrarian Reform in Mexico." In *Reforming Mexico's Agrarian Reform,* ed. Laura Randall. Armonk, NY: M. E. Sharpe.

Osterling, Jorge P. 1985. "The Society and Its Environment." In *Mexico: A Country Study,* ed. James D. Rudolph. Washington, D.C.: American University.

Otero, Gerardo. 1996. "Neoliberal Reform and Politics in Mexico." In *Neo-Liberalism Revisited. See* Gates 1996.

Quintanilla, M. Juan, and Mariano Bauer E. 1996. "Mexican Oil and Energy." In *Changing Structure of Mexico: Political, Social, and Economic Prospects,* ed. Laura Randall, pp. 111–26. Armonk, NY: M. E. Sharpe.

Riding, Alan. 1984. *Distant Neighbors: A Portrait of the Mexicans.* New York: Alfred A. Knopf.

Teichman, Judith A. 1995. *Privatization and Political Change in Mexico.* Pittsburgh, PA: University of Pittsburgh Press.

Chapter 4

Allensworth, Diane DeMuth, and Andres G. De Wit Greene. 1990. "Mexico: Perspectives in School Health." *Journal of School Health* 60(7), pp. 337–41.

Barkin, David. 1990. *Distorted Development: Mexico in the World Economy.* Boulder, CO: Westview Press.

Bennett, Vivienne. 1992. "The Evolution of Urban Popular Movements in Mexico Between 1968 and 1978." In *The Making of Social Movements in Contemporary Latin America: Identity, Strategy, and Democracy,* ed. Sonia Alvarez and Arturo Escobar. Boulder, CO: Westview Press.

Cornelius, Wayne. 1996. *Mexican Politics in Transition: The Breakdown of a One-Party-Dominant Regime.* San Diego: The Center for U.S.–Mexican Studies, University of California.

Felix, David. 1982. "Income Distribution Trends in Mexico and the Kuznets Curve." In *Brazil and Mexico: Patterns in Late Development,* ed. Sylvia A. Hewlett and Richard S. Weinert. Philadelphia, PA: Institute for the Study of Human Issues.

Gollás, M. 1994. "México 1994. Una Economía sin Inflación y sin Crecimiento." Documento de Trabajo, CEE, El Colegio de México, Mexico City.

Graizbord, Boris, and Crescenio Ruiz. 1996. "Recent Changes in the Economic and Social Structure of Mexico's Regions." In *Changing Structure of Mexico: Political, Social, and Economic Prospects,* ed. Laura Randall. Armonk, NY: M. E. Sharp.

Krooth, Richard. 1995. *Mexico, NAFTA and the Hardships of Progress.* Jefferson, NC: McFarland & Company, Inc.

Lomnitz, Larissa. 1984. "Horizontal and Vertical Relations and the Social Structure of Urban Mexico." *Latin American Research Review* 17(2), pp. 51–74.

Lustig, Nora. 1992. *Mexico: The Remaking of an Economy.* Washington, D.C.: The Brookings Institution.

———. 1996. "The 1982 Debt Crisis, Chiapas, NAFTA, and Mexico's Poor." In *Changing Structure of Mexico. See* Graizbord and Ruiz 1996.

McKinley, Terry, and Diana Alarcón. 1995. "The Prevalence of Rural Poverty in Mexico." *World Development* 23(9), pp. 1575–86.

"Mexico: Survey." 1995 (October 28). *The Economist* (special supplement).

Nash, June. 1995. "The New World Dis-Order: A View from Chiapas, Mexico." *Indigenous Perceptions of the Nation State in Latin America* 56, pp. 171–95.

Chapter 5

Arrom, Silvia M. 1994. "Changes in Mexican Family Law in the Nineteenth Century." In *Confronting Change, Challenging Tradition: Women in Latin American History*, ed. Gertrude Yeager, pp. 87–102. Wilmington, DE: Scholarly Resources.

Baud, I. S. A. 1992. *Forms of Production and Women's Labour: Gender Aspects of Industrialization in India and Mexico.* Newbury Park, CA: Sage Publications.

Chant, Sylvia. 1994. "Women, Work and Household Survival Strategies in Mexico, 1982–1992: Past Trends, Current Tendencies and Future Research." *Bulletin of Latin American Research* 13(2), pp. 203–33.

Dubois, Jill. 1993. *Women in Society.* New York: Marshall Cavendish.

Epstein, Nadine. 1988. "Mexico's First Woman for Prez." *Ms Magazine* 16(9), p. 68.

Fernandez-Kelly, Maria Patricia. 1983. *For We Are Sold, I and My People.* Albany: State University of New York Press.

GENESYS. 1994. *Gender and Sustainable Development: A Training Manual.* Washington, D.C.: U.S. Agency for International Development.

Gutmann, Matthew C. 1996. *The Meanings of Macho: Being a Man in Mexico City.* Berkeley: University of California Press.

Hall, Sandi. 1987 (May). "Little Progress for Mexico's Women." *World Press Review*, pp. 53–54.

Hellman, Judith Adler. 1994. *Mexican Lives.* New York: The New Press.

Inter-American Development Bank (IDA). 1995. *Women in the Americas: Bridging the Gender Gap.* Baltimore: The Johns Hopkins University Press.

Janofsky, Michael. 1996 (November 7). "Women Make Only Moderate Gains Despite Many Contenders." *New York Times* 146(50604), p. B2.

Kopinak, Kathryn. 1996. *Desert Capitalism: Maquiladoras in North America's Western Industrial Corridor.* Tucson: University of Arizona Press.

LeVine, Sarah, with Clara Sunderland Correa. 1993. *Dolor y Alegría: Women and Social Change in Urban Mexico.* Madison, WI: The University of Wisconsin Press.

MacLachlan, Colin M., and Jaime E. Rodriguez O. 1980. *The Forging of the Cosmic Race.* Berkeley: University of California Press.

Miller, Francesca. 1994. "The Suffrage Movement in Latin America." In *Confronting Change*, pp. 157–176. *See* Arrom 1994.

Moghadam, Valentine M. 1995. "Gender Dynamics of Restructuring in the Semiperiphery." In *EnGENDERing Wealth and Well-Being: Empowerment for Global Change*, ed. Rae Lesser Blumberg, Cathy A. Rakowski, Irene Tinker, and Michael Monteon, pp. 17–37. Boulder, CO: Westview Press.

Monteon, Michael. 1995. "Gender and Economic Crises in Latin America: Reflections on the Great Depression and the Debt Crisis." In *EnGENDERing Wealth and Well-Being*, pp. 39–62. *See* Moghadam 1995.

Moser, Caroline. 1993. "Adjustment from Below: Low-Income Women, Time and the Triple Role in Guayaquil, Ecuador." In *Viva: Women and Popular Protest in Latin America*, ed. Sarah A. Radcliffe and Sallie Westwood. London: Routledge.

Skidmore, Thomas E., and Pete H. Smith. 1992. *Modern Latin America*. New York: Oxford University Press.

Soto, Shirlene Ann. 1990. *Emergence of the Modern Mexican Woman: Her Participation in Revolution and Struggle for Equality, 1910, 1940*. Denver, CO: Arden Press.

Stern, Steve J. 1995. *Women, Men, and Power in Late Colonial Mexico: The Secret History of Gender*. Chapel Hill: The University of North Carolina Press.

Stevens, Evelyn P. 1994. "Marianismo: The Other Face of Machismo." In *Confronting Change*, pp. 3–17. *See* Arrom 1994.

Vasquez, Josefina Zoraida. 1994. "Women's Liberation in Latin America: Toward a History of the Present." In *Confronting Change*, pp. 18–25. *See* Arrom 1994.

"Women—The Invisible Victims of the '90s." 1995 (June 26). *LatinAmerica Press* 27(23), p. 4.

Chapter 6

Bartra, Roger. 1977. "The Problem of the Native Peoples and Indigenist Ideology." In *Race and Class in Post-Colonial Society*, pp. 341–354. UK: UNESCO.

Beals, Ralph. 1969. "Amerindian-Mestizo-White Relations in Spanish America." In *Comparative Perspectives on Race Relations*, ed. Melvin N. Tumin, pp. 239–257. Boston: Little, Brown.

Cornelius, Wayne A. 1996. *Mexican Politics in Transition: The Breakdown of a One-Party-Dominant Regime*. San Diego: The Center for U.S.–Mexican Studies, University of California.

Davis, Darién J. 1995. "Introduction: The African Experience in Latin America—Resistance and Accommodation." In *Slavery and Beyond: The African Impact on Latin America and the Caribbean*, ed. Darién J. Davis. Wilmington, DE: Scholarly Resources.

Dubois, Jill. 1993. *Women in Society*. New York: Marshall Cavendish.

Hill, Jane. 1991. "In Neca Gobierno de Puebla: Mexicano Penetrations of the Mexican State." In *Nation-States and Amerindians in Latin America*, ed. Greg Urban and Joel Sherzer, pp. 72–94. Austin: University of Texas Press.

Knight, Alan. 1990. "Racism, Revolution, and Indigenismo: Mexico, 1910–1940." In *The Idea of Race in Latin America, 1870–1940*, ed. Richard Graham, pp. 1–5. Austin: University of Texas Press.

LeVine, Sarah, with Clara Sunderland Correa. 1993. *Dolor y Alegría: Women and Social Change in Urban Mexico*. Madison, WI: The University of Wisconsin Press.

Lumsden, Ian. 1991. *Homosexuality: Society and the State in Mexico*. Toronto: Canadian Gay Archives.

MacLachlan, Colin M., and Jaime E. Rodriguez O. 1980. *The Cosmic Race: A Rein-terpretation of Colonial Mexico.* Berkeley: University of California Press.

Nash, June. 1995a. "The Reassertion of Indigenous Identity: Mayan Responses to State Intervention in Chiapas." *Latin American Research Review* 30(3), pp. 7–41.

———. 1995b. "The New World Dis-Order: A View from Chiapas, Mexico." *In-digenous Perceptions of the Nation-State in Latin America* 56, pp. 171–95.

Payne, Douglas W. 1996 (Summer). "Between Hope and History: Mexico's Indi-ans Refuse to Disappear." *Dissent,* pp. 61–66.

Psacharopoulos, George, and Harry A. Patrinos. 1994 (March). "Indigenous Peo-ple and Poverty in Latin America." *Finance and Development,* pp. 41–43.

Riding, Alan. 1984. *Distant Neighbors: A Portrait of the Mexicans.* New York: Alfred A. Knopf.

Salloum, Habeeb. 1996. "The Mayan Ruins." *Contemporary Review* 268, pp. 248–52.

"This Land Is Our Land." 1995. *LatinAmerica Press* 27(36), p. 3.

Toplin, Robert Brent. 1974. "Introduction." In *Slavery and Race Relations in Latin America,* ed. Robert Brent Toplin, pp. 3–12. Westport, CT: Greenwood Press.

Tresierra, Julio C. 1994. "Mexico: Indigenous Peoples and the Nation-State." In *Indigenous Peoples and Democracy in Latin America,* ed. Donna Lee Van Cott, pp. 187–212. New York: St. Martin's Press.

Van Cott, Donna Lee. 1994. "Foreword." In *Indigenous Peoples and Democracy,* pp. 1–23. *See* Tresierra 1994.

Vigil, James Diego. 1980. *From Amerindians to Chicanos: The Dynamics of Mexican American Culture.* Prospect Heights, IL: Waveland Press.

Chapter 7

Camp, Roderic Ai. 1993. *Politics in Mexico.* New York: Oxford University Press.

———. 1982. "Family Relationships in Mexican Politics: A Preliminary View." *The Journal of Politics* 44, pp. 848–62.

Carlos, Manuel L., and Lois Sellers. 1972. "Family, Kinship Structure and Mod-ernization in Latin America." *Latin American Research Review* 7(2), pp. 95–124.

Dubois, Jill. 1993. *Women in Society.* New York: Marshall Cavendish.

Economic Commission for Latin America and the Caribbean (ECLAC). 1995. *Family and Future: A Regional Programme in Latin America and the Caribbean.* Santiago, Chile: United Nations.

González, Mercedes de la Rocha. 1994. *The Resources of Poverty: Women and Sur-vival in a Mexican City.* Oxford, UK: Blackwell Publishers.

Gutmann, Matthew C. 1996. *The Meanings of Macho: Being a Man in Mexico City.* Berkeley: University of California Press.

Hall, Sandi. 1987 (May). "Little Progress for Mexico's Women." *World Press Re-view,* pp. 53–54.

Hellman, Judith Adler. 1994. *Mexican Lives.* New York: The New Press.

Kuznesof, Elizabeth Anne. 1989. "The History of the Family in Latin America." *Latin American Research Review* 24(2), pp. 168–88.

LeVine, Sarah, with Clara Sunderland Correa. 1993. *Dolor y Alegría: Women and Social Change in Urban Mexico*. Madison, WI: The University of Wisconsin Press.

Lomnitz, Larissa. 1984. "Horizontal and Vertical Relations and the Social Structure of Urban Mexico." *Latin American Research Review* 17(2), pp. 51–74.

MacLachlan, Colin M., and Jaime E. Rodriguez O. 1980. *The Forging of the Cosmic Race*. Berkeley: University of California Press.

Miraftab, Faranak. 1994. "(Re)Production at Home: Reconceptualizing Home and Family." *Journal of Family Issues* 13, pp. 467–89.

Moore, Molly. 1996 (December 10). "Mexican Waifs Ply Meanest of Streets." *Washington Post*, p. A23, col. 1.

Murphy, Arthur. 1991. "City in Crisis." *Urban Anthropology* 20(1), pp. 1–13.

Olivera, Mercedes. 1976. "The Barrios of San Andrés Cholula." In *Essays on Mexican Kinship*, pp. 65–95. *See* Nutini 1976.

Riding, Alan. 1984. *Distant Neighbors: A Portrait of the Mexicans*. New York: Alfred A. Knopf.

Selby, Henry A. 1991. "The Oaxacan Urban Household and the Crisis." *Urban Anthropology* 20(1), pp. 87–98.

Selby, Henry A.; Arthur D. Murphy; and Stephen A. Lorenzen. 1990. *The Mexican Urban Household: Organizing for Self-Defense*. Austin: University of Texas Press.

Staudt, K. 1993. "Gender Inequality and Industrial Development: The Household Connection." *Journal of Comparative Family Studies* 24(1), pp. 1–21.

Winter, Mary. 1991. "Interhousehold Exchange of Goods and Services in the City of Oaxaca." *Urban Anthropology* 20(1), pp. 67–85.

Chapter 8

Berryman, Phillip. 1994. "The Coming of Age of Evangelical Protestantism." *NACLA Report on the Americas* 27(6), pp. 6–10.

———. 1980. "What Happened at Puebla." In *Churches and Politics in Latin America*, ed. Daniel H. Levine, pp. 55–86. Newbury Park, CA: Sage Publications.

Blancarte, Roberto J. 1993. "Recent Changes in Church-State Relations in Mexico: An Historical Approach." *Journal of Church and State* 35(4), pp. 781–805.

Braden, Charles W. 1966. *Religious Aspects of the Conquest of Mexico*. New York: AMS Press, Inc.

Camp, Roderic Ai. 1994. "The Cross in the Polling Booth: Religion, Politics and the Laity in Mexico." *Latin American Research Review* 29(3), pp. 69–100.

Cleary, Edward L. 1985. *Crisis and Change: The Church in Latin America Today*. Maryknoll, NY: Orbis Books.

DePalma, Anthony. 1996. "Let the Heavens Fall, Mexicans Will Revere Virgin." *New York Times* 145(50465), p. A4.

Dixon, David. 1995. "The New Protestantism in Latin America." *Comparative Politics* 27(4), pp. 479–92.

Drogus, Carol Ann. 1995. "The Rise and Decline of Liberation Theology: Churches, Faith, and Political Change in Latin America." *Comparative Politics* 27(4), pp. 465–77.

Dubois, Jill. 1993. *Women in Society*. New York: Marshall Cavendish.

Floyd, Charlene. 1996. "A Theology of Insurrection? Religion and Politics in Mexico." *Journal of International Affairs* 50(1), pp. 142–65.

Ingham, John M. 1986. *Mary, Michael and Lucifer*. Austin, TX: University of Texas Press.

Levine, Daniel H. 1986. "Religion, the Poor, and Politics in Latin America Today." In *Religion and Political Conflict in Latin America*, ed. Daniel H. Levine, pp. 3–23. Chapel Hill, NC: The University of North Carolina Press.

———. 1980. "Religion and Politics, Politics and Religion: An Introduction." In *Churches and Politics in Latin America*, pp. 13–16. *See* Berryman 1980.

MacLachlan, Colin, and Jaime E. Rodriguez O. 1980. *The Forging of the Cosmic Race*. Berkeley, CA: University of California Press.

MacNabb, Valerie Ann, and Martha W. Rees. 1993. "Liberation or Theology? Ecclesial Base Communities in Oaxaca, Mexico." *Journal of Church and State* 35(4), pp. 723–49.

Mainwaring, Scott. 1990. "Democratization, Socioeconomic Disintegration, and the Latin American Churches after Puebla." In *Born of the Poor*, ed. Edward L. Cleary, pp. 143–67. Notre Dame: University of Notre Dame Press.

McGuire, Meredith B. 1992. *Religion: The Social Context*. Belmont, CA: Wadsworth Publishing.

Metz, Allan. 1994. "Protestantism in Mexico: Contemporary Contextual Developments." *Journal of Church and State* 36(1), pp. 57–78.

Montgomery, T. S. 1980. "Latin American Evangelicals." In *Churches and Politics*, pp. 87–108. *See* Berryman 1980.

Nicholson, Irene. 1967. *Mexican and Central American Mythology*. London: Paul Hamlyn.

Renato, Poblete. 1970. "The Church in Latin America: A Historical Survey." In *The Church and Social Change in Latin America*, ed. Henry A. Landsberger, pp. 39–52. Notre Dame: University of Notre Dame Press.

Stewart-Gambino, Hannah. 1994. "Church and State in Latin America." *Current History* 93(581), pp. 129–33.

Chapter 9

Albornoz, Orlando. 1993. *Education and Society in Latin America*. Pittsburgh, PA: University of Pittsburgh Press.

Arizpe, Lourdes. 1993. "An Overview of Women's Education in Latin America and the Caribbean." In *The Politics of Women's Education: Perspectives from Asia, Africa and Latin America*, ed. Jill Kerr Conway and Susan C. Borque, pp. 245–58. Ann Arbor: The University of Michigan Press.

Arnove, Robert F.; Alberto Torres; Stephen Franz; and Kimberly Morse. 1996. "A Political Sociology of Education and Development in Latin America: The Conditioned State, Neo-Liberalism and Educational Policy." *International Journal of Comparative Sociology* 37(1–2), pp. 140–58.

Arnove, Robert F., and Carlos Alberto Torres. 1995. "Adult Education and State Policy in Latin America: The Contrasting Cases of Mexico and Nicaragua." *Comparative Education* 31(3), pp. 311–25.

Camp, Roderic Ai. 1980. *Mexico's Leaders: Their Education and Recruitment.* Tucson: The University of Arizona Press.

Epstein, Erwin E. 1985. "National Consciousness and Education in Mexico." In *Education in Latin America,* pp. 50–78. *See* Brock 1985.

Gimeno, José Blat. 1983. *Education in Latin America and the Caribbean: Trends and Prospects, 1970–2000.* UK: UNESCO.

Inter-American Development Bank (IDB). 1995. *Women in the Americas: Bridging the Gender Gap.* Baltimore: The Johns Hopkins University Press.

Izquierdo Munoz, Carlos, and Sylvia Schmelkes. 1992. "Mexico: Modernization of Education and the Problems and Challenges of Basic Education." In *Education, Policy and Social Change: Experiences from Latin America,* ed. Daniel A. Morales-Gomez and Carlos Alberto Torres, pp. 57–69. Westport, CO: Praeger Publishers.

Kent, Rollin. 1993. "Higher Education in Mexico: From Unregulated Expansion to Evaluation." *Higher Education* 25, pp. 73–83.

Levy, Daniel. 1980. *University and Government in Mexico: Autonomy in an Authoritarian System.* New York, NY: Praeger Publishers.

Lorey, David. E. 1992. "Universities, Public Policy and Economic Development in Latin America." *Higher Education* 23, pp. 65–78.

———. 1994. *The Rise of the Professions in Twentieth-Century Mexico: University Graduates and Occupational Change Since 1929.* Los Angeles: UCLA Latin American Center Publications.

———. 1995. "Education and the Challenges of Mexican Development." *Challenge* 38(2), pp. 51–56.

Osborn, Thomas Noel, II. 1976. *Higher Education in Mexico.* El Paso: Texas Western Press.

Palafox, Juan Carlos; Juan Prawda; and Eduardo Velez. 1994. "Primary School Quality in Mexico." *Comparative Education Review* 38(2), pp. 167–80.

Reimers, Fernando. 1991. "The Impact of Economic Stabilization and Adjustment on Education in LA." *Comparative Education Review* 35(2), pp. 319–53.

Riding, Alan. 1984. *Distant Neighbors: A Portrait of the Mexicans.* New York: Alfred A Knopf.

Torres, Alberto. 1991. "State Corporatism, Educational Policies, and Students' and Teachers' Movements in Mexico." In *Understanding Educational Reform. See* Ginsberg et al. 1991.

"Two Teens: Different Lives." 1988 *Scholastic Update* (November 18): 13–14.

Vaughn, Mary Kay. 1990. "Primary Education and Literacy in Nineteenth-Century Mexico: Research Trends, 1968–1988." *Latin American Research Review* 25(1), pp. 31–66.

Chapter 10

Alba, F. 1978. *La Población de Mexico: Evolución y Dilemas*. Mexico, D.F: El Colegio de México.

Centro de Estudios Económicos y Demográficos. 1981. *Dinámica de la Población en México*. México: El Colegio de México, 2a. edición.

Dirección General de Planificación Familiar (DGPF). 1988. *Encuesta Nacional de Planificación Familiar*. México, D.F.: Secretaría de Salud.

Durand, Jorge, and Douglas S. Massey. 1992. "Mexican Migration to the United States: A Critical Review," *Latin American Research Review*, 27:2, pp. 3–42.

Grindle, Merilee. 1988. *Searching for Rural Development: Labor Migration and Employment in Mexico*. Ithaca: Cornell University Press.

Ham-Chande, Roberto, and John R. Weeks. 1992. "A Demographic Perspective of the U.S.–Mexico Border." In *Demographic Dynamics of the U.S.–Mexico Border*, ed. John R. Weeks and Roberto Ham-Chande. El Paso, TX: Texas Western Press.

Jiménez, R. G. Vera, and G. Ruiz. 1986. *Factores Sociodemográficos Asociados a la Mortalidad Infantil en México*. Paper presented at the Third National Conference on Demography, Mexico.

Jiménez Ornelas, René A. 1992. "Los Cambios de la Mortalidad en México (1900–1987)." In *Poblacion y Sociedad en Mexico*, ed. Humberto Muñoz Garcia. México, D.F.: Miguel Angel Porrua, Grupo Editorial.

Martin, Philip. 1996. "Mexican–U.S. Migration: Policies and Economic Impacts." In *Changing Structure of Mexico: Political, Social and Economic Prospects*, ed. Laura Randall, pp. 145–56. Armonk, NY: M. E. Sharpe.

Massey, Douglas; R. Alarcón; J. Durand; and H. González. 1987. *Return to Aztlan: The Social Process of International Migration from Western Mexico*. Berkeley: University of California Press.

Minujin, A.; G. Vera; R. Jiménez; and G. Ruiz. 1984. *Factores Sociodemográficos Asociados a la Mortalidad Infantil*. Memorias del Congreso Latino-americano de Población y Desarrollo. México: Instituto de Investigaciones Sociales, UNAM, and Banco de México.

National Center for Health Statistics. 1994. *Health United States, 1994*. Washington, D.C.: Government Printing Office.

Oxford Analytica. 1991. *Latin American in Perspective*. Boston: Houghton Mifflin Company.

Palma Cabrera, Yolanda, and Carlos Javier Echarri Cánovas. 1992. "La Fecundidad en México: Niveles Actuales y Tendencias." In *Población y Sociedad en México. See* Jiménez 1992.

Schteingart, Martha. 1989. "The Environmental Problems Associated with Urban Development in Mexico City." *Environment and Urbanization* 1:1 (April), pp. 40–50.

Siembieda, William, and Ramon Rodríguez M. 1996. "One Country, Many Faces: The Regions of Mexico." In *Changing Structure of Mexico*, pp. 351–64. *See* Martin 1996.

SSA. 1988. *Encuesta Nacional sobre Fecundidad y Salud 1987*. Mexico, D.F.

United Nations. 1993. *Population, Social Equity and Changing Production Patterns*. Santiago, Chile.

———. 1993. *Internal Migration of Women in Developing Countries.* ST/ESTA/SER.R/127. New York.

Weeks, John R., and Roberto Ham-Chande, eds. 1992. *Demographic Dynamics of the U.S.–Mexico Border*. El Paso, TX: Texas Western Press.

Chapter 11

Allensworth, Diane DeMuth, and Andres G. De Wit Greene. 1990. "Mexico: Perspectives in School Health." *Journal of School Health* 60(7), pp. 337–41.

Angotti, Thomas. 1995. "The Latin American Metropolis and the Growth of Inequality." *NACLA Report on the Americas* 28(4), pp. 13–18.

Bagley, Bruce Michael. 1989. "The New Hundred Years War?: U.S. National Security and the War on Drugs in Latin America." In *The Latin American Narcotics Trade and U.S. National Security*, ed. Donald J. Mabry, pp. 43–58. Westport, CT: Greenwood Press.

Barkin, David. 1993. "Environmental Degradation in Mexico." *Monthly Review* 45(3), pp. 58–77.

Barry, Tom; Harry Browne; and Beth Sims. 1994. *The Great Divide*. New York: The Grove Press.

Bennett, Vivienne. 1992. "The Evolution of Urban Popular Movements in Mexico Between 1968 and 1988." In *The Making of Social Movements in Latin America*, ed. Arturo Escobar and Sonia E. Alvarez, pp. 240–59. Boulder, CO: Westview Press.

Blake, Donald R., and Sherwood Rowland. 1995. "Urban Leakage of Liquefied Petroleum Gas and Its Impact on Mexican City Air Quality." *Science* 269(5226), pp. 953–56.

Bongaarts, John. 1996. "Global Trends in AIDS Mortality." *Population and Development Review* 22(1), pp. 21–45.

Collins, Charles O., and Steven L. Scott. 1993. "Air Pollution in the Valley of Mexico." *The Geographical Review* 83(2), pp. 119–34.

Council on Scientific Affairs. 1990. "A Permanent U.S.–Mexico Border Environmental Health Commission." *JAMA, The Journal of the American Medical Association* 263(24), pp. 3319–21.

Craig, Richard B. 1989. "Mexican Narcotics Traffic: Binational Security Implications." In *The Latin American Narcotics Trade*, pp. 27–42. *See* Bagley 1989.

Del Villar, Samuel I. 1989. "Rethinking Hemispheric Anti-narcotics Strategy and Security." In *The Latin American Narcotics Trade*, pp. 105–22. *See* Bagley 1989.

DePalma, Anthony. 1995 (May 13). "The Mexicans rise up against fiscal terrorism." *New York Times* 144(50060):4.

Dillon, Sam. 1997. "Mexico and Drugs." *New York Times* 146, p. 5(L), col. 5.

Dubois, Jill. 1993. *Women in Society.* New York: Marshall Cavendish.

Economic Commission for Latin America and the Caribbean (ECLAC). 1995. *Family and Future: A Regional Programme in Latin America and the Caribbean.* Santiago, Chile: United Nations.

Feldstein, Mark, and Steve Singer. 1997. "The Border Babies." *Time* 149(21), p. 72.

Floyd, Charlene. 1996. "A Theology of Insurrection? Religion and Politics in Mexico." *Journal of International Affairs* 50(1), pp. 142–65.

González, Mercedes de la Rocha. 1994. *The Resources of Poverty: Women and Survival in a Mexican City.* Oxford, UK: Blackwell Publishers.

Guendelman, Sylvia, and Monica Jasis. 1990. "Measuring Tijuana Residents' Choice of Mexican or U.S. Health Care Services." *Public Health Reports* 105(6), pp. 575–83.

Gutmann, Matthew C. 1996. *The Meanings of Macho: Being a Man in Mexico City.* Berkeley: University of California Press.

Hamill, Pete. 1993. "Where the Air Was Clear." *Audubon* 95(1), pp. 38–50.

Hellman, Judith Adler. 1994. *Mexican Lives.* New York: The New Press.

Honey, Martha. 1994 (September 26). "Mexico's Open Secret." *The Nation* 259(9), pp. 310–12.

Inter-American Development Bank (IDB). 1995. *Women in the Americas: Bridging the Gender Gap.* Baltimore: The Johns Hopkins University Press.

Langewiesche, William. 1993. *Cutting for Sign.* New York: Pantheon Books.

LeVine, Sarah, with Clara Sunderland Correa. 1993. *Dolor y Alegría: Women and Social Change in Urban Mexico.* Madison, WI: The University of Wisconsin Press.

Levy, Daniel. 1980. *University and Government in Mexico: Autonomy in an Authoritarian System.* New York: Praeger Publishers.

McKinley, Terry, and Diana Alarcón. 1995. "The Prevalence of Rural Poverty in Mexico." *World Development* 23(9), pp. 1575–85.

Melendez, Michelle, and Franc Conteras. 1997. "Dateline Chiapas: After Three Years of Rebellion, the Zapatistas Continue to Battle for Indigenous Rights in Mexico." *Hispanic* 10(1–2), p. 28.

"Mexico under Fire for Rights Abuses." 1995. *LatinAmerica Press* 27(44), pp. 1–8.

Nash, June. 1995a. "The Reassertion of Indigenous Identity: Mayan Responses to State Intervention in Chiapas." *Latin American Research Review* 30(3), pp. 7–41.

———. 1995b. "The New World Dis-Order: A View from Chiapas, Mexico." *Indigenous Perceptions of the Nation-State in Latin America* 56, pp. 171–95.

Olavarrieta, Claudia Diaz, and Julio Sotelo. 1996. "Domestic Violence in Mexico." *JAMA, The Journal of the American Medical Association* 275(24), pp. 1937–41.

Oppenheimer, Andres. 1996 (June 17). "Guerillas in the Mist." *New Republic* 214(25), pp. 22–23.

Oxford Analytica. 1991. *Latin America in Perspective.* Boston: Houghton Mifflin Company.

Payne, Douglas W. 1996 (Summer). "Between Hope and History: Mexico's Indians Refuse to Disappear." *Dissent* pp. 61–66.

Pinheiro, Paulo Sergio. 1996. "Democracies without Citizenship." NACLA Report on the Americas 30(2), pp. 17–23.

Preston, Julie. 1997. "Drugs Connect Mexico Leaders to Abductions." *New York Times* 146, S1, p. 1 (N), p. 1 (L), col. 3.

"Rescuing the Tunnel Rat: The Mexican Border." 1997. *The Economist* 342(8002), p. 29.

Reyna, José Luis. 1989. "Narcotics as a Destabilizing Force for Source Countries and Non-source Countries." In *The Latin American Narcotics Trade*, pp. 123–38. *See* Bagley 1989.

Reynolds, Lloyd G. 1996. "Some Sources of Income Inequality in Latin America." *Journal of Interamerican Studies and World Affairs* 38(2–3), pp. 39–46.

Riding, Alan. 1984. *Distant Neighbors: A Portrait of the Mexicans.* New York: Alfred A. Knopf.

Selby, Henry. 1990 (March 21). "Mexican Household Response to Economic Crisis." Paper presented at the Latin American Conference, Baylor University.

Solis, Dianne. 1995 (September 1). "In Mexico, a New Kind of Rebel Emerges." *The Wall Street Journal*, Eastern Edition 226(44), p. A4.

"Special Issue: The Face of AIDS in Latin America." 1996. *LatinAmerica Press* 28(9), pp. 1–5.

"Special Issue: Mexico." 1988 (November 18). *Scholastic Update.*

"The Poor Man's Superman." 1988. *Scholastic Update* (November 18), p. 10.

Tresierra, Julio C. 1994. "Mexico: Indigenous Peoples and the Nation-State." In *Indigenous Peoples and Democracy in Latin America*, ed. Donna Lee Van Cott. New York: St. Martin's Press.

Warner, David C. 1991. "Health Issues at the U.S.–Mexican Border." *JAMA, The Journal of the American Medical Association* 265(2), pp. 242–47.

INDEXES

NAME INDEX

Sellers, Lois, 102, 103, 109
Sherman, William L., 8
Sherzer, Joel, 207
Siembieda, William, 5, 142
Sims, B., 159, 160, 168, 171–173
Singer, Steve, 169
Skidmore, Thomas E., 9, 19
Solis, Dianne, 178
Sotelo, Julio, 162, 163
Soto, Shirlene Ann, 74–76, 80
Stannard, David E., 10
Staudt, K., 105
Stern, Steve J., 74, 80

Stevens, Evelyn P., 71, 72
Stewart-Gambino, H., 114, 117, 119, 120, 123, 124
Szelkey, Gabriel, 5
Taggart, James M., 209
Teichman, Judith A., 45
Tinker, Irene, 206
Toplin, Robert Brent, 87
Torres, A., 128, 132, 135, 138
Tresierra, J. C., 88, 90, 97, 173, 176
Tumin, Melvin N., 207
Urban, Greg, 207

Valdes Ugalde, F., 36, 37
Van Cott, Donna Lee, 88, 95
Vasquez, Josefina Zoraida, 80
Vaughn, Mary Kay, 128
Velez, Eduardo, 133
Vera, G., 150
Vigil, James Diego, 85, 86
Warner, David C., 164
Weeks, John R., 153
Weinert, Richard S., 205
Westwood, Sallie, 207
Winter, Mary, 102
Yeager, Gertrude, 206

SUBJECT INDEX

Horizontal kinship networks, 102
Household labor, 80
Household work, 80
Housing crisis, 169–171
Huerta, Victoriano, 18
Huipils, 94
Human rights, 22
  suppression, 26
ICA, 55
Illegal migration, 6
Illiteracy, 65, 135
Import substitution industrialization (ISI), 36, 146, 151
Import-export economic structure (Latin America), 43
Independence, 13–15
Independence wars, 43, 88, 115
Independent unions, 23
Indigenismo, 89, 90, 97
Indigenistas, 90, 91
Industrias Unidas Sociedad Anonima, 59
Industry, 46–51. *See also* Government-owned industry groups, 59
Inequality, 65–66. *See also* Social inequality
  Mexican woman, 75
  regional patterns, 64–66
Infant mortality, 148–149, 155
  rates, 149, 164
Inflation, 44
Informal economy, 159
Informal polygamous relationships, 109
Informal sector, 81
Initiating role, 78
Integral Family Development (DIF) institutions, 164
Integrationist education, 133
Interamerican Convention to Prevent, Sanction, and Eradicate Violence against Women, 163
International Monetary Fund (IMF), 25, 44, 45, 51
International trade, 42
Internationalization, 21
Irrigation, government-subsidized development, 2
Jefe de familia, 71
Jefes, 138
Job security, 61
Joseph, Ferdinand Maximilian (Austria), 15
Juarez, Benito, 16
Keynes, John Maynard, 63
Kinship relations, 112
Kinship ties, 107
Labor. *See* Child labor; Household labor; Wage labor; Women
  discipline, 24
  division, 42
  force, 35
  legislation, 37
  officials, 35

Labor market. *See* Binational labor markets
  discrimination, 97
  distribution, 93
Labor relations, 144
Labor unions, 77
Land and liberty (Tierra y libertad), 90
Land owners (hacendados/finqueros), 12
Land redistribution, 49, 90, 175
Land tenure, 62
Large-scale commercial agribusinesses, 49
Large-scale infrastructure development, 44
Large-scale plantations, 48
Las mujeres abnegadas, 69
Latent function, 133
Latin America, general information, 184–185
Latin American Bishop's Conference, 116, 117, 124
Laws of Reform (1859), 33
Legal migration, 6
Liberal clergy, 118
Liberalism, 16
Liberation theology, 33, 117–119
Licenciados, 131
Life expectancy, 164
Llosa, Mario Vargas, 23
Long-distance trade, 9
Lower class, 61–62
Loyalty-resource exchanges, 28
Machismo, 72, 73, 166
  cult, 71, 163
Macho image, 166
Macho men (machos), 71, 78
Macroeconomic policies, 82
Madero, Francisco I., 18
Magic, 94
Male-dominated workforce, 70
Manifest destiny, 15
Maquila Industry Association, 81
Maquiladoras, 51–55, 81, 105, 152, 168, 171
Maquila-lined border, 169
Maquilas, 81, 105, 108, 169
Mariana, 71
Marianismo, 71, 72
Marital infidelity, 165
Market deregulation, 42
Market reforms, 42
Market-based institutions, 41
Marriage, 109–110. *See* Endogamous marriages; Exogamous marriages
Marriage rites, 109–110
Mass-produced consumer products, 151
Mayas, 87, 88, 96
McDonalds, 6
Medicine, 94, 136
Mercantilism, 12
Mestizaje, 89
Mestizo culture, 10, 89, 90, 133
Mestizo customs, 94

Mestizo landowners, 95
Mestizo nation, 4
  Amerindian assimilation, 88–89
  survival, 93–95
Mestizo population, 123
Mestizo race, 91
Mestizos, 5, 12, 14, 65, 67, 85–87, 89. *See also* Non-Mestizos
Mexican American War, 88
Mexican border communities, 173
Mexican Businessmen's Council (CMHN), 36
Mexican Constitution (1917), 19, 24, 27, 46, 49, 119, 122, 128, 157, 163, 169
Mexican daily newspapers, 183
Mexican economy, 41–56, 136
Mexican education, 127–140
  nationalist function, 133
Mexican educational system/Mexican economic system, interrelationship, 136
Mexican family, 99–112. *See also* Modern Mexican family nuclearization, 100–101
Mexican government, 165, 166, 173
  corruption, 26
  websites, 185
Mexican manufacturing, 51–55
Mexican migration, 152
Mexican mobility, 57–67
Mexican National Dance Theater, 91
Mexican people, Catholic church, 120–122
Mexican Petroleum Company (PEMEX), 47, 168, 169
Mexican politics, 26, 32. *See also* United States
Mexican Revolution (1910-1917), 17–19, 38, 46, 48, 60, 61, 91, 176
Mexican solution, 102
Mexican state, Roman Catholic church, 115–116
Mexican stratification, 57–67
Mexican-American War, 2, 26
Mexican-U.S. migration pattern, 171
Mexico
  general information, 184–185
  miracle, 19–20
Microplots, 65
Middle class, 60–61, 75
Middle-class women, 82
Middle-income countries, 63
Migration, 62, 150–153. *See also* Cross-border migration patterns; Illegal migration; Legal migration; Mexican migration; Rural-to-urban migration patterns.
Military, 37–38
Mining, 48
Ministry of Health, 164